Legend Keeper:
More Trails and Tales

Bud Cheff Jr.

With a Foreword by Dale A. Burk

Legend Keeper: More Trails and Tales

By Bud Cheff Jr.

With a Foreword by Dale A. Burk

Copyright 2012 by Bud Cheff Jr.

ISBN 1-931291-98-5 (hardcover)
ISBN 1-931291-99-3 (softcover)

Library of Congress Control Number: 2012944048

Published in the United States of America

Second Printing, December 2012
First Edition, October 2012

ALL RIGHTS RESERVED

No part of this publication may be reproduced in any retrieval system, or transmitted in any form or by any means without the prior written permission of the copyright holder or the publisher.

STONEYDALE PRESS PUBLISHING COMPANY
523 Main Street • P.O. Box 188
Stevensville, Montana 59870
Phone: 406-777-2729
Email: stoneydale@stoneydale.com
Website: www.stoneydale.com

On Becoming a Legend Keeper

Publisher's Note: *This item is excerpted from Chapter Six, where you'll read it in context, that of a young boy coming to grips with the fact that the stories, the legends, of history surrounding the place where he lived involved real people using real tools (we call them artifacts) in the process of going about their daily lives. We believe this excerpt sets a perfect tone for the theme of this book, that of recalling the legends of those who passed through our part of the world in years before it became, for us, our time and place. The boy in this story is, of course, Bud Cheff Jr., the author of this book and his recalling of these two incidents gives us perfect perspective of what, for him, became a lifelong passion – that of loving the legends of those who came before him and then doing something to keep them, to share them with others.*

"In 1946 when I was ten years old, the family was going from Ronan to Martin City when we had a flat tire going through Bad Rock Canyon. This was a usual thing in those days – every one always had flats. While Dad changed the tire my sister Ola and I climbed up the side of the canyon. We found a cave-like rock crevice which we crawled into, and in the back sticking partially out from under a packrat nest Ola found a war club. To me, this was a special find, as I had heard the story the year before of the battle here. That war club made my imagination run wild with visions of the battle.

A few years later my brother Kenny and I were rummaging around at an old burned-down trading post. Most of one log wall was still standing and under some of the debris along that wall we found many treasures including arrowheads, spear points, a calvary buckle, knives, axe heads, a buffalo horn, and other things. Most of it had been ruined by age and fire but some things were as good as new, and I was hooked forever on western history, and collecting."

Cover Photos: *The montage on the front cover exemplifies the broad dimension of legend keeping the author explores in his book. Clockwise from top left, the photos are of the author, astride a favorite horse, in 1965; the author's wife, Laurie, as a newlywed at their first home near Ronan; Becky, a grizzly that lived on the Cheff's ranch along the Mission Mountains; some of the Cheff family, Laurie Jo, Jim, Buddy III, and Laurie at Mollman Lake in the Mission Mountains; Michel, Eneas Conko's father, circa 1865; and (center) Marissa, Eneas Conko's great-great granddaughter.*

FOREWORD

Sometimes the trails one takes to achieve a lifetime of experiences and involvement in a wild land are over the tracks left by others who, before him, had already traveled similar trails, particularly those close to him; sometimes, though, they're not. Most of us follow the footsteps of those of our kin whose heritage we share; we most often go, simply, where the daily demands of our life takes us. But, occasionally, other trails beckon, even demand that we take, or even make, new trails into places and experiences both unknown and familiar. But in thinking of this, consider that unto each person, each individual, unique experiences arise even when they walk in, or alongside, the footsteps of those who've trod such trails before them. In the process, even though much of what one encounters lies in the tradition of those whose footsteps they follow, the experiences, the comprehensions, the rewards, and the remnants of those travels may be similar but they're not the same. Each person's travels, their trails, accordingly, become a rich, unique, tapestry of life experienced, and then shared in the telling of the tales of what that person experienced in having trod those trails. Such is the case of a man named Bud Cheff Jr. of Ronan, Montana, the author of this book.

Bud Cheff Jr. enjoys both the privilege and the peril of growing up in and living in the footsteps of a famous father. His dad, Bud Cheff Sr., became a living legend in the Mission Valley of northwestern Montana by the time he'd reached mid-life and that standing only grew as he lived into his eighties and nineties before passing away in 2011 at the age of ninety-six. A master woodsman, a master horseman and cowhand, an internationally acclaimed wilderness outfitter, author of a book about his life in the wilderness titled *"Indian Trails and Grizzly Tales,"* and another book on back country survival the old-fashioned way, *"The Woodsman and His Hatchet,"* Bud Cheff Sr. was also the scion of one of Montana's most well-known and respected families, so renowned, in fact, that the elder Cheff was elected to the Montana Cowboy Hall of Fame in 2012 for his many accomplishments.

Which brings us to a key point about the what and the why of this book – *"Legend Keeper: More Trails and Tales."* Given the reality of his situation, of knowing from an early age that he walked in the footsteps of a famous father, Bud Cheff Jr. – known as Buddy to those of us whose lives he's touched over the last several decades – could have simply stayed in the shadow of his father's fame and not struck out to accomplish a few things on his own – of pursuing, in his own right, an endeavor out of covering many of those same trails and tales his father had experienced with others. Instead, Buddy became an accomplished woodsman himself, a rancher, a wilderness guide, an ironworker whose skills took him to many other places in the American West, a businessman, and, significant to our story, the founder of the Ninepipes Museum of Early Montana along Highway 93 south of Ronan. But early in life, as our author shares in his story in Chapter Four titled "The Start of a Legend," he encountered something, at the age of ten, that changed his life, and in the process enriched ours. He realized that it was within his grasp to become a definer and a keeper of legends. He took on, at that tender age, a task he now realizes he won't be able to complete in a lifetime. Or even two! But from that day in 1946 to the present, Bud Cheff Jr. kept a promise he made to himself: to seek out, research, keep and then share the stories of the legends of his land.

From then, to now, Bud Cheff Jr. has been a keeper of legends, not only of those retold in the form of cold artifacts but close, live, heart-pounding personal relationships with many of the actual makers of those legends, friendships that transcend generations and cultures and well as peoples. Over the years, our author cherished the fact that he'd grown up in the Mission Valley where he and his family shared – actually share is the proper word here because those relationships continue to this day – a close kinship with the Salish and Pend d'Orielle peoples, with the wild, mostly undeveloped landscape, and the constant interplay with the wildlife found in that natural environment. Thus, like his father but in a very different, second generation way, Bud Cheff Jr. related personally to the people and places and things that he found along the trails of his life. The result is, of course, this book, a treasure trove of looking into the lives, indeed many of the legend makers he encountered in his lifetime. And, in the process of comprehending what he's put together in this book, we come to realize that Bud Cheff Jr. has, in a very real way, become a legend in his own right. The legend keeper's story thus brings us to a perfect ending – legends have, sometimes, a way of becoming real right before our eyes. That is, indeed, what we encounter in following the trails and tales found within these pages. Bud Cheff Jr., without realizing it, herein created a legendary classic of his, and our, time and place in history.

Dale A. Burk, Stevensville, Montana, July 10, 2012

TABLE OF CONTENTS

Foreword 5

Introduction 11

Chapter One: My Early Years
- The Sentinel of The Mission Valley 16
- Hijacked at Mollman Lake 17
- Spook Lake 19
- The Jail Break 21
- Christmas With Old Bob 24
- The Raven 26
- Dad Saved The Day 27
- Get a Bigger Stick 28
- Keep Your Head Down 29
- I Fall On a Grizzly 30
- A Close Call 31
- The Coach 34
- Going Duck Hunting 36
- Memories of Days in Montana's Wilderness 37
- Riding The Rails 41
- Scarface Peak 46
- The Barefoot Bride 50
- Moose Creek Adventure 56
- Mick, Me and a Mountain Goat 62

Chapter Two: Family Tales
- A True Montana Ranch Family 64
- Spotlighters 65
- The Start of a Legend 66
- Mollmans 68
- More Than Just a Mirror 70
- A Boy and His Chaps 72
- A Moonshine Run 72
- Post Creek Rustler 78
- Hector McCleod 80
- New Year's Eve, 1926 83

- The Secret 84
- The Dixon Mines 90
- The Passing of a Legend 91
- A Really Big Soul 94
- Cowboy Hall of Fame Citation....................................95

Chapter Three: Stories from the Past
- Lost Gold Mine 98
- The Fight Between Sum-a-Kaa and Dave Finley 102
- The Deer Child 107
- The Pend-d-Orielle Camp Meets The Famous
  Harry Morgan 114
- Winter Medicine Dance, 1924 118
- Montana's First Recorded Marriage 125
- And Then There Were Bootleggers..........................128
- War Song 130
- The Old Wagon Trail Incident 131
- The Blacksmith's Daughter 132
- Angeline By The Lake 136

Chapter Four: Bear Stories
- The Sheep Killer 144
- A Grizzly In the Trap 146
- A Blond Grizzly 147
- Observations of Ranch Bears 148
- Bear Romance 151
- Fall, 2008 152
- Spring, 2010 153
- Fall, 2010 154
- Josie and Her Cubs 154
- Spring, 2011 155
- My First Encounter With Becky 157
- My Second Encounter With Becky 160
- Bear Scare At The Eagle Tree 162
- Rocks and Bears 163
- Shadow 165
- Another Shadow Story 166
- A Chance Meeting With Shadow 168
- Our Ranch and Bears 169

- So Long Shadow 170
- February 2012 171
- A Lion By the Tail 173
- Katie and the Grizzly 178

Chapter Five: Cowboys & Longhorns
- The Longhorns 179
- Longhorns and Bears 180
- Old Blue 182
- The Cowboys 184
- Billy Schall, A Montana Cowboy 188

Chapter Six: Unwritten Indian Stories
- The Bee Tree 191
- Mary Catherine's Place 191
- Eneas Conko 192
- Traditional Medicine Ceremonies 195
- The Bravest of the Brave 198
- The Flathead War Chief of the 1800's 201
- Jacques Houle (Hoole) 202
- Flathead Indians and Amazing Tales of Horsemanship ... 204
- Jackson Sundown and the Nez Perce War 206
- Major Owen 211
- The End of a Way of Life 213
- The Blackfeet Winter Raid at Wild Plum Camp 221

Chapter Seven: Wrapping It Up
- Wrapping It Up 221

Afterword 223

Bud Jr. family, Donna holding Garrett, Jim, Bud Jr., Laurie, Jo, Sheri, and Bud III.

INTRODUCTION

I dedicate this book in loving memory of my mother and father, Bud and Adelle Cheff, who could not have been better parents. Mom taught me the love of books and history, while Dad taught me to be at home in the wilderness as well as the value of hard work. They showed my brothers and sisters, and me, how to enjoy life and love each other. I can see them now, dancing around on the rough board floor of our small log cabin, looking into each other's eyes with love. They both had good singing voices and would sing in duet. We had no electricity in those days, or even a battery radio, so we made our own music. Dad was an expert mouth harp player and that was our only music.

I also dedicate this book to my family and wonderful wife, Laurie. She did all the proofreading and editing of this book, and all my work. Laurie and I live here on the Mountain Shadow Ranch, the same property on which I was born seventy-five years ago. Our son, Buddy III, and his two boys run the ranch, along with our daughter, Laurie Jo and husband, Yo. Son Jim, with his wife Donna and family, live east of Ronan where they raise horses. Jim has a construction company and Donna is a teacher. With two sons and a daughter, they give a hand on the ranch when it's needed. We live on the south part of the ranch, which is a prime grizzly bear and wildlife habitat. We are blessed with an almost daily wildlife show. Many of the bear instances in the book are taken from my daily log.

I was born September 8, 1936, in my grandparents' log house on this ranch. I was the oldest of five boys with one younger and one older sister. A younger brother died at birth when I was five. My dad, my sister, Ola, and little brother Kenny and I buried him on the ranch. We had a ceremony with Dad and Ola saying prayers. My mother was in the Sisters' hospital at St. Ignatius, near death from a burst appendix.

We lived in a log cabin my father built at the foot of the Mission Mountains, eight miles southeast of Ronan, Montana. We did not have electricity or running water in the house, and all the ranch and farm work was done with horses. We had a car, but no truck for hauling. We used a team and wagon in the summer, and a sleigh in the winter. Dad got his first tractor in 1954, a little Ford 8N. It was a hard life for my parents, but it was paradise for me and my siblings.

Bud (Dad) holding Ola, Adelle (Mom) holding Buddy Jr.

In 1996 my wife Laurie and I, with the help of my mom and dad, Bud and Adelle Cheff, built the Ninepipes Museum of Early Montana. It is located on Highway 93 seven miles south of Ronan. It is a nonprofit 501(c)3 museum depicting early Montana Indians, settlers, and wildlife. Many of the stories in this book were originally written for the museum's quarterly newsletters. They are taken from the reflections of my life, and from others in my early years to the present. The stories are meant to give a little information on local and Montana history. Even the animal stories will give you a taste of living in rural Montana. As a boy growing up, I loved to be around the elders and listen to them. My grandparents, my uncles, and my aunts had a special way of holding the listeners interest with their colorful verbal descriptions and French accent. Both my grandfather and grandmother were of French, and Mohawk-Iroquois descent, often called Metis. Most of our friends and neighbors were Indian families, and some of the real old full bloods were still living then. Some people think of these old Indians as being a stern, stoic people. This was true if you were a stranger or if they did not trust or like you. Once you got to know them, they were wonderful people, easy to laugh, and they loved to play a joke on each other. Life was real hard for them, with no money or income, but then it was about the same at that time for their white neighbors. When they would come to visit Dad or we would go visit them, it was a special thing for me. There was always storytelling, as they liked to talk of the past, and I listened to every word. If they talked only in Salish I would have Dad explain some parts of it to me. Most of the time they spoke in broken English, with some French and Indian mixed in. Some of them spoke pretty good French, learned from the Black Robes, the Sisters, and trappers. Some of the stories in this book came from these wonderful times in my young years.

Our family moved to Martin City when I was in the fifth grade, and I graduated from high school at Columbia Falls, Montana, in 1955. The town of Martin City was named for my great-aunt and uncle, Joseph Gaspard and Malvina Martin. The town was built on their homestead. Dad worked on Hungry Horse Dam, but continued to outfit and guide big game hunters on the side. We were never without cows and horses, even when living at Martin City. We had about a hundred head of horses at the Ronan ranch, and would bring young horses up to break, and then sell some of them. I spent every minute I could in the mountains hunting, trapping, fishing, and on a horse. I was always trying to follow in my dad's footsteps, but he made big tracks that were sometimes hard for me to follow.

In my own life I witnessed my grandmothers, my mother and countless other neighbor women working so hard, and doing so much with so little; keeping a home, warm meals for the family, tending a garden, canning over a hot stove, sewing new clothes, some out of flour sacks, and patching old ones. The household work was enormous but they were still always ready to drop everything and help their man get a crop seeded or the hay up before a rain; to move cows or horses, to help in the branding, lambing, or calving. Then they had to get supper for the tired crew, no matter how tired they were themselves. On Sunday they would be up extra early to get morning chores done, the kids clean and dressed in their best, and usher the family off to church. I had a most wonderful childhood, but I was aware of the hardships my mother endured to make it happen. I saw her knuckles bleeding from hours of washing clothes on the scrub board, saw her fall on the ice while carrying buckets of water from the creek, and the beads of sweat on her face from working over the hot stove, canning food or rendering bear or pig fat for lard. Then, at the end of the day, fix herself up so she would look nice when Dad came home.

My wife, Laurie, is no different than my mother. Even though she has many of the modern conveniences of today, she still works so hard. I think women are just born with this inner strength. I am definitely aware that she is the wind under my wings.

Many of the stories in this book were written or co-written by my daughter, Laurel Josephine, under her pen name Josephine Chevre, which was our family name before it was changed to Cheff in the late 1700's. I would rough out a story and have her rewrite it, or just orally relate the story for her to write. She has been a blessing to me and the museum for her work on the newsletters. I am expecting a lot more help in the future, now that she is living back on the ranch.

At the end of the day I hope I will be remembered for being hard working and honest, for holding all family dear to my heart, and for loving the wilderness and wildlife. I inherited some of my parents' strength and integrity, even though I stepped off the winding trail numerous times on the way. I do believe my sister, Ola, will be the first to greet me as I cross over. She and I were very close all her short life. She became ill with sugar diabetes at the age of eight, and died when she was twenty-five. In our teen years she couldn't climb the mountains like I could so I would pay close attention to everything I saw. Then at home she would have me tell her what I had seen in minute detail. She was my guiding star growing up.

Now that I am on the last leg of my journey through life I feel compelled to record some of the stories I learned as a boy before they are lost. For me, and I hope for others, they bring the real life history in early Montana a little closer.

Chapter One

THE EARLY YEARS

THE SENTINEL OF THE MISSION VALLEY
It was over three hundred years ago that this great Ponderosa, or yellow pine, emerged from the fertile soil at the base of the Mission Mountains. Its parent, a large yellow pine, had dropped the seed a couple years earlier on ground that had been blackened by a lightning-started forest fire. The tree was about thirty-five years old in 1728 when it looked down on the first horses in the valley. From then on, it would see many horses. The Upper Pend d'Oreille Indians' lifestyle was experiencing a big change as they learned how to utilize the strength and intelligence of this wonderful new animal.

Throughout the years the tree observed Blackfeet war parties sneak into the valley to steal the Pend d'Oreille's horses and women. It also watched the horses carrying the women and children up the mountain to the huckleberry patches, and the hunting and gathering parties returning with roots and meat. It looked on as the women and children gathered in the meadow below, blue with camas blooms, to dig the plump bulbs. It saw the tipi village being taken down as the Indians prepared to move across the mountains to the plains for their annual spring buffalo hunt.

In about 1790, it saw the first white man, and by 1810 it was seeing these strange white men more often. It was standing tall in 1845 as the Hudson's Bay Company men built Fort Connah, five miles to the south of the tree. Then, in 1854 Father Hoecken and other Black Robes started the construction of the St. Ignatius Mission. In 1855 it watched the Indians trailing by to join the Bitterroot Salish, and meet Governor Isaac Ingalls Stevens at Hellgate, for the famous signing of the Hellgate Treaty.

The tree was surprised in 1860 when two Indians, Charley and Louie Mollman, and their families moved in around it. They brought their horses and their small herd of cattle. The tree had never had cattle grazing around it before. In 1874, it witnessed Walking Coyote leading his little herd of buffalo calves into the valley, the start of the great Allard and Pablo herd. It also started to see more dust as the old trails turned into wagon roads. By 1885, it was a common sight to see the smoke and hear the whistle of the steam engines from the new railroad across the valley.

From its lofty height, in 1910 it could see the dust in the west from the buffalo roundup, making room for the swarms of settlers coming into the area. It listened with pleasure to the singing and the beat of the drums at the Mollmans' annual Winter Jump Dance.

Brothers Bud & Vila Cheff standing at the Sentinel tree.

In 1920 the tree saw its first sheep when the Cheff family joined the Mollmans and built a house just a couple of hundred yards from it. And it smiled at the children playing at its base, knowing it was too big for them to climb up to it's lofty branches. It worried when Polley Lumber Co. built railroad tracks and started logging within a half-mile of it. The tree was glad it stood out in the meadow by itself, too far and maybe too big to be of interest to the loggers.

It witnessed the dust from the first automobiles as they replaced the horse and wagon. It heard the roar and saw the shadow of the first airplane flying over its head. In 1936 it heard another new baby cry in the Cheff home when grandson, Bud Jr., was born. Then in 1938 it saw the valley light up with electricity from the new Kerr Dam, just built on the Flathead River near Polson and south of Flathead Lake. It looked on as Gene Allard, standing proudly on the back of his tractor, drove into the meadow below. It was the first tractor in the area, and the beginning of the end for the teams of horses, the noble animals that helped conquer the frontier.

In the early 1960's Mother Nature injured the tree with a lightning strike, but the tree lived on. Then in 1974 it was hit by lightning again. This hit was a hard one, but not fatal. The great tree struggled on until 1986 when lightning again struck it. This time it knocked the top fifty feet of the tree off. It could not withstand this hit and was dead in two years.

At this writing, January of 2008, this great tree, this valley sentinel, is still standing. Much of its bark is gone and many of its massive limbs, some over twelve inches in diameter, have fallen. The trunk has dried and shriveled, but the tree still stands, watching the world change. I often look at this great tree, and let my mind drift back in time, seeing the changes in the land the tree has seen in it's long life; knowing it was here to witness history unfold. "If it could only talk!" The tree is now six feet four inches in diameter at the base, nineteen feet around, and ninety feet tall, no longer the towering one hundred forty feet it was before its top was knocked off. After every storm or strong wind, I look out with fear that it will be gone. When it does go down, it will take a part of me with it.

HIJACKED AT MOLLMAN LAKE

In 1942 my folks were taking a group of people into the Mission Mountains. They had a lady staying at our house to look after us and a couple other kids whose parents were on the trip. I was six years old and had been insisting I should be able to go with them. Dad let me know this was a trip for grown-ups, and I could not go this time. Being a very stubborn kid I decided to follow them, figuring when I showed up at their camp they would have to let me stay. It never entered my mind what a stressful burden I would be putting on the babysitter.

The horses and pack string were barely out of sight when I started after them on foot. I couldn't find my shoes, but I was out-growing them anyway, and they hurt my feet. I hardly ever wore shoes in the summer time, and I was usually barefoot or in moccasins. The shoes were for school. But I knew I needed something on my feet in the mountains. I

Adelle Cheff, son Buddy Jr. at their home.

had one moccasin, I had lost the other, or maybe the dog had dragged it off. I put an overshoe on the other foot and it worked fine, as neither one had a heel and I was the same height on both feet. I took off after the folks but never did catch up, or see them again. This was all right as I didn't want them to see me and send me back home. I trailed them to Mollman Lakes, about six miles or more from home. I knew the way to the lakes as I had been there with the folks, and the year before my sister Ola and I had tagged along with some of our uncles, who were four or five years older.

Jo, Jim, Buddy and Laurie at First Mollman Lake.

I was just getting to the second lake when I ran into some older boys who lived a few miles from us, Chuck Olson, and three brothers Glen, Don, and Ted Shepard. They knew me, and wanted to know where I was going. I must have been a sight to see; a wild-haired little kid covered with dust and sweat, my face smeared with berry juice. I had on bib overalls, which I hated. I couldn't wait to be old enough to wear pants and a belt. I must have really looked like a lost waif with my fancy foot gear. I told them I was following my mom and dad. They said they had been camped here for two days and my folks had not come by here. I told them, "Yes they have, I am following their horse tracks!" The boys told me they were going home, and I must go back down the

Ola at age seven.

mountain with them. I said, "No I won't!" and ran around them. They caught me, and I fought tooth and nail, kicking and biting, but they overpowered me and dragged me along. Every time they let their guard down I would make a run for it. We were just below the Granite cliffs when I got away again. I curled up into a ball and rolled down off of the trail through a patch of stinging nettles, thinking they wouldn't follow, but they caught me and dragged me back up to the trail. They had pretty much run out of patience with me when one of them offered me his yellow bone-handled pocket knife if I would come with them and not fight. I could not resist that pretty knife. I surrendered and went with them, but they kept me in front so they could watch me. When we got down the mountain they let me go on home by myself, which was only about three-quarters of a mile, and they went on down the road towards their place. When I got home I was going to show Ola my knife, but was heart-broken, for I had a hole in my pocket, and I had lost it! I never was punished for my caper; losing the knife was my punishment.

SPOOK LAKE

Spook Lake in the Mission Mountains was named by my dad, Bud Sr., in the late 1930's, after hearing a tale told by Ed Sias about the lake. When I was a boy, Ed and his family lived about a mile and a half south of us on the Charley Brush place. Dad often hired Ed and his partner, Leo David, as guides. They also helped him build and clean trails in the Bob Marshall Wilderness and in the Missions. Both men were part Indian, good hunters, and at home in the mountains.

In 1943, when I was seven years old, I went on a trip with Dad, Ed, and Leo into the Missions. Dad had hired the men to help him build a trail over Elk Creek to the Swan Valley. In those days before trucks and trailers Dad trailed the horses from our place in the Mission Valley to his hunting camp in the wilderness, packing all his hunting gear and supplies on pack horses. It was a job getting across the Missions without a good trail, and the old Indian trail had become impassable with down timber and boggy ground in places. I knew this firsthand, as I had helped Dad take the horses across the Missions the year before. It was my first time helping Dad with this. He was leading a string of pack horses, and I was hazing the loose horses behind him when we got caught in an early snow blizzard. I can still hear the wind moaning through the dead snags in the old burn area. When Dad stopped to camp for the night he told me to get off my horse, but I was too cold to move. I just leaned over and fell head-first into the snow. Dad got a fire going and thawed me out and everything in the world was good again.

On this trail building trip, although it was summer and warm I insisted on wearing my white mountain goat fur-out chaps. Dad had made them for me for Christmas, and I was so proud of them I would have worn them to bed if Mom had let me. This trip was a dream come true for me as I was in my beloved mountains, helping build trail, doing my favorite work. The evenings were special, sitting around the camp fire, listening to the men tell stories. Ed was a great story teller and he was known to stretch them to his liking. To a young boy, everything a grown-up said was bound to be true, and I was certain everything Ed said was "the sure enough truth."

I show off my mountain goat chaps to my Dad, hunter, Joe Forte, hunting camp.

He told a number of stories, but the one that had me sitting on the edge of my log was the one that earned Spook Lake its name. Few people have been to Spook Lake as it's a high mountain lake, and not in the heavily traveled hikers route. It's been many years ago that I heard Ed telling this tale, but its still vivid in my mind. You had to be seven years old, sitting by a camp fire, surrounded by darkness and night sounds with an occasional scary call of a loon from the pond down below to really appreciate it. Across the fire from me with the fire light playing tricks on his features, sat Ed. He was fairly tall, a slim man with a full black beard and a beat-up old Stetson cowboy hat on his head.

The story went like this. Ed started talking: "We, Leo and I, were camped at Spook Lake. Of course it didn't have a name then. We let the horses graze around a while, then tied them up and gave them a bit of oats. We knew they would leave us afoot if we left them loose all night. We had finished cooking some supper, and had set back to enjoy a smoke. The sun had went down and it was getting dark. It was a clear night, but no moon or stars were out yet. Then out of nowhere there was a loud roar of thunder from across the lake. It was followed by a big gust of wind coming across the lake scattering our stuff around. Then every thing was quiet, and we heard a voice call out 'H-e-y Ed!' I asked Leo, 'Who was that?' He was just staring out across the dark lake."

I glanced up at Dad and scooted a little closer to him, and wondered why he had a twinkle in his eyes. Ed continued, "The voice called again but louder, 'H-e-y Ed!' The voice called out four or five more times, each time getting louder. The last time it was so loud it echoed back and forth off the cliffs above the lake. Then there was a loud, roaring noise like a forest fire, and a big ball of fire lit up the lake. The ball of fire came rolling across the lake on top of the water towards us. The horses were pulling back trying to get away, but Leo and I were froze in our tracks. We had our guns in our hands but there wasn't anything to shoot at. When the ball of fire got to our shore it exploded into nothing. Leo and I had our gear packed up and horse saddled in nothing flat. We traveled clear to Summit Lake in the dark before we stopped. It was a good thing horses can pick their way in the dark, as we sure weren't about to spend the night at Spook Lake!"

That night I dreamed of a voice calling "H-e-y Buddy!" and a ball of fire chasing after me as I hunkered way down in my sleeping bag.

In later years Ed Sias's son, Herby, worked for us as a hunting guide. Herby was a favorite around camp. The hunters loved him and Mom made sure he always had plenty of food on his plate. He thought the world of Mom and Dad, and they always had a good word for him. Herby passed on this past year and left behind a lot of friends.

Herb Sias in hunting camp.

THE JAIL BREAK
by Bud Cheff Jr. as told to Josephine Chevre.

In 1948 I was a husky, dark-haired kid with a fast horse and a head full of romantic notions. The construction of Hungry Horse Dam was in full swing, and Martin City, the last of the old-time boomtowns, was in its heyday. There were fights every day and shootings were common. *Life Magazine* published a story about Martin City called "The Wildest Dam Town in the U.S.A." Naturally, my brothers and I did our best to

Brothers Mick & Buck Cheff, Martin City, 1954.

live up to this title.

My great-great uncle and aunt, Gaspard Joseph and Malvina Martin, came into the Flathead Valley in about 1883 by wagon train. The wagon boss was another three "greats" back, uncle Joseph Tetrault, and also on the trip was Josephat Cheff. He built the first hotel and saloon where the town of Columbia Falls now stands. My great-great grandmother, Edna La Forge, was living at the town site of Demersville at this time. She was born in 1823, died in 1900 and was buried at Columbia Falls.

As the wagon train wound its way along the west shore of Flathead Lake the boss decided they would stay the night near what is now Big Arm. It had been raining but that night the sky cleared and it froze hard. In the early morning Joseph Tetrault aroused the camp for a early start. Aunt Vina, who was 16 years old and just newly married, awoke with her long black hair frozen to the ground. Joseph, being an impatient man, took out his hunting knife and cut off her beautiful hair.

Aunt Vina said she never quite forgave her uncle for this. Her house at Martin City was built overlooking Abbot creek. When I was a boy fishing along the creek, she would sometimes see me and invite me up to the house to have tea and cookies with her.

On one occasion I saw her standing on her porch veranda, combing her hair in the morning sunlight. It made me think of the wagon train incident, but her hair was now snow white and hung below her waist. She always wore her hair in a bun, and I had never seen it down before. This beautiful scene is etched in my mind.

At this time the town supported two grocery stores, a service station, a soda fountain, a barbershop, a shoe store, a pool hall, and a church in a tent house. A building with wooden benches served as a theater while the real one was being built. There were also thirteen saloons and three cat houses; Sugar Hill, Sugar Valley, and the M&M. Most of the businesses were on Main Street, which was graveled and sported wooden sidewalks. The rest of the streets were dirt. In later years the main street was paved and some businesses poured concrete sidewalks.

I had a paper route, passed on to me from my cousin, Vern Byrd, which I later passed on to my brother, Kenny. Now this was not a good town to carry a paper route. People were always coming and going, and with all that activity, seemed to forget to pay the paperboy. I would sell my extra papers in the bars. Sometimes the ladies would tease me and give me sips of their drinks.

Aunt Vina Martin, age 16, when she came to the Flathead.

Mabel, the Madam of Sugar Hill, would always give me a tip, saying it was so far to come up the hill. She was a nice, generous lady with red hair and a matronly manner about her. Mabel closed her house on Sundays and she and her girls would dress up real fancy and tour the valley in her Lincoln convertible, hitting Columbia Falls, Kalispell and Whitefish.

In the 40's the Martin City bars stayed open all night if they wanted to. Some had swinging doors, and they all kept their doors open in good weather so it was easier to stagger in and out. The Hungry Horse Bar had horse tracks imprinted on the sidewalk leading into the bar. One day my brothers Mick and Buck, who were only about six or seven years old, rode by the Hungry Horse. Some of the inebriated patrons showed them the tracks of other horses that had gone inside, and talked the boys into riding their horses into the bar. Their horses were slipping and sliding, while the patrons hooted and laughed, encouraging the boys on, and enjoying the entertainment mightily.

My little brother, Kenny, was running with some older, very wild kids. They were keeping Mom and Dad real busy with their capers. One day the town law, Vern Greene, had them locked up. Dad was tired of chasing after Kenny, so he told Vern to keep him there overnight. When I found out Kenny was in jail, I decided to ride my horse down to visit him.

No one was at the jailhouse, so I rode around to the back where there was a barred window, with no glass, about six feet up the wooden wall. I called out and Kenny's towhead popped up to the window. He was looking pretty woebegone. He did not like jail one bit, he told me, and he wanted me to help him break out. Now I had seen enough cowboy movies to know how to do that, and it seemed like a heroic gesture on my part, what with Kenny's ten-year-old face pressed up to the bars in such a miserable fashion. I rode my horse up to the window, tied my lariat to a bar, and took three or four dallies around the saddlehorn. Kenny watched me, and a look of pure, joyous hope lighted his sad little face. I felt proud to be able to rescue my little brother from his awful fate.

My horse was a Thoroughbred racehorse with a really fast start. I pursed my lips, the signal for him to go. When he hit the end of the rope he was going full out. The next thing I knew, I was sitting on the ground, still in my saddle. The latigo had broken on my cinch. I looked up at Kenny, framed in the barred window, and he had the most crestfallen, despairing look on his face that I had ever seen. He knew he was going to have to stay there until Dad gave the okay for his release. So much for being the hero of the day. The jailbreak didn't work like it did in the Roy Rogers movies!

CHRISTMAS WITH OLD BOB

As a boy in Martin City in the late '40's I came to know an old hermit who lived back in the trees near our house, which was the last house on our road. We called the hermit "Old Bob." He was a husky, barrel-chested man, and a loner. He had no house, just a board lean-to, open on the front. A big log he had hewn flat on top served as a bench and bed. He slept on that hard log with just an old army blanket under him, and one to cover up with.

Bob had a flat-topped stove that he used for cooking and heat. He would cut dead trees about twelve inches in diameter into lengths about twelve feet long. Bob would carry these logs on his shoulders, up the river bank to his camp, then saw them into blocks with his crosscut saw. Most men couldn't have picked these logs up!

Old Bob lived here the year around, even when the temperature dropped to 40 below. His camp was not cluttered, but could have been fixed up a lot better. He didn't seem to want to make it more comfortable for himself. Bob's main diet was pine squirrel, sometimes grouse or venison. He had a medium-sized dog, black and long haired, that was well behaved. He was probably a spaniel and shepherd cross. The dog never barked except when he had a grouse or squirrel treed for Bob to shoot, or when a bear would come into camp, which was quite often. Bob's only gun was a single-shot .22 rifle.

He was well educated, but would not talk of his past. The kids liked him, and he seemed to enjoy them more than the grown ups. I sometimes went by his camp on my way hunting or fishing, and we talked quite often. He liked to talk about politics, and knew what was going on in the world.

Bob sometimes dug ditches for water and sewer lines by hand, for Mr. Joe Weedning, a developer who had bought a lot of land from my Aunt Vina Martin. Joe had a limp and walked with a cane, and Old Bob called him Limping Jesus. The ditches had to be below the frost line, four or five feet deep. Bob's ditches were perfectly straight, and the sides vertical and all the same width. He was a perfectionist in his work, but not at his camp.

Ola at Martin City, age fourteen.

My Uncle Herman and Aunt Bernida Byrd were always trying to give him things from their store, but Old Bob would not take handouts. On real cold nights, Dad would sometimes check on him. On some cold mornings Mom would have Kenny and me go check on him. Mom always had us kids take a big plate of our dinner to him on holidays, as he would not come and eat with us. On Christmas we kids would take him a little gift of something, sometimes gloves or wool socks. He did not like taking the gift, but he would, mostly, I think, so he wouldn't hurt our feelings. I remember going over to his camp one Christmas day. It was a beautiful day, the snow was over two feet deep and his camp looked so cozy and cheery in the snow. Ola said, "It's just like going to the stable in Bethlehem to see Jesus." I think God was smiling on Old Bob and us kids that Christmas Day.

THE RAVEN

My head is ringing with the frantic cries of eight ravens, two adults and six young ones: the low, hoarse calls of encouragement from the parents and the frantic high-pitched calls of the young. This distracting noise goes on from daybreak to sundown for about three weeks. The young ravens are going through flight training and a crash course on food source and survival. This has been happening here every spring for thirty years.

The pair nests a few hundred yards back in the tall timber southwest of the house, and uses the back yard and surrounding meadows for their training grounds. I dread the day they leave the nest, but I would miss them if they were not around. As a boy at Martin City, I thought ravens were the most disgusting birds in the world. I watched them feeding at the city dump, eating until the food would run back out of their mouths. They would regurgitate what they had eaten and then eat some more. As I learned more about them I realized they were very smart birds even if they were gluttons.

They had a roosting ground about a half-mile west of old trapper Mickey Wagner's homestead. There were hundreds of them roosting there at night, or just resting there in the day. I would play that they were the enemy and I was a Flathead scout sneaking into their camp. I never made it in without them catching me. They had sentries posted all around the roosting ground and every once in a while one of the sentries would make a reconnoitering flight around the area. If they saw anything amiss they would give an "alert" call and if it looked threatening, they would give the full alarm and all of them would take to the air. They are a very smart bird, they have their own language and I think they can reason some things out. They never miss an opportunity for food, and there is very little they won't or don't eat. They are an important part of nature in Western Montana and can teach you a lot about what's happening in the woods if you watch and listen to them.

DAD SAVED THE DAY

In the fall of 1947, I persuaded my folks into letting me take a week off from school to help Dad take a hunting party into the Missions. I had turned eleven years old the week before, and this was kind of a birthday present for me. At eleven, I wasn't the best help but I could lead the pack horses and help with camp chores. I was in charge of getting in wood and doing dishes while Dad was doing the cooking, guiding and all the real hard work. There was nothing he could not do, and in the mountains he was a Superman. Some days Dad would take the hunters horseback up to a divide, and I would bring the horses back to camp, leaving the men to hunt back to camp on foot.

I had a lot of time for myself and, with my .22 rifle, I did a lot of grouse hunting. One day I heard two bull elk bugling, and I snuck up close to them to watch them fight. They went at it for a long time. It was a special thing for me to watch, and it's embedded in my memory. A young boy alone with two big bulls grunting, horns clanking, dirt and sod flying; it was a little bit scary when they came close to me. One finally fell to his knees, and got up and ran. The winner bugled a short bugle and went up the hill to some cows.

One morning we woke up to snow on the ground. Dad and the hunters went out from camp, hunting on foot. A little later I took my .22 and went down the canyon the opposite way from where the hunters had gone. When I was about a mile and a half from camp I ran into a big grizzly bear track that was real fresh. It was going back up the canyon and to the east side. I decided to follow it and if I got the chance, kill it. I was a good shot, and had figured out in my mind how I would do it. I had that youthful self-confidence that I could do most anything, and I was immortal. The hard knocks and reality of life hadn't caught up to me yet. I had trailed the bear for about a half mile when the tracks went into some thick brush and trees. I knew he was just ahead of me and I was going real slow, looking and listening carefully. All of a sudden I was startled by a loud rifle shot. Then I heard a voice say, "Here comes another one!" Then Dad's voice saying, "Don't shoot in the brush, let it come out in the open. We don't want to kill another one if we don't have to."

About that time I walked out of the brush. Dad and the hunter were astonished to see me come out right behind the big grizzly. I was peeved because they had shot my bear. Dad said, "How were you planning on killing this big old boar grizzly with that .22 rifle?" I told him I was going to shoot his eyes out, and if that didn't kill him, I would shoot him in the heart. Dad had taught me as a small boy, you don't shoot at the animal, you shoot at a specific part of the animal. At the time I never realized how lucky I was to be alive. There was a good chance the bear might have killed me, and it was even more certain that the hunter would have shot me if Dad hadn't grabbed his arm and told him not to shoot. This would not be the last time my dad saved my life. Thanks Dad, for all you have done for me in my life.

(*Note: When I came out of the mountains a neighbor boy a few years older than me went in and took my place helping Dad for the rest of the trip. That boy and his wife are now members of the Ninepipes Museum, ranchers Phil and Diane (Allard) Grant.)*

GET A BIGGER STICK

In the fall of 1948 I was elk hunting with my dad in the lower South Fork of the Flathead. We were hunting for ourselves, after our winter meat. This was special to me, as we didn't have to worry about making sure one of dad's hunters got his elk. We boys were not supposed to shoot any big bulls; they were for the paying hunters. I did shoot a few through the years, but their horns always ended up going back east with a hunter. On this day I heard three spaced shots up the canyon from me, and I knew it was Dad's old single-shot .30-30. I was surprised for I had never known Dad to shoot more than once to get his game. This was something I always tried to follow in his footsteps. I was careful never to shoot unless I could make a kill with one shot, especially if Dad was within hearing. I started up to where the shots had been fired, and found Dad butchering a spike bull elk. He was feeling bad because he had shot three spike bulls. He thought his gun sights must have gotten knocked off as he had missed the elk twice before it went down. He had been shooting uphill, and the elk was in the trees with tall snow brush so he could not see it too well. When he got up to it, he realized he had killed three of them.

The next day Dad, my younger brother Kenny, who was nine years old, and myself (I had just turned twelve a few weeks before) went up to pack out the elk. We only had three pack horses so Dad would have to make two trips to get the meat down to the road. When we got to the elk, there was a big grizzly there, working on them. He had already buried one of the elk. Grizzly bears will often dig a shallow hole, drag the kill into it and cover it with dirt, sticks, pine needles, or what ever. Mountain lions will cover their kill also, with needles, sticks, and hair they pull off the dead animal. They do this to keep the birds off. It was lucky the elk wasn't already skinned, or it would have been ruined. We loaded the horses and Dad headed down the mountain with the first load, leaving Kenny and me to clean the dirt and sticks off the elk the bear had buried. Dad told us to make some noise and scare the bear off if it came back.

None of us had brought a gun that day because with the three elk, we had all the meat we needed. It was only a short while after Dad left that the grizzly showed up. He grumbled around us, going back and forth. Kenny and I each had a stick and we were beating on a log, singing Indian war songs to the bear. This went on for quite awhile. The bear started coming a little closer and making more noise. It seemed like Dad would never get back! Time goes slow for kids and it was an eight mile trip down to the road and back. I told Kenny, "You need to get a bigger stick, the grizzly is getting meaner." Kenny found a bigger stick and we were really beating the log, and singing at the top of our lungs. This worked for awhile, but I could see the bear was about ready to run us off, or worse. It was getting close to dusk when Dad heard us yelling, and came hurrying up, riding a packhorse. The bear backed off a little but he didn't leave. We packed up the rest of the elk and left. This was the same grizzly that killed the hunter the next fall. I killed that same grizzly two years later.

KEEP YOUR HEAD DOWN

When I was about fourteen years old – old enough to know better but still doing dumb things – my brother Kenny (three years younger than me) and I were camping up the North Fork of the Flathead River, close to the U.S. and Canadian border. We did not have a tent, just a canvas fly stretched over a ridge-pole like a tent, open at both ends. We were spending a few days of fishing and picking huckleberries. The fishing was so good it was almost to the point of being boring, as you caught a fish with just about every cast. We had hiked up a ridge to check for huckleberries, and ran into a big old silvertip grizzly. It wasn't alarmed by us, but moved on up the ridge a ways. That evening, after a fried fish supper we crawled into our sleeping bags. Our heads were facing opposite directions with his head on one end and mine at the other end of our shelter. In the middle of the night I was awakened by something moving near me. I thought of the big grizzly we had seen earlier that day, thinking maybe it had smelled our fish and was looking for a meal. I reached over slowly and got my pistol. I could hear a rustling sound at Kenny's end of our fly. I saw a grey shadow moving, then the moon came out from behind a cloud and I could see it was a big porcupine, and he was on top of Kenny's sleeping bag. The movement and weight of the porcupine was waking Kenny up. He was a sound sleeper and slept with his head down in his sleeping bag. He mumbled something and started to stir. I hollered to him, telling him, "Keep your head down and don't raise up!" I drew a bead on the porky and shot it, nearly scaring my little brother to death. Waking up with something on his sleeping bag and a loud gunshot in the night, he thought for sure the big grizzly was about to eat him. He was in real danger though. If he had stuck his head out of the bag the porcupine would have, for sure, slapped his face full of quills. It was real dumb of me to shoot it while it was on top of him. His sleeping was over for the night. It's a wonder that he ever went camping with his big brother again.

I FALL ON A GRIZZLY

When I was about fourteen years old, I was helping Dad pack a couple of elk out of a high mountain basin. We had the elk loaded on the pack horses, and were coming back down the mountain when the tracks of a large grizzly crossed our trail. I told Dad I wanted to try and get the bear, as it was such a fresh track. He told me, "Go ahead, I'll take the elk on down and you can catch up, but don't follow him too far, it's getting late." I said, "If I don't catch up to him in a hour I'll head on down the mountain."

The snow was about ten inches deep and soft, so it was quiet and easy tracking. I had followed the bear about a mile when the track led into a heavy yew brush area. A low-growing evergreen, yew brush grows in the moist shady canyons of western Montana. The Indians used it to make their bows, as it was hard and strong. The bow makers were very fussy in their selection. The stem had to be straight with no blemishes. I came to a cut, or ravine, about thirty feet across and ten feet or so deep filled with yew brush that the bear had gone down into. It was too brushy to see where the he'd come out. I just assumed he had gone on through and out the other side. I did not want to claw my way through the brush-filled ravine. There was a dead snag that had fallen a little ways below, and it made a nice bridge, but a slippery one. I started across it, pushing the snow off with my feet as I went. I was going slow and careful so I wouldn't slip and fall off the log. Unbeknownst to me that bear had come down the draw, and laid down for a nap right under the log I was walking on! When I was about half way across, a patch of snow fell onto the sleeping bear. The grizzly came boiling up out of the yew brush, scaring the devil out of me. I lost my balance and fell off the log, with a yell, right on top of the bear. This scared the bear as much as he had scared me. A yelling human jumping on him from nowhere was too much for the grizzly. The last I saw of that bear was his big butt going up over the bank. I'd had all the bear hunting I wanted for that day, and the bear probably never felt safe sleeping in the yew brush again. Dad thought it was funny when I told him what happened, but cautioned me again not to be walking wet logs. I knew better, but often did it, and took some hard falls as a result.

Looking back, some people have told me that my parents, especially my dad, let me do things way beyond my age. Dad was a good teacher, and knew what my brothers and sisters and I were capable of. We grew up taking some responsibility for ourselves at a young age. Also, the way of life for everybody was a lot different than it is now.

A CLOSE CALL

On a Friday morning in 1951, the Columbia Falls High school principal came to my freshman English class and had me come with him to his office. I thought I was in trouble, as I had been there before, but I didn't know why this time. Before we got to his office he told me, "Buddy there are a couple of hunters from back East here, and they want to hire you to help them get an elk. You are excused for the day; it will give you a chance to make some spending money, but be back here Monday morning."

That principal, Mr. Dulane Fulton, would be promoted to superintendent of schools the following year. Although I loved high school and my classmates, I was not the best student. It was hard to keep my mind on school work and not on the mountains, and hunting and fishing which was so dear to me. My saving grace was my love of history, and I read every book in the school library that pertained to it. I credit Mr. Fulton for keeping me in school. He understood me and had enough confidence in me to overlook some of my shortfalls, and I didn't want to let him down.

The two hunters were young men and seemed like nice fellows. That afternoon I helped one of the guys get an elk. The next day I took two pack horses and two saddle horses, and the hunter and I went up the mountain to pack the elk out. It was a miserable day with cold, drizzling rain. We left the saddle horses on top of the ridge. The elk was down in a steep canyon, and I led the pack horses down on foot. The hunter had a rifle with a scope on it which had fogged up, so he left it with the saddle horses. I was carrying my .30-30 carbine rifle, in case we saw another elk. When we got about a hundred yards from the elk, a real big grizzly bear stood up, grunting and popping his teeth. He dropped down on all four feet and started up the mountain in our direction at a slow lope. I had been raised around bears and I had respect for them, but no fear. I thought this bear had just heard our horses and didn't know where we were for sure, and was coming toward us by mistake. So I hollered and waved my arms to let it know where we were.

Instead of changing its course, it started bellowing, and came at us at a full charge. The pack horse bolted, as did the hunter. He had no gun! I jacked a shell into the chamber of my gun, and the bear was already there. It only took him a few seconds to get to me. Bears are amazingly fast when they want to be; I would be finding this out on several occasions in the future. I shot the bear between the eyes when he was about eight feet from me. He went right down, and I thought in my mind, it was just like shooting a pig, which I had helped Dad do a number of times. I was so sure of myself, I didn't get rattled at all at such a close encounter. I stepped up to him to nudge him with my foot to see if there was any life in him. I never had a chance to nudge him as he jumped up as fast as he had gone down. I really don't remember anything after that moment, except him knocking me down, but some way, I shot him again and broke his neck. It was lucky for me that I had a short carbine rifle as I probably couldn't have shot him again with a long rifle. I was not really hurt, just bruised, but I sure had the cockiness in me knocked out. It took a few minutes for it to sink in just how lucky I had been! The forehead is flat on a grizzly bear skull and slopes steeply back. My first bullet had not penetrated the skull but glanced off, only stunning him.

When we got the horses caught and settled down we loaded the elk. Then I put the bear hide I had skinned on top of the elk. It was a job getting it on! The hide was so heavy the two of us could hardly lift it.

This grizzly was huge, in the 800 to a 1,000 pound range. The hunter wanted the bear, but I didn't want to give it up. It was so big, and my first grizzly. He told me, "You live out here where you can always kill a grizzly." That was true but probably never one this big, and one that had almost killed me. He finally persuaded me, just a dumb kid, to give it to him for $10.00. I was even more sorry when Dad scolded me for it, and told me this was the same bear that he, my brother Kenny, and I had encountered two years before, in this same canyon. He said he was also certain this was the same bear that killed a hunter in that drainage the year before. Dad and my uncle Chris had searched for the missing man that fall but a snowstorm had covered his remains and he was not found until spring.

I was back in school Monday as I had promised Mr. Fulton, but only by luck, and the Lord looking out for me. Mr. Fulton died in 2011 at a Kalispell rest home. I went to see him a few months before he passed on. We had a great visit with a lot of laughs; his mind was sharp as a tack! I was so glad I had gone to see him, and he seemed awful happy to see me. What a grand old gentleman.

I spent most of the first half of my life working as an outfitter and big game guide in the fall, and as a steel or ironworker the rest of the year. I worked

Principal at Columbia Falls, Dulane Fulton.

all over the United States, from the east to the west coast. In 1956, when I was nineteen years old, I was working in Northern Minnesota for Bethlehem Steel on a big structural steel project. A old ironworker there called Jonesy nicknamed me Montana, and the name followed me around the country. In 1958 I was working on a uranium mill in New Mexico. One day in the lunch shack a crane operator was telling a story about a grizzly bear up in Montana that had killed a man, and how a kid named "Buddy Cheff" killed the big grizzly with a hunting knife. He said he had worked with the kid's uncle. He had the story mixed up. The man killed by the bear had fought him with his knife before he was killed. It was the next year that I had killed the bear, but with a gun. Curly, an ironworker I had worked with in Colorado the year before, was in the shack eating his lunch. He yelled across the room, "Hey Montana, that's your real name. Was that you?" I said, "yes" and tried to explain what really happened without making the operator sound like a liar. But they didn't buy it, and I was known as the kid that killed a grizzly with a knife. (Curly was killed on that job a few weeks later).

THE COACH

My years in high school were probably the most fun and carefree years of my life. The Columbia Falls school was well run, with good teachers and a wonderful bunch of talented kids in the classes. The principal, Carl Launer, ran a tight ship. I had a lot of friends, boys and girls, and I can't think of a single kid that I did not like. I hope the feeling was mutual.

There was one teacher that gave me a hard time whenever he got the chance. The head coach, Bud Beagle, was a young handsome guy with a good athletic build. He was a little on the cocky side, but really just a kid himself. We became good friends and have remained friends throughout our lives. I played three years of football for him, playing defense and offense in every quarter of every game, except one.

My junior year I had a good paying summer job ironworking and I hated to quit. I started school a week late, and had missed the early football practice. Coach Beagle was unhappy with me for missing the first two weeks of practice. During our first game of the season I sat, warming the bench through the first quarter. At the start of the second quarter, assistant coach Ralph Barnaby said, "Cheff, get in there." I lucked out and sacked the quarterback on the first play, and I was forgiven. I loved football, I guess because of the rough and tumble part of it. To me it was fun! If I had taken it a little more seriously I might have been a

Coach at Columbia Falls, Bud Beagle.

better player. Beagle called me the team clown, and chewed me out sometimes, and twice he benched me for part of a quarter.

One time when we were playing Kalispell he got pretty mad at me. I had a real big guy playing opposite me who weighs about two hundred eighty pounds. I was at one hundred seventy-five. When the ball was snapped I was faster than he was, and I jerked him forward so he was on his hands and knees. I swung on to his back, grabbed his jersey, leaned back and started to spur him, like riding a bucking horse. This caused our team a fifteen yard penalty, an unhappy coach, and I sat the rest of the quarter on the bench.

Beagle and I were always wrestling and he often played tricks on me. I was so gullible that it was easy for him to do. The best trick he played would have gotten him fired if it had taken place in today's world. During my senior year we were out on the field, starting practice. I was standing, talking to my buddy Roger Christensen, who was our team center, and a darn good one, when Beagle walked up to me. He had a wild look on his face and he hollered in a loud voice, "Cheff, I have taken all the shit I'm going to take from you." All the team stopped to see what was going on. He pulled out a pistol and shot me in the chest. I grabbed my chest and fell over backwards, thinking I was dead. Roger and my teammates

Football photo, Bud Cheff Jr. in front of Columbia Falls High School.

were in shock, also thinking I had been shot. The whole team thought it was for real because they knew we were always scuffling, and they thought, as I did, the coach had finally snapped. If this had happened during track season the joke would not have worked so well. He shot me with a blank starter pistol! When I finally realized I hadn't been shot and got to my feet, Beagle had tears running down his face from laughing.

That same year I went out for the boxing team. I didn't know sickum about boxing, but had been in a lot of street fights. We had two good boxing coaches, brothers George and Marvin Ingraham. They spent a lot of time with me, trying to refine me a little. I learned a lot from them and was ready for my first smoker. Coach Bud Beagle had come to the smoker to see me fight. He was setting in the first row right below me. When the bell rang and we came out fighting I forgot everything the coaches had taught me. I came out swinging and never stopped until I had knocked my opponent out of the ring. He wouldn't get back in, he said, "I'm not going to fight that guy, he's crazy!" Embarrassed, I looked down at Coach Beagle, who was laughing so hard he fell off his chair.

My next smoker went a little better; we were boxing the Ronan, and, I think Kalispell teams. Henry Camel was our neighbor, and a friend, from Ronan. He was a Ronan boxing coach and had been a professional boxer. He boxed an exhibition match that night, and when it was my turn he came to my corner and coached me. His son, Marvin, became the cruiserweight world champion.

Beagle later quit coaching and became a much-loved principal at Target Range school in Missoula, Montana. We have remained good friends all these years, and he has been a supporter of the museum since it started in 1996. The summer of 2011, he and a friend were going through the museum with me when he told me, "Buddy, you have really done a great job here." It was a special compliment coming from him. Thanks, Coach, for all the good memories.

GOING DUCK HUNTING

Life in the 1950's and first half of the 1960's in the small towns of Montana was nothing like the life of today. There were no drugs in the towns or in schools, and although there was under-age drinking, the parents kept a tight handle on in it. The worst violence you might find in the school would be a black eye or bloody nose after school. No one would think of threatening someone with a knife or gun, but every boy had a knife in his pocket. During hunting season most boys had a rifle or a shotgun in their car in the school parking lot. It would not be unusual for some to have a box of shells in their locker to trade with some one.

I had a funny experience related to this, although I didn't think it was funny at the time. In my junior year of high school my buddy Hugh Adams and I decided to skip school and go duck hunting. We were just heading out in my '46 Mercury when Hugh realized he didn't have his shotgun shells. They were in his school locker. I drove around back of the school on the south end so Hugh could go in the door that went to the shop building. He had to go upstairs to his locker. He had only been gone a minute when the door opened and out came Mister Launer, the school principal, who was heading out to the shop. I tried to scrunch down to the floor board so he wouldn't see me in the car. The car had a starter button on the dashboard, and when I scrunched down my knee hit the starter button. The car jerked forward, and in my panic, my knee hit twice more. The car went erunt, erunt, erunt, and then everything was quiet except for my heart pounding. Then there was a tapping on my car window. I looked up and Mister Launer was standing there. He beckoned me with his finger to get out of the car. I had just stepped out when Hugh came out the school door with his shells. We were both caught by a darn starter button. Mr. Launer said, "Put the shells in the car and get to your classes." He had no problem with the guns and shells but he did with skipping school. I could see a sliver of a smile on his face and thinking about it now, I bet he chuckled all the way out to the shop.

MEMORIES OF DAYS IN MONTANA'S WILDERNESS

Some memories stay trapped in your mind, vivid and alive as if you had experienced them only yesterday. One particular December day in 1955 holds such a memory for me; I can still feel the complete stillness of the snowy canyons and the edges of the moonlit sky. I was trapping in the South Fork of the Flathead River drainage, primarily for marten, but also for mink, fox, coyote, ermine, and beaver.

The winter before I had a permit to catch fifty beaver between Spotted Bear and Big Prairie, but it had not been very profitable, as the price of beaver had dropped. This winter I had fifty miles of line out, too much for one person, but at nineteen I was still young and thought I could do anything. It took three days on snowshoes to cover my line one way. This was before four-wheel drive pickups and snowmobiles. I had a small makeshift cabin on both ends of the line and a lean-to in the middle. One of the lines went up the mountain from the first camp, making a loop up one ridge and down the next, then back to camp. I would spend the first day on this line and the second day work up the river to the lean-to camp. On the third day I would continue up river to my main camp. The fourth day I worked a short line up the mountain that took about three hours to run, round trip. I would spend the rest of the day working on skins and resting, and on the following day, start back down again.

Part of the winter catch, snowshoes and furs.

Winter had come early and hard that year; the snow was about four feet deep at the river level and seven to ten feet higher on the mountain. The temperature had dropped way below zero and stayed there for a number of weeks. The trees were still full of sap when this cold snap hit and for days it sounded like a war zone. The cold would split the trees, which were mostly spruce and some fir. When the trees split it sounded like a rifle shot in the cold clear air. This loud booming went on for several days. It didn't kill the trees but ruined the quality of lumber from them. The creeks started freezing from the bottom up, making the big ones hard to cross. One afternoon I was crossing a large creek that was frozen from the bottom up, carrying my snowshoes since my trail was beat down hard enough to walk without them. There was a kind of snow and ice bridge formed over the main channel of the creek. As I walked across this, it gave way, dropping me into the creek. The water was swift and deep, and I had trouble getting out onto solid ice.

I managed to hold onto my snowshoes, but I was soaked from head to toe. It was way below zero and I was still three miles from my cabin. My mind was going a mile a minute on how best to save myself. My hands were already so numb with cold I could barely move my fingers, and I doubted if I could get a fire going before I froze. I decided to try to make it to my camp, where I always kept my pitch shavings ready to light a match to them. I started running, thinking the exertion would generate enough heat to keep me from freezing.

Everything I had on was wool, my long johns, pants, shirt, socks, and coat. That's what saved me, along with the running, even though my wool clothes were heavy, water soaked, and frozen stiff on the outside. On the inside, even being wet they held some of my body heat. My beard was frozen, my face was caked with ice and I could barely see, as my eye lashes froze together. I made it to camp exhausted, but alive, and got the fire going with the first match. I looked at my thermometer. It read 22 below. I was lucky to have made it, and being in good physical shape helped the luck along.

One clear, cold December morning I left my lean-to camp before daylight. The snow reflected the bright moonlight and I could see quite well. This camp was cold and uncomfortable, and I was anxious to get moving on the trail and warm up. I didn't have any marten in my sets, only one mink and an ermine. When it's really cold, the marten don't move around very much. I had been trapping for several weeks and was getting hardened in, and my trail was well packed so I was making good time. I could run most of the day on snowshoes, only stopping at a set when it needed attention. When I say run, I don't mean bolting through the woods, but sort of moving at a running walk.

I reached my upper camp early that day, with a couple of daylight hours left, so I decided to run the short line that afternoon, instead of waiting until morning. The weather had changed during the day, warming up and clouding over, and now it was starting to snow. I had gone about two miles up the mountain when I saw a grizzly track crossing my line trail. As I studied the tracks I was amazed at the huge feet this bear had! It was snowing hard and I knew that it had only been a few minutes since the grizzly had been there. I continued up my line, wondering what this big fella was doing, still out. He should have been denned up four or five weeks earlier. I got to the end of the line and started back down with only one marten. When I reached the spot where the grizzly had crossed the trail, I realized that he had come back, and was following my tracks, backtracking me toward camp. I followed and saw that he had stopped at each set, tearing it up and eating the bait. I used sockeye salmon, catching them at the end of their spawning runs up the river earlier in the season, and freezing them for my winter trapping. These runs are a thing of the past now.

It was getting dark fast and I was anxious to get to camp, but I didn't really want to rush right into that big bear's arms. I had a .22 pistol, but it seemed pretty puny and didn't offer much comfort at the thought of meeting such a big grizzly in the dark. I caught up with the bear about seventy-five yards from camp. I didn't see him until he huffed at me, and even then I could just make out his outline in the darkness.

I had my pistol in my hand for what little help it would give me. I didn't stop, just kept on walking at the same pace, right by him, with only twenty five or thirty feet separating us. As I passed him, I could feel the hair on the back of my neck standing up. The bear didn't move.

I strained to hear something, but there was utter silence, except for the soft scrunch of my own feet on the snow. It was hard not to hurry, but I did not want to do anything to break the spell of truce that seemed to hang in the air. I got to the cabin and lit my lantern, since I had no flashlight, then dug my salmon cache out of the snow and took it into the cabin with me. The salmon runs were over and there would be no chance to get more if the bear ate them. I built a fire in the stove, took the bucket and axe to chop the ice, as well as the lantern, and started down to get some water. The creek was about seventy yards away, and I didn't want to leave the cabin and have the bear rob my fish and grub, but I told myself he had probably gone on about his business. When I got back with the water, I set the bucket down to open the door.

Suddenly I caught a movement to my left at the same time I heard something. I raised the lantern up in time to see the big fellow walking away from the cabin. He stopped and stared at me, but didn't seem to be

Winter in Montana.

a bit scared, or for that matter, aggressive. I told him to go to bed, and went in to start my supper. As the cabin warmed up the food odors must have enticed the bear, and it wasn't long before I heard him sniffing around the cabin. He stood up and leaned against the wall several times. If he had taken a notion to, he could have demolished my flimsy cabin in a few minutes. I told him what a good shot I was with my pistol and all the things I would do to him if he tried to come in. He must have believed me because he quit pushing on the cabin wall. The last thing I heard as I drifted off to sleep was his nose sniffing around the cabin. The next morning he was gone and I never saw him again. He must have gone back to his winter den, leaving me with the memory of that exciting night. In my lifetime I had had many encounters with these beautiful but dangerous bears, and my admiration for them increases with each incident.

I had a number of other exciting experiences that winter, some not so good, but they all ended well. The best thing of all for me was knowing that I was the only person in that wilderness that winter. To know that I was totally dependent on myself in this beautiful but rugged paradise was a feeling beyond what I could ever describe.

RIDING THE RAILS

In 1955 I graduated from high school. That spring I went to work for Chester Brown, (Brownie) building two bridges on the new highway up the Middle Fork of the Flathead River. It was the most fun job I ever had. I thought the world of Brownie and he liked me, so we had a lot of fun as we worked. Some days we were the only two ironworkers on the job. We started early, worked like the devil to get way ahead in our work so we could go fishing in the afternoon. That summer I stayed in Martin City with my sister Ola and her husband, Don Lietz. Mom and Dad had already moved back to the ranch at Ronan.

When the job was finished that fall the fur prices on marten and mink were good so I laid out about fifty miles of trap line and spent the winter trapping in the South Fork of the Flathead. In March I came out and shopped my furs, but the market had dropped and I only received half of what I had expected. I left my traps and gear in my trapper line shack, planning on going back for them when the snow melted. It was wet and sloppy when I came out, and was very hard traveling on snowshoes but the snow was too deep without them. I brought out some of my traps, but I had a ninety pound pack of furs and gear, and I could not manage any more.

After I got back to Martin City, the business agent, Warren Aycock told me ironworkers were needed on a new taconite plant near Aurora, Minnesota. I decided to go, and never had time to go back for my traps. I often wonder who ended up with them, about one hundred fifty traps, stretchers and camp gear.

My brother Kenny came with me to Belton (now called West Glacier) in my '46 Mercury. I gave Kenny my car, waved good bye and hopped a freight train headed east. There were no empty cars on the train, it was fully loaded and all the boxcars were locked. I got into an open gondola loaded with machinery. There were two bums already on it, the only place on the whole train with room enough to ride.

Right after I got on, a storm hit. The bums had a jug of wine, which they shared with me, and this warmed me up for the next hour or so. Because the train was fully loaded with about a hundred cars, it was moving slowly. We reached the summit about midnight. The temperature had dropped to zero, and my new friends and I were almost frozen. The train pulled onto the siding to let another train go by, and while we were stopped, one of the bums went over to the station house and bummed a jug of coffee. I didn't drink coffee at that time, but I was so cold I drank some with relish as the train started off again. The bums had a big wool blanket that they were wrapped in, and they invited me to join them. I

Bud Jr., brother Kenny behind him, connecting.

crawled in with them gratefully, and we cuddled up for body heat. It's funny how circumstances can change your thinking. The day before I would never have dreamed I would be gratefully drinking and sleeping with two quite dirty and unpleasant smelling hoboes. After that trip, I looked at hoboes with a different light.

I had been told not to carry any money on the train, or I would be rolled or killed for it. Since I had about two hundred dollars in my duffle bag, this warning was always on my mind, but these two were pretty nice and caring guys. The train stopped again on a siding near Cut Bank, Montana, to let other trains pass, and then continued on to Havre, Montana. The two hoboes were heading back east, but when the train stopped in Havre, the temperature was way below zero. They got off and said, "No one can live riding in an open car in this kind of cold." They tried to get me to get off with them, but I said I was going on. They said "So long, Kid, you're going to die on this train!" and they were almost right. In a few hours I was wishing I had gotten off at Havre, it was so cold! I had not realized how much the two hoboes and their blanket had helped in keeping me from freezing. I started Indian dancing to keep my blood pumping. I danced most of the day until I played out. I probably hold the record for Indian dancing the most miles; it must have been over two hundred.

Bud Jr. on steel column, connecting a girder.

I remembered Dad talking about guys putting paper in their clothes and covering up with newspapers to keep warm during the Depression. The car right behind me had some big machinery in it, covered with heavy paper. I climbed back to the car with great difficulty, as I was so cold I could barely move, and I almost fell between the cars. Using my pocket knife, I cut off a big piece of paper and took it back to my car. I rolled up in this paper, and it helped a lot, especially keeping the wind out. The train never stopped in the towns we passed. I would have gotten off if it had.

Finally it stopped on a siding, and I was getting desperate. I could see lights a long way off, but I had no idea where we were. The wind and snow was blowing and I was so cold I had a hard time getting my mind to work. I felt I probably would not survive much longer. A brakeman with a light came down the track and I thought maybe he would let me get in the caboose with him. I hollered at him when he came back, but he shined his light on me and never said a word, just ran back down the tracks and the train took off again.

I was so cold I forgot how hungry and thirsty I was; all I wanted to do was to go to sleep. Looking back it seems I was lacking in good sense, but I did know enough that if I went to sleep, I would never wake up again. Rolled up in that paper, I counted, and at each count I would wiggle my fingers and toes. I would drift off and then remember I could not sleep! And then I would start counting again. I was so tired and numb from cold I could barely move my arms and legs. It seemed this went on forever. Finally the train slowed down, entering a big town and I thought it was going to stop. It went through the town slowly, then started to pick up speed. I was desperate to get off; I managed to get my duffel bag and push it over the side of the car, then pushed myself over headfirst. The fall and activity kind of revived me and I picked up my duffel bag and walked back into the town.

Everybody stared at me and acted like they didn't want to get too close. I went into a bathroom at a service station and when I looked in the mirror, I couldn't believe it was me. My face was swollen up and it was a bluish-black color, smeared with blood from a cut on my forehead, as well as one of my hands, bleeding from my dive off the train. I hadn't felt anything when I fell. I washed up as best I could and started on into town. My hands and feet were thawing out and hurting like the devil. I also had something in my eye that was really bothering me. I rented a hotel room above a restaurant and bar, took a bath and changed my clothes, then went down and ordered a big plate of ham and eggs. Boy, they tasted good! Next I found an eye doctor and he took a piece of steel out of my eye but had a hard time, it was so deep, and a part broke off. He had to leave that part in. I was ugly enough before, now I had a patch on my eye too.

The next morning I bought a Pullman train ticket to Virginia, Minnesota. I was completely broke now. I had been on that freight train from Sunday afternoon until mid-morning Tuesday. It took about two weeks for my body to get back to normal. My face peeled and my feet were so sore it was painful to walk. I would have saved money and time if I had bought a ticket from the start, but I had always wanted to ride a freight train. If it had been summer it would have been okay but the train was traveling with that blizzard all the way.

When I got to Virginia, Minnesota, I went right to the bank to cash a check, planning to draw money from my account in Columbia Falls, Montana. They wouldn't cash my check. My looks and a patch on my eye didn't help. Finally I convinced the banker to call my bank, and the person who answered said it couldn't be me because I was in Martin City. I told him to ask for Donna, a girl who worked there that I knew well. I got on the phone and she recognized my voice, and said, "Buddy, what are you doing in Minnesota?" The bank would only let me cash a check for $30.00; they still didn't trust me.

I got directions to the job site and was told it was near Aurora, to the north. While hitchhiking from Virginia to Aurora my luck changed for the better. A Bethlehem Steel pick-up stopped and gave me a ride. The driver was the head superintendent for Bethlehem Steel, Mr. Gibson. I don't remember his first name, as I never used it. In those days, you did not greet your elders by their first name, it was always Mister or Mrs. He was not bothered by my eye patch, he also had a black patch over one of his eyes. Later on he told me how he had lost his eye. He also got a piece of steel in it when he was a young man, and had gone to the company doctor. The doctor was drunk and put acid in his eye by mistake, and burned his eye out. He took me to the job and got me signed in with the company and with the union steward. When we drove in at the job site, I was surprised to see the main office building had a Montana Anaconda Copper Company sign on it. Next Mr. Gibson took me to the construction camp where I signed into the barracks. He gave me a ride to and from work for the next four days, until I got settled in and found a ride to work. He told me stories of how they put up steel when he was young, using guy derricks powered with horses and steam donkey engines. I will never forget that busy but kind man, who took the time to help a dumb country boy. Sometimes when I get disillusioned with mankind, I think back through my life and remember so many good and caring people that I have met along the way, and I say a prayer of thanks to them for helping me on my journey.

SCARFACE PEAK

While guiding hunters for my dad in the fall of 1957 I had one of my most hair-raising experiences. I have had numerous narrow escapes throughout my life, most of them on bridges and high steel structures. But they usually happened so fast, and I was so busy trying to save myself that I did not have time to get scared. This time was different. I had plenty of time to pray and do some repenting.

Every year I took a leave from my ironworker job, wherever it might be, and worked as a big game guide for my dad. I was an ironworker connector, which required me to be in top physical shape. Climbing the steel columns with thirty pounds of tools and bolts hanging from your belt required you to be strong in the shoulders, arms and hands. There were two connectors on each job, and they were considered the top dogs on the job. There were a lot of guys that wanted to be connectors and I worked hard to stay in top shape. I always wanted to be the best, and my life often depended on it. If you got too tired you were at risk of falling.

The year this incident happened we were camped at our upper Holbrook campsite in the Bob Marshall Wilderness. It was a beautiful fall day. I was guiding two hunters for elk and mountain goat, both in their late thirties, and nice guys. We left camp that morning, climbing to the top of the Holbrook and Burnt Creek Divide, which is about seven thousand feet in elevation. I was checking the high pockets along the divide for elk. There was also a chance for goats in this area. We followed the ridge to Scarface Peak with no luck. We were a long way from camp and the hunters were getting a little tired. I suggested the hunters take a rest, and I would climb the peak and look at the backside for goats.

I noticed one of them was limping a little. I didn't know until that night that he had a very deformed leg. He was a tough, gutsy guy to have made the hike we took on that leg, and never complain a bit.

From where we were, it was an easy climb up Scarface, following a goat trail to the area I thought we might find some goats. I decided to

Bud Jr. on Chimney Rock, Mission Mountains.

climb around the north face of the peak, so I could look down on any that were there. It is hard to sneak up on a goat from below, but it's easy to sneak down on them. They are generally looking down, and the breeze is usually going up. If I spotted any Billy goats I would go back, get the hunters and take them up the goat trail.

    I started up and around the north face of the peak, carrying my octagon-barreled 1894 .32 Special Winchester. When I was fifteen years old I had traded my Uncle Chris my .30-30 carbine for this gun. He had let me take it to use deer hunting one day. I came upon several deer, and one was a big buck, so I shot it. When I got to it, I could see the bullet had gone through the buck and killed another one. "Two in one shot," I thought. "This gun has special powers." Because the gun did not have a sling, I always carried it in my hand or the crook of my arm. In those days I was seldom without my gun. I needed it in case a hunter crippled an animal, and some of the hunters insisted I carry a gun, being a little leery of grizzly bears, since there were a lot of them in our area. I personally had no fear of a grizzly, but I had a lot of respect for them. I have seen hundreds in my lifetime and I still get a thrill each time I see one. On this day we saw a lot of bear sign, but no bears, just a few mule deer. Thinking back now, I don't know why I didn't leave my gun with the hunters while I checked for goat. At the age of twenty-one years, I did not have the wisdom of an older person, even though I thought I did at the time.

I don't think I realized that I had my gun in my hand until I needed that hand for climbing. I had been guiding since I was twelve, and I did know the mountains. My dad, the best mountain man in the Northwest was my teacher. I had never tried to climb this side of the peak before, and it was a lot harder that I expected. I worked around the face quite a ways until I could not see the ridge or the hunters. I should have turned back then, but I didn't. On the difficult places I tied my gun to the back of my belt with a leather thong so I could use both hands freely. I thought I could get to the top and come back down the goat trail. I came to some very difficult places and knew I was past the point where I could turn back. Anyone who has done mountain climbing knows it's a lot harder to go down than to go up, unless you are using a line. Going up you can see and test your hand and foot holds, but going down you can't see where to step. When I'm climbing peaks for fun I carry some chalk so I can mark my steps at the bad spots.

It was easy going for a while, and I was getting close to the top. Then it got bad, and I started to worry. Finally I got stuck on a narrow ledge and knew I couldn't go back down. There was another ledge about seven or eight feet above me. It stuck out further than the one I was on, and I couldn't see what was above it. I didn't know if I could go any farther if I did get on it. I knew if I committed to trying to pull myself

Laurie Cheff on Charlotte Peak, Bob Marshall Wilderness.

up to the next ledge and didn't make it, I wouldn't be able to get back to the one I was on. I would fall at least five or six hundred feet before I hit the first ledge or out-cropping.

There was a lot going through my mind. I thought of trying to call to the hunters to go back to camp and get my dad, but I didn't know if they would hear me. It would be dark before they got to camp, and Dad was guiding hunters in another canyon, and probably would not get back to camp until late. My mom, who was cooking in camp, would be worried sick. She might encourage Dad to climb the mountain in the dark and my foolishness might get him killed. I was also wrestling with my pride. The thought of Bud Cheff's son having to call for help was a crushing thing for me. I had spent my whole life trying to make him proud of me and to live up to his reputation. I just could not make myself call out. I thought of untying my gun from my belt and leaving it, but I decided if I was going to die I wanted to die with my gun with me.

I had to stretch to reach high enough to get a hand hold. I knew when I took my weight off my feet, my body would swing out into space and I wouldn't be able to get back on the ledge. I spent a lot of time feeling and testing my hand holds, all the while cussing myself, repenting, and hoping God would forgive my sins. I sure had a sick feeling in my stomach. I knew my chance of making it up onto the ledge was very slim. I thought of all my loved ones and prayed for strength. It was really hard to take my weight off my feet. I can feel it all over again right now, just writing this. As my body swung out over space, I thought it was my end. The next thing I remember, I was pulling myself onto the ledge.

I could hardly believe I had made it. The world never looked so good as it did right then. The rest of the climb to the top was easy. As I looked down, the only goats I saw were a nanny and two kids. I was glad, as I did not feel like doing any more climbing that day. When I got back to the hunters I didn't say a word about my close call. I didn't tell my dad about it until three or four years later. Even now, fifty-five years later, I get a knot in my stomach thinking about hanging in space from that ledge.

Daughter Jo on McDonald Peak.

THE BAREFOOT BRIDE

In 1958 while I was working as a ironworker on the construction of a uranium plant in New Mexico, I received a draft notice from Uncle Sam to report for a physical at Butte, Montana. This was not welcoming news to me. I had a good paying job and a new '58 Ford hard-top car. My lifelong buddy, Webb Garey, and I started out in my new car to go to the Mardi Gras in New Orleans, but we never made it. We ended up broke in New Mexico, but we had a lot of fun getting there. There were two big uranium mills being built near Grants, and I went right to work as an ironworker connector. Webb went to work as a millwright a week later. We almost starved the first week, until I got a paycheck. The first thing we did was go to the store to get groceries, and there was a cute girl working there. We both wanted to ask her for a date, so we flipped a coin and Webb won the flip. Her name was Addie Lou. I think Webb cheated on the flip, but he denied it, and it's hard to argue with a six-foot-six guy like Webb. This turned out to be his lucky day. Addie was the love of his life and they ended up getting married, and fifty-three years later, still are.

I went to Butte and took my physical. I rodeoed for a couple months until I got orders to report to Fort Ord, California. Before I left, my uncle Junior said he knew the perfect girl for me, a daughter of some friends. He wanted to arrange a date between us, but I wasn't very interested, and neither was she, so it never happened. I went on to the army, but before I left I traded my '58 Ford in on a 1960 Ford Starliner, so I would have a new car when I got out.

I got home from the army just in time to help Dad with the fall packing. It was good to be home and back on a horse again, and in my beautiful mountains. After hunting season ended we pulled the horses shoes, and they were put on winter pasture. Then I went to work, ironworking on the new addition being built at the Missoula-Frenchtown pulp mill. Again, Uncle Junior told me he wanted me to meet this girl, Laurie Kopelman, the same girl he had wanted me to date before I got drafted. He said, "You have to meet her." So I agreed to go on a date with her.

The new 1960 Ford Starliner that I had ordered when I got home from the service had not been delivered yet, so I borrowed my friend Terry Stiner's new Pontiac. Terry came with me to pick up my blind date. The plan was to drop him off at the Kings Inn Bar, where all the ironworkers hung out, after we picked up my date.

I was really nervous. I had gone on a blind date while I was in the army, but I saw her picture before hand. I had no idea what Laurie looked like, only that uncle Junior said she was real pretty, and I would like her. Terry and I found the house and her mother let us in. She seated us on the couch, and said Laurie would be out soon. A few minutes later a young woman came out, and I sighed in relief, as she was good looking and seemed nice. But she said, "I'm Sharon, Laurie's sister. She will be right out."

Now I was scared again, thinking, "Why did I agree to this date?" Terry was not helping any, whispering sly comments.

About five minutes later, Laurie came out in a form-fitting white dress. She had beautiful dark hair and a face like an angel, with deep sky blue eyes. I was at loss for words. Terry hit me in the ribs with his elbow, and whispered, "You lucky S.O.B.!" It surely was the best day of my life!!

This was a busy time for me. I was helping Dad and Mom on the ranch, ironworking all day, and riding saddle and bareback broncs in rodeos every weekend that I could. I had just started to compete in rodeos when I was drafted, and I was anxious to get back into it. Besides all these activities, I was trying to romance this lovely young woman who was stealing my heart. I never got more than four or five hours of sleep a night. I finally asked Laurie to marry me, but she said no, that she wanted to but she was not sure that she should. She had been married before and had a little baby. She went to Idaho to live with her married cousins for a while so she could sort things out. I was heartbroken; for some reason I had always thought when I found the right one and fell in love, the girl would just naturally be in love with me too. It wasn't that I thought I was so great that a girl would fall in love with me, it was just the way I thought love worked. I guess seeing how Mom and Dad always loved each other made me think love was always like that.

At this time Dad was also ironworking at the pulp mill, and was my foreman on the raising gang, I had gotten pretty reckless up on the iron, and one day Dad told me, "If you don't quit taking so many chances up there I am going to fire you. I don't want to see my son fall to his death while working for me." I slowed down some, but was still a little wild up there. One day I was sitting on top of a steel column about ninety feet above the ground waiting for the next beam to be raised up to me. It was a nice day and I was feeling strong and invincible. I had the urge to do a handstand on top of the column. As I started to raise my body up, a voice of reason whispered, "Are you crazy? You can't do this on the ground without going over backwards half the time!" I let my body gently back down to the safety of the steel column, not feeling quite so invincible.

About the end of June, Laurie came back to Missoula from Idaho. One Sunday Uncle Junior, who was going to Polson to see his daughter,

Connecting iron, brothers Buck & Bud Jr. climbing column.

Yvonne, asked her if she would like to go with him, since he would be stopping off at the ranch on his way. Laurie accepted his offer, but when they got there, she was very nervous, not knowing what my folks would think, or what I would think. I was gone to a rodeo, but Mom welcomed Laurie, and invited her to stay until I returned. She knew I would be glad to see her. When they saw me driving up, Mom told Laurie to go into the bedroom and wait, since I always went in there first to hang up my hat and coat. Then we would have some privacy to greet each other. Mom was so wise, and always knew what was in people's minds and hearts. I had been dating another girl from Missoula and she and her girl friend had been up to the ranch to see me, but Mom knew she was not the right one, and did not invite her to stay. She knew that Laurie was the one in my heart.

I went into the bedroom and hung up my hat, and when I turned around Laurie was standing there. She looked like a scared rabbit ready to cry or run. I was at a loss for words so I didn't say a thing, I just took her in my arms and kissed her. A couple weeks later I took her horseback riding over on the big ridge by McDonald Lake, to watch the sunset. Mother Nature was on my side and it was a beautiful evening, made extra special with a wonderful display of the Northern Lights. You just could not have found a lovelier view, or evening, and I asked her again to marry me. She said yes as I held her tight in my arms, with her head on my shoulder. Even the horses seemed to know it was special, they softly blew their approval as I kissed her under the spectacular sky, with the lights blinking in the valley below. It was a happy ride back to the ranch for both of us.

We planned an August wedding and I gave Laurie an engagement ring. On Sunday, the week before our wedding, I was riding in a rodeo. It was a two-day show but I had to work on Saturday so Bob Schall, who was putting the rodeo on, let me ride all my horses Sunday. I was setting in first place on my Saturday's bareback ride, and I had drawn Yellow Gold, a good bucker, for my second horse. I was setting tight in perfect time with the horse, spurring every jump and racking up points. Billy Schall, my rodeo hero, would have smiled and given me the thumbs up right then. I heard one of the Schall girls hollering, "Ride him Buddy!" Just before the whistle blew my rigging came loose and I was bucked off, plus the horse kicked me in the head. I usually put my rigging on myself, and check my cinch. This one time I had not, and was out of the money. On my wedding day I had the back of my head shaved and stitched up. My lovely bride didn't seem to mind, her eyes shined with love when she looked at me that day, and said, "I do."

We rented my Uncle Vila's house, at the foot of the mountains, for our first home. Laurie spent the night before our wedding there by herself. Her mother and sister Sharon were supposed to come in

Sharon, Laurie, Bud Jr. and Don Lietz.

the morning, and help her get ready, then take her to the St. Ignatius Mission where we were to be married. Unknown to all of us, Laurie's family and a lot of others coming from Missoula had gotten hung up for more than a hour in road construction near Evaro. When Laurie didn't show up, my Mom sent my brother Mick and sister Roxy over to Vila's house to check on her, as there was no phone in the house. They met Laurie walking down the road in her wedding dress, barefooted, carrying her shoes. The hitch-hiking bride! I wish we had a picture of her then. On the way to the Mission, Laurie told Mick, "It's okay if you go faster." Mick was just learning to drive and said afterward that he was already going faster than he felt was safe! Although the wedding was held up, it all turned out well, even if I wondered for a while if I was getting jilted. After the reception we went to Polson for dinner and then came back to our new home. I thought it was never going to get dark. I finally asked Laurie, "Do you think it's dark enough to go to bed?" She bashfully said, "I think so."

Laurie and Bud, leaving on honeymoon.

The next morning we

were up early and got the horses ready to go into the Missions on our honeymoon. We camped at Summit Lake and had beautiful weather for the whole trip. The first morning we looked out of the tipi and there were eleven elk grazing with our horses. We spent the first day fishing, skinny-dipping and enjoying the mountains and each other. The second day I took Laurie on the old Indian trail over Goat Foot Pass. I wanted to check the elk sign in Crazy Horse for the fall hunting. I left Laurie in a high alpine meadow on the Crazy Horse Divide, as she was getting a little saddle sore. I went on down into Crazy Horse and was gone about three hours. When I returned, I looked down at the meadow and there were twenty-seven mountain goats in a half-circle around Laurie, wondering who this strange girl was sleeping in their meadow. As I approached the goats moved back. I woke Laurie, and told her, "Look, you had some

Laurie, fishing on our honeymoon.

Laurie at Uncle Vila's, our first home.

visitors while you were sleeping." It was a lovely sight, seeing her sleeping on that warm sunny day with the goats looking on. It made me think of the story book of Heidi.

The honeymoon ended too soon, and we had to head back to the real world. On the way out we were crossing a rock slide and I stirred up a hive of rock bees. They took out their anger on Laurie's horse as she came by, and Laurie got bucked off in a jumble of boulders. She wasn't hurt bad, just a couple cuts and bruises. She took the mishap right in stride, and I knew then, I had picked the right girl to be my partner.

MOOSE CREEK ADVENTURE

In 1964 I was offered a job outfitting and running a hunting and fishing lodge in the Selway Wilderness in Idaho. I flew my family and gear, plus horse grain, in an old DC-2 from Johnson's Flying Service from Missoula to the Forest Service landing strip at the Moose Creek Ranger Station. It was too big a plane for that narrow canyon and short landing strip. We had a hair raising flight, but Cookie, the man flying it, was the best bush pilot in the country and got us there safely. It was a mile to the ranch lodge, located across the river, and we hauled our gear in the ranch's jeep and trailer. Laurie and the kids walked across the swinging bridge while I put our gear in the trolley beside it, then pulled it across.

The plane had to stay the night, and wait for the heavy morning air to fly out. I left Laurie and the three kids, Jim, five years old, Buddy the Third, four years old, and Laurie Jo, one, alone at the lodge while I rode back to Missoula on the plane. Then I went to our Ronan ranch, loaded up the horses and hauled them by truck to Elk Summit

Buddy III and Jim holding their fish.

in Idaho. I trailed them the thirty-five miles to the hunting lodge at Moose Creek.

It was not a profitable year for us, but an interesting one. There were a lot of rattlesnakes there and I had several close calls with them. Laurie was kept busy watching out for the kids, with the river by the door and the worry of snakes. She

Laurie catching big fish.

really had her hands full, cooking for everyone, cleaning the guest rooms, and doing the laundry. Once in a while between parties she managed to do a little fishing, which she loved.

We got busy with summer guests and the baby, Jo, got the German measles so Laurie's mother came in by plane to help with the kids. She stayed about two weeks; then we had the plane come pick her up and fly her back to Missoula. I had hired a young man from Orofino, Idaho as a guide and wrangler, as he was familiar with the area. I was short on horses and had brought a four-year-old mare in to break, and she turned out to be a real outlaw. I had to rope her every morning, snub her tight to the post and tie a foot up to saddle her. She was bad for biting, striking, and kicking so you really had to watch her. I would untie her from the post after I got in the saddle, and let her buck. She never bucked me off but she never gave up trying. After her morning buck, she was pretty good the rest of the day, nice soft riding, and tough.

Moose Creek rattlesnakes.

The wrangler was watching me one day after a couple of weeks of this morning battle. He said, "You know Bud, you are nuts, only a crazy man would ride a horse like that."

The Moose Creek Ranch and lodge was about four miles upriver from us. It was a pretty big dude ranch, and several times Laurie rode her horse there to visit the women. It was a treat for her to get away from the men and talk to women for a change. The ranch boss asked me to break a couple of horses for them which I did, and I was able to use them for a while. I finally had to go back to Ronan and bring in more horses.

It was a long, three day trip for me. I left early in the morning riding a strong, fast-traveling Thoroughbred gelding I called Spook. He had a tendency to always find something to shy away from. At one point I was trotting across a long meadow when a cow moose joined us. She seemed to really like Spook and was trotting along, right close to him. I kicked Spook into a gallop and the moose stayed right with us until we got back into the woods, and then she quit. I just got to the top of Elk Summit, about a mile from my truck, when Spook bogged his head and went to bucking. He caught me completely off guard, riding with loose reins and my mind wondering if the truck would start. He was a hard bucker and jarred me loose in the saddle on his first jump, and I couldn't quite regain my seat. I did not want to get bucked off in all the rocks and he was bucking down hill, which makes it even harder. I was pulling leather for all I was worth. I didn't want to be laying up on the divide all busted up. I finally got him under control, got to the truck, and it started right up. I never did figure out what made him buck like that after a thirty-five mile ride. I got home about two in the morning, slept a few hours, got horses and rigging loaded up and headed back. I was tired when I reached the lodge the next afternoon.

We had some amusing experiences and some not so amusing during the time at Moose Creek. One that comes to mind happened in the early fall. I had a party of hunters at our spike camp and we were heading back to the ranch. Two hunters were riding in front of me and I was leading the packstring. The wrangler would be coming in that evening with the rest of the hunters. My horses were heavily loaded and the two hunters had gotten several miles ahead of me. I was about half-way from the divide to the ranch when I heard two rifle shots. I thought, "That sounds like it's right at the ranch. What would they be shooting at, there aren't any elk around there!" Then I thought of Bonnie, the moose, and her calf, surely they wouldn't shoot them. Bonnie and her calf were the ranch pets. The kids had named them Bonnie and little Bonnie.

When I got to the ranch my worst fears were true. There, in the corral by the salt block, lay the calf moose. They had shot Bonnie, too, but she got away. I was so mad I came close to beating them up. Nobody had a moose permit, and I could lose my outfitting license. I was frantic! I told the hunters to dress the calf out. I grabbed my gun and went after Bonnie, following her blood trail. I went about a quarter of mile before I found her and put her out of her misery. Then I ran back to the barn to get the tractor and trailer. My son, Jamie (Jim), was there and he wanted to go with me. I never thought ahead and said okay. Working as fast as I could I skinned and quartered the moose, and loaded her on the trailer. All the time I was skinning her, Jamie kept telling me, "This is Bonnie the moose!" And I would tell him "No, this is an elk." I got back to the ranch, quartered the calf and put both of them in meat bags, then hung them on the meat pole. I had been working as fast as I could, trying to get them covered and hung before the rest of the party got in. I had made the two hunters put their elk tags on the animals, and cautioned them not to say a word about the moose. The wrangler spent a lot of time over at the ranger station and I was afraid he would spill the beans. That night as everyone was sitting at the supper table Jamie proclaimed, "I helped my daddy skin Bonnie The Moose." You could have heard a pin drop. Laurie ushered him away, but the cat was out of the bag. Jamie knew that it was Bonnie The Moose, and nothing I had said was going to change his five-year-old mind.

One other time we had a large party of ten hunters. They had flown in on a twin engine plane that was way too big and fast for this little mountain air strip. I don't what kind it was, but it was about the size of a DC1 and more sleekly built. I took the hunters up to the spike camp while the pilot stayed at the lodge. About the third day he flew the plane to Missoula to fuel it up, and came back the next day. Several of the hunters and I watched him from the top of the mountain. He had to drop down into the narrow canyon and fly up the river to make a left turn onto the runway. He made four false tries before he got enough nerve to drop into the canyon. The plane was too fast for this kind of flying; it would stall out if he flew at the speed of the bush planes. He had been smitten by Laurie and when he came back from Missoula he brought her a bouquet of a dozen red roses. Of course I was a little jealous as all I was giving her was hard work. The day before they left, the pilot paced back and forth with the worry of getting the plane out of this 'hell-hole' as he called it.

The hunting party left in the early morning to utilize the heavy morning air. The plane was loaded with about a twelve hundred pounds or more of meat, the hunters and their gear. The pilot was worried sick, and I was getting that way. I think the hunters had all taken a few nips of the bottle to settle their nerves. It did not help your fear when you had seen the remains of several wrecked planes of the past strewn around the area.

The forest ranger and his assistant were there from the ranger station. We moved the plane as far back on the landing strip as we could to gain more distance, clear back into the stumps. We looped a rope to the plane, then back to a stump and put chalks in front of the wheels. The pilot tested everything out about ten times. The forest ranger said "They're never going to get out of here in this plane." Finally they told us to take the chalks out from in front of the wheels, and when they gave us the signal to cut the rope, the pilot revved the engine until the plane would start jumping, then he would chicken out. Then try it again. He finally had it wound up until it was just dancing, then he gave us the signal to cut the rope. They went screaming down the runway, but not getting off the ground. At the end of the runway the tops of the big trees from the river bank stuck up about thirty feet above the runway. They had to turn right down the canyon. The ranger kept saying, "They'll never make it. They're going to go right into the river." All three of us were holding our breath. There must have been a breeze coming up from the river because as they left the runway the plane raised up and just skimmed the tree tops. It disappeared down the canyon and we never saw or heard of them again.

A bush pilot named Larry, a swell guy from Kamiah, Idaho, flew supplies and mail into us every week. He had three other outfits he also supplied, and he was putting in a lot of long hours. He had a Cessna 185 plane with a lot of power and extended wing flaps, allowing him to be airborne in just a few hundred feet. When he got to us, Larry would buzz the ranch and I would cross the river on the swinging bridge, get in the jeep and drive up to the landing strip to meet him.

It was getting late in the fall and starting to freeze at night with snow on the peaks. On this day it was late when he buzzed us, and as usual, I went up to meet him, and unload my stuff. It was so late and he looked tired, I asked him, "Larry, why don't you spend the night with us and go on to the Fish Lake camp in the morning?" He said he had to be back at Kamiah early the next day to take a load to the Selway Lodge that morning. He would go on to Fish Lake tonight and stay there so he could get back to Kamiah early. The next morning when he took off from Fish Lake, his plane iced up and he crashed into the mountain. He left behind a wife and some small kids. It was a shock to us, and very sobering, as we depended so much on planes. We were just about to close the lodge for the season, and I was not planning to come back next year as it wasn't cost effective for us.

    We had to go to the ranger station to call for a plane from Missoula to come in to get Laurie and the kids. The pilot was an excellent, experienced bush pilot, and I had a lot of faith in him but the weather had turned bad and I was worried for them, and with Larry's death fresh on my mind it made it worse yet. I was wishing I had sent them out the week before, but my hired man had quit two weeks earlier and I really needed Laurie for the last party. About a hour after I got back to the ranch from their takeoff, I heard a plane coming from the north, and it was my family. I hurried back to the landing strip, getting there just as they taxied up. The pilot said they couldn't make it over the divide as every pass they tried was socked in. He said he would stay the night at the lodge and hope for better weather in the morning.

    The next morning it was still drizzling rain but with a little higher ceiling. The pilot said he thought he could make it out all right. I took them back to the plane and watched them leave again. I felt awful lonely standing there. The ranger station had closed the week before and even my ranger friends were gone. My stomach had a knot in it as I watched the plane disappear into a rain cloud with my beloved family. I knew if they didn't get over the divide this time the plane wouldn't have enough fuel to get back to the ranch again.

Our 35th Anniversary, flight, gift from Nels and Cathy Jensen.

    My younger brother, Mick, brought another truck to Elk Summit, then walked in to the lodge to help me pack up and bring the horses home. I was glad to see him! We kept busy the rest of the day and the next, getting the ranch closed up for the winter. On the third day we headed out with the horses for Elk summit. This was the hardest part as sitting in the saddle I had a lot of time to think. I wouldn't know if my family had gotten home safe until the next morning. I had been doing a lot of praying, and blaming myself for putting them at risk. At Elk Summit we loaded the horses into the trucks and took off for home.

We got home the next morning, not having been to bed yet. I was met with a happy kiss from Laurie and warm hugs from my three little ones, and my world was wonderful again.

MICK, ME AND A MOUNTAIN GOAT

As I sat in the intensive care waiting room waiting for my second youngest brother, Mick, to wake from open-heart surgery, my mind wandered back through the years, reliving experiences we had shared, some fun and some pretty serious. Mick, like all my brothers, is very strong but more than that, he's just plain tough. He is a soft-spoken, easy-going man, but you don't want to push him. When he tells you something it's worth listening to. In our April 2006 Museum newsletter I gave tribute to the old-time cowboys; now I want to pay tribute to as good a cowboy that ever forked a horse. From an outlaw horse to a mean, angry cow he can handle them all.

One memory that crossed my mind happened about twenty-five years ago. I was no longer involved in the outfitting business, but I did go into camp occasionally and guide hunting parties in the Bob Marshall. On this occasion, I had some hunters on Charlotte Peak goat hunting when one of the hunters killed a goat on the north rim of the peak. The goat fell onto a shale rock chute and slid over the cliff to a spot where we could not get down to retrieve it. Early the next morning Mick and I rode our horses up to the timberline and hiked around the north rim, then back below the peak where the goat was laying. We were sure we'd be able to get to it by climbing up from below and we found the goat without too much difficulty. We took the head, hide and hindquarters, and left the rest, as the meat was spoiled from lying there all night. We started back on the long, six-mile hike around the rim. It was only about one and one half miles up over the rim to our horses and we decided to climb in a likely looking spot. I was about forty-five years old then, past my prime, and spending a lot of time behind a desk. Mick was nine years younger and still in top shape. He tied a long rope around his waist so his hands were free for climbing, and took the lead. He would use the rope to pull the goat up when he got to a safe spot; it would also help me up a bad place if I needed it. We were close to the top, going up a very bad spot when Mick hollered to me that he could not make it. I was on a sloping ledge about two and a half feet wide and four feet long. I could not see him from my spot, but from the trickle of rocks coming down I knew he was right above me. He said to get back as much as I could so he wouldn't knock me off when he fell. I yelled back to him, "You have to make it or we are both going down. I'm not moving, I'm gonna try and stop you if you fall."

It was a tense couple of minutes as I frantically tried to find some way to snub the rope and break his fall. I guess he did not want to take his older brother down with him, and he managed to make it up to the next ledge. He pulled the goat up and then, with his help on the rope, I made it up to his ledge. We were silent for the rest of the climb, both thinking we should have gone around.

At the top Mick said, "You know you couldn't have stopped me, I would have knocked you off too!" I said, "Probably so, but I would have had to try, you would have done the same if it had been me falling." With a twinkle in his eye he laughed and said, "Nah, I would have let you sail right on by!" I don't think there is a mountain or a horse that Mick couldn't handle, but he's sure enough got a handful right now. Hang tough, Mick!

Chapter Two

FAMILY TALES

A TRUE MONTANA RANCH FAMILY

Today another hard-working ranch lady, Dorothy Allard passed on. She was ninety years old. You might have seen her helping out in the field, or doing chores, but no matter what she was doing, she was always a lady. Gene and Dorothy Allard were our neighbors and friends when I was growing up. Their daughter, Diane, who was a few years younger than I was, seemed more like a cousin than a neighbor. I have a lot of fond memories of this family. Gene's parents, Mr. and Mrs. Joe Allard were good friends of my grandparents. My grandmother and Mrs. Allard were best friends. The Allard family, like the Cheff family, are of French and Indian descent. Gene's grandfather, Charley Allard, along with Michel Pablo, had the famous last buffalo herd in the U.S.

When I was twelve years old, I spent several days looking for a bunch of our horses. I finally found them east of Ronan. There were not many fences then and if a gate was left open the stock could wander off a long ways. When I found them they were about ten miles from home. I had more than a little trouble getting them back, as some of them kept trying to cut out and leave the herd. There were thirty-five or forty head of our horses in the bunch, plus six belonging to our neighbors. One of the neighbor's horses caused most of the trouble, trying to get his pals to quit the herd. It was a good thing I was riding a fast horse that knew more about running horses than I did. When I got them in the corral my younger brother, Kenny, who was nine years old, helped me cut out the neighbors' horses and we took them back to their owners. Two belonged to Gene Allard and the other four troublemakers belonged to a wealthy "hobby" rancher. We met Gene on the road and he opened the gate to his pasture so we could put his in. He asked us where we had found them and when I told him, he thanked us and gave us each a silver dollar. That was a lot of money then, and he did not have any to spare. I never forgot his generosity. Then we took the other four horses to the wealthy neighbor's place. He never even said thank you, and acted as if it was our fault his horses had been gone. I was wishing I had cut them out and left them where I had found them. Gene died in 2002 at the age of ninety-seven and has been waiting for his lifetime partner, Dorothy, to join him.

SPOTLIGHTERS

A few nights ago my brother Buck had a cow illegally shot and butchered. He will probably never find out who did it. This made me think of my many losses throughout the years. The two-legged predators are worse than the four-legged ones; the four-legged ones don't know any better, they are just following their natural instincts. We have been plagued by spotlighters for many years. I have lost count of how many cows have been shot on our ranch. Most all of them were longhorns and none of them were butchered, just shot and left to rot. One year we had three killed in a two-month period. Frustrated, as it did no good to call the sheriff, I put a piece in the paper telling the spotlighters what I thought of them. The next week, for spite, they gut-shot my main saddle horse and left it to die.

Some years ago I had one special longhorn cow that was sort of my pet. She was a white and black speckled cow with beautiful long black horns, a perfect mother who raised a calf every year. Some of the longhorns will calve until they are twenty years old, while other breeds of cows are usually only good for ten to twelve years. She had a sweet disposition and knew how to work me into giving her a bite of grain. If she saw me around the barn or corral she would leave the others and come to me and beg. She would hook one of her longhorns around me and pull me in close, then give me a lick like she was licking her calf.

One day I was out riding, checking the cows. My grandson, Buddy IV, who was about three and a half years old, was riding behind my saddle. He liked to ride with me and I would often feel his head against my back. I would look back and he would be sound asleep. I guess the rhythm of the horse rocked him to sleep. On this day I spotted a cow laying down and I could tell it was dead. As I drew closer I got a sick feeling in my stomach as I realized it was my favorite cow. I rode up and got off my horse, taking Buddy off also. The cow had been shot in the head by a spotlighter. As I was standing there looking at her I must have had a pretty sad look on my face, because Buddy took hold of my hand and said, "Papa, does seeing your cow dead make you sad?" I said "yes it does, Buddy." He said "Me too." I looked down and he had tears in his eyes.

Riding back home I thought of how my grandfather must have felt some eighty years ago when he looked at his dead sheep killed by the bears and coyotes. I was the last Cheff baby born in his house and his first grandson born with the Cheff name. He gave me a filly colt born that spring to celebrate my birth. The colt's mother was a descendant of Marcus Daly's race horses and the sire was Eneas Conko's best race horse. This colt would be the main brood mare for our horse herd for years to come. I wondered if grandfather was watching this day as I rode with my grandson on a descendant of the colt he had given me, plus riding on the same ground he had ridden so long ago. My conclusion was there will always be heart wrenching losses in every generation; it just goes with ranching.

Bud Cheff IV and his granddad.

THE START OF A LEGEND

One particular birthdate, April 2, 1915, is very important to the Ninepipes Museum of Early Montana and to me. The following incident is taken from our family history.

Marie Cheff knew it was very close to the time. This would be her fourth child, and there would be ten more in the future. She had previously given birth to Leo, Joseph and Bernida. She did not expect trouble, but thought it was time to send Ovila to get her good friend, Mrs. Joe Allard, who was to be the mid-wife. The Allards lived just two miles southeast of the Cheff home, across Post Creek. At that time the Cheffs were living near Finley Creek on the Antoine Finley Place. Mrs. Allard hurried to the Cheffs' in the horse and buggy, accompanied by one of her sons, Irvin, on horseback. After several hours of labor, Mrs. Allard became alarmed, and told Irvin to go get old Mrs. Deschamps, and if she was not home, to go on to the Tom McDonald place and get

Mrs. McDonald.

Irvin kept his horse at a fast gallop the three miles to Mrs. Deschamps. He helped her hook up her horse and buggy, then went on to his home, only a mile away. Mrs. Deschamps went west across Post Creek and picked up Mrs. McDonald, and they headed for the Cheff house at a fast trot. These two elderly frontier ladies were sisters, having lived through many hardships, and were up to most any task.

The Deschamps family, like my family, were early Frenchtown, Montana, settlers, and had moved west from Ontario, Canada, in the 1800's. My friend, Bob Deschamps and I both laughingly claim our great grandmothers were the King's Daughters. My great-grandfather, Robert Caron, was with the French explorer Champlain when they started the settlement of Quebec in the early 1600's. His name is on the plaque in Old Quebec City to honor those early explorers. The king of France sent a ship to New France with orphan girls to be their wives. These girls were referred to as the King's Daughters.

A young Mrs. Tom McDonald.

The birth ended well with the three very capable midwives overseeing it, and Vern Edmond (Bud) Cheff Sr. was born. Mrs. Allard was his Godmother, and always made a special gift for him on his birthday. She was a wonderful and gracious lady. Bud got his name from his sister Bernida, who was two years old when he was born. She was speaking in French, trying to say baby (be'be'), and called him Bu' de', which evolved into Buddy.

With Dad's parents both being of mixed blood descent, and the family speaking French and Indian, he was easily accepted into the home and lives of their Indian neighbors. He learned the old ways from those that had actually lived it, valuable knowledge that stayed with him all his life. Both his parents were hard workers and they instilled this trait into their children. Ovila, Buddy's dad, was good at everything he did. He was an excellent shot with a shotgun and rifle. He was interested in past history, and this accounted for him allowing Buddy go on extended trips with their Indian friends. He would tell Buddy, "You need to carry a pencil and paper in your pocket and write things down so you don't forget." Growing up, Buddy's passion was for horses and hunting, a passion that stayed with him throughout his life. All of these things helped to form young Bud Sr. into the extraordinary man that he was to become.

Ovila and Marie Cheff in their later years.

MOLLMANS

The name Mollman to most people today refers Mollman Lakes or the Mollman Trail. They know nothing about the two great old warriors for which they are named. According to my grandfather, the name Mollman came from the Jesuits, calling them in French "the Molleman Brothers," which roughly translated meant they were quick learners and easy to work with. The Indians pronounced it Molt-le-men. Charles was born about 1833 and died in 1926, and Louie was born about 1836 and died in 1929. Their mother was a Pend d'Oreille, and their father, Peter, was a Mohawk Iroquois who had migrated to the Bitterroot from Ontario, Canada, in about 1828. He had learned how to farm at a Catholic Mission in his youth. Louie and Charley learned their farming skills and work ethic from him. Peter could talk French, and the boys learned some from him. When Peter was killed on a hunt in the Big Hole in 1856, his wife and family moved to the Mission Valley to be close to her people.

The Mollman's settled at the foot of the Mission Mountains in the natural meadows there. They did not do any crop farming, but had a garden. They fenced off some of the meadows to save the grass for winter pasture for their cattle and herd of horses. They built miles of split rail fences, dug extensive irrigation ditches, and did flood irrigating. They did an amazing amount of this kind of work, which was very uncommon at the time.

Both men were bow and arrow makers for the tribe. They, along with the tribe, crossed the mountains to the plains twice a year to hunt buffalo.

The old-timers said Louie's arrows would go clear through a buffalo. According to Dad, he would jump on his buffalo horse and race around the meadow when he was ninety years old. Louie and Charley both wore leggings and a breech cloth, winter and summer. Louie never had a pair of pants on in his life and died in his breech cloth.

Charley was short like his father, and Louie tall like his mother. Louie and my grandfather, Ovila, were good friends. Louie called Ovila "My little cousin from Canada." Ovila was from Ontario, as was Louie's dad. My uncle Charley (Vila) Cheff was born in Charley Mollman's house and was named for him. My uncle Louie Cheff, who was taller than Vila, was named after Louie Mollman. Philomie, Louie's wife, would laugh and put

Louie Mollman.

Charlie Mollman.

her hands on the two boys heads, and say, "Sh-aut-ley! Charley and Louie! Short and tall."

What I wouldn't give to have been able visit with these old ones. Their knowledge of early Montana history would have filled volumes of books. Now it is mostly all lost. If I had just had the foresight to question my grandfather, he could have told me many of their stories, as he also spoke both French and Indian, and he often visited with them.

The next time you see the Mollman Trail road sign, I hope you think of these two old warriors.

Louie Mollman sitting at his cabin.

MORE THAN JUST A MIRROR
The story below is based on events told to me by my father, Bud Cheff Sr., and put in story form by Josephine Chevre.

The mountains were still softened by a delicate, blue mist on what promised to be a fine morning, when Ovila Cheff hitched up his team and started out to plow the field below old Louie Mollman's cabin. The clean smell of new earth turning under his plow, and the noisy cacophony of bird song intermixed with the rattle of harness and soft blowing of the horses lifted his spirit, and he hummed snatches of French tunes under his breath, his eyes peaceful in spite of the drudgery of the work. Up the hill he could hear, faintly, the tap... tapping of Louie's hammer as the old man worked at patching his roof.

Of Iroquois and Pend d'Oreille descent, at ninety-two Louie Mollman still had the carriage of a fierce and powerful warrior, and his intelligent face was chiseled into a severity that mapped the intense struggle of his life. It was a face that caused the white passerby to feel uneasy, and the younger generations speak of him in respectful tones.

Famous for his expert skill with horse and bow, today Louie noted his own diminishing agility with a twinge of regret as he worked loose a rotten shingle. Only yesterday he had leapt upon the smooth back of his favorite horse and raced across the meadow, his mind's eye once again seeing the dark shapes of bison through the dust, bow taut in his hands, his whole being melded with the animal carrying him across the short grass country. The spirit inside of him felt ageless, but the stiffness of his body confirmed the truth his heart knew. He glanced down the hill to where Ovila trudged behind the plow, tiny in the distance, and further out in the valley where wagon trails now snaked across the broad expanse, and was relieved his time was almost over.

Ovila wiped the sweat from his face with his sleeve. The sun was climbing overhead and the warming air wafted the scent of pine down to him. He rounded the corner of the field when bright sunlight hit his face. He glanced around, wondering what had caused the light to flash at him so. He came around the field again, and the light flashed in his eyes as he rounded the corner. The third time he located the flash of light as coming from Louie's place, and it dawned on him that Louie was signaling him. Suddenly concerned for his old friend, he stopped the team.

Louie was lying next to the rock he had fallen on when he slipped off of the roof. Next to him a small, polished metal mirror winked up at the sky from the intricately decorated frame that contained it. Made for the reticule of some European lady many decades before, it had served Louie well, nestled in a little buckskin pouch inside the pipe bag that always hung on his belt. Fighting to remain consciousness, he had managed to position himself so he could reflect light into one corner of the field where Ovila would see it when he came around. Louie's face was drawn with pain, but he still managed to grin at Ovila as he knelt down by him.

"*Le tetit ami,*" Louie's voice was like parchment. "The sun is unusually bright this morning, eh?" Relief and amusement warred in Ovila's eyes as he said tenderly, "*Oui, mon vieux,* but what were you thinking, to make your face pretty up there on the roof?"

The mirror was an important item to the Indians. The western nations first obtained mirrors through trade from the Hudson's Bay Company in the 1700's, and by the 1800's most families had at least one in their possession. Warriors carried a mirror in their tobacco or medicine bag, and used them for plucking whiskers and decorating themselves as well as for more utilitarian uses, such as signaling. Some mirrors were made of metal and carried in a buckskin pouch; glass mirrors were carried in rawhide bags to keep them from breaking. The bags were usually lavishly decorated, often with horsehair drops. Hard to obtain, mirrors were highly prized until around the 1890's, when they became a common household item.

A BOY AND HIS CHAPS

Hector McCloud was feeling parched, but it wasn't the sweet glacier water of the Missions that he was wanting on this particular spring day in 1923. No, he had a yen for something with more kick to it. Well, he though to himself, it's a fine day to visit an old friend. So he turned his horse toward Mount Harding Peak.

Ovila Cheff's ranch was nestled in the shadow of the glacier-studded mountain, and his bootlegging still was nestled even deeper in the woods that covered the mountain's feet. Ovila had become friends with Hector on the buffalo roundup where Hector was one of the cowboys, and he greeted Hector warmly. Rex, the oldest living child of Ovila and Marie's fourteen children, was standing near his dad, all ears to hear the men talk. He was in awe of this both famous and infamous cowboy. Hector looked at the handsome, young thirteen-year-old, remembering how a much smaller Rex had run out in front of his team in Ronan and nearly been trampled. Rex was openly admiring Hector's beautiful white angora chaps. He sighed wistfully, saying, "I hope I have a pair of white chaps like that some day." Now Hector had a special fondness for Rex. He rubbed his chin, and looked at Rex thoughtfully.

"Rex, I'll sell you these chaps," Hector said. Rex's eyes got bigger.

"But I don't have any money."

"Well, if you work and save your money for a year, I bet you can earn enough to buy them. I'll sell them to you for $23.00." Hector stuck his hand out. "Is it a deal?"

"Yes sir!" Rex grinned from ear to ear and shook Hector's hand so hard that Hector had to cough and hide a grin. Rex could hardly believe that Hector would really sell him his chaps. But when Hector was leaving, he turned and called out to Rex, "Save your money, son, and I'll be back in a year with your chaps."

Rex went to work. He caught fish and sold them in town. In the fall he shot, plucked and sold ducks, and in winter he walked the long miles of his trap line on Post Creek relentlessly. He put his earnings in cans and hid them in the woods.

True to his word, exactly one year later Hector came riding up with the chaps hanging on his saddlehorn. "Well, Rex, here's your chaps.

Have you got my money?" Hector asked?

"I don't know if I've got enough," Rex stammered.

"Fetch it, and let's see." So Rex headed to the woods and came trotting back with three heavy cans full of coins. He counted all his money and found he had $27.00. Hector took $23.00 and said, "You're sure better at saving than I am, son. You worked hard for this money, and we are going to put it where it will do some real good. There's a family northeast of Ronan with a whole lot of little kids. Their house just burned, and they lost everything. I think they could sure use this $23.00 more than I can."

Hector McCloud was as wild as they came; there was no end of tales of his deeds and misdeeds. This story shows his softer side. Hector had an arm shot off at St. Ignatius in an altercation with a moonshiner. His colorful life ended April 23, 1936, when he was shot and killed during a card game in Nevada.

Rex Cheff has led a colorful life of his own, ranging from bush pilot to chiropractor and naturopathic doctor. In 2002, at ninety-two years, he lived near Ronan at the old homestead where he continued to practice the healing arts, still as handsome as ever.

Rex Cheff, eighty-eight years old.

A MOONSHINE RUN

Ovila had the Model-T loaded with his latest batch of whiskey when Rex and little Bud squeezed into the car, fairly bursting with excitement. They were going with their father to make a delivery to the Daly Ranch in Hamilton, almost a hundred miles away to the south in the Bitterroot Valley. Built by the famous Copper King, Marcus Daly, now dead some twenty years, the ranch was known to have some of the best Thoroughbreds in the world, and many of the fine-blooded horses in the Mission Valley came from this stock. Rex tried to impress upon his young brother how rich and famous the Copper King had been, but the seven year old was only interested in the racehorses. He looked dreamily out the window, imagining himself on the back of the winner as it pounded across the finish line, the astonished crowd roaring at the sight of such a young jockey. Rex sighed and slumped back in the seat. He might as well be talking to a stump when Buddy got that glazed look on his face.

At twelve, Rex was becoming more aware of Ovila's business practices. He had gotten an inkling that something exciting might be happening when he saw his father talking with Jim Green, the Missoula County Sheriff, Dwight Mason, the County Clerk, and Dan Heffner, the County Attorney. It was known in certain circles that the Metis Frenchman from Ronan made top quality moonshine. All good friends and customers of Ovila's, they had likely helped set up the secret delivery to the Daly ranch. Ovila himself had ties to the Anaconda Company and the residents of that area. He had come West from Ontario, Canada, at age seventeen in the late 1800's to Anaconda, where he had two uncles living at that time. He stayed with Josephat Cheff and his sons, who were tunnel builders for the Anaconda Company. Ovila had relatives scattered over western Montana, many in the Frenchtown area. His grandmother lived in Demersville in the Flathead Valley, and he was also related to the Demers.

With the coming of the Great Northern Railroad, the Flathead Lake steamboat business died, and with it the settlement of Demersville. The new town of Kalispell, three miles up the river, replaced it. Both of Ovila's parents were of French and Mohawk Iroquois descent and were sometimes called Metis, meaning mixed blood. Ovila worked that first year as a ranch hand at the Grant-Kohrs Cattle Ranch.

He then went to work for the Anaconda Copper Co. on construction and maintenance. In 1903 the Anaconda Company sent him to Cuba as superintendent to erect a smelter. When he finished the project in Cuba he went home to Ontario and married Marie Caron, returning to Montana with her in 1906. The Anaconda Company wanted to send him out of the country on another job but he did not want to leave Montana, so he quit the company and moved to the Mission Valley. He worked for Andrew Stinger on his ranch located west of Ronan, where the Mission Mountain

Golf Course is now located. Eventually, along with ranching on his own place, Ovila started a soda pop factory and mint distillery. When prohibition was enforced, ever the entrepreneur, he branched out into the illegal moonshine industry. His uncle, Calix Dugas, owned a hotel and saloon in Eureka, Montana, where Calix was also the sheriff. He ran whiskey from Canada to Butte, Helena, and Missoula, on the side. Moonshine was the business of the day, and taking his two sons on this run provided a cover.

Ovila was not anticipating any trouble along the way, and he knew the boys, who had never ridden to Missoula in a car before, would have a fun time. Ovila stopped at his friend, Alex Morigeau's place on Valley Creek to visit for a few minutes as was the custom for many of the local folk. The Morigeau ranch had functioned as an informal way-station for years and was a good place to exchange information.

They continued on, eventually heading down the Coriacan Defile, which is now called Evaro Hill. Rex pointed out the log chute, explaining to Buddy that the hill was too steep for the logging wagons, and that the horses could not hold the heavy loads back, so a chute was built out of logs which were then greased. The teamsters unloaded the logs from the wagons at the top of the hill and rolled them onto the chute. The logs slid down the chute to the bottom of the hill, where they were reloaded onto the wagons and hauled to the mill. Rex explained the chute to his little brother every time they made a trip to Missoula by wagon, but Bud didn't mind; it always fascinated him. He and Rex discussed how much fun it might be to slide down that chute if they built a special toboggan to take them down it.

Soon they passed the Marent Trestle, coming to the Baron O'Keefe Ranch with its big apple orchard. Whenever they went to Missoula with the team and wagon they always camped at the bottom of Evaro Hill, just above the orchard. Now, with the car they didn't need to camp, they could make it to Missoula and back in one day if they didn't have too many flat tires.

The ranch was impressive and Bud always insisted that when he grew up he would have a ranch just like the Baron's. One of Montana's most colorful early settlers, the Baron started his ranch in 1861, selling fruit and vegetables to the early mining camps. He was famous for his fiery temper, which resulted in him being the defendant in the first civil trial in Montana Territory in 1863.

There are many versions of this event. It seems that a Frenchman known as Tin Cup Joe let his horse get into the Baron's seed oats while he was camping on the ranch. Tin Cup Joe accused the Baron of causing the horse's death when he chased it over the top of his root cellar and it fell through the roof. Tin Cup wanted recompense for his horse, so a trial was held in Bolte's Saloon. A fellow named Brooks was the judge, and Frank Woody represented Tin Cup. O'Keefe naturally represented himself. When the judge declared that the Baron owed $40.00 for the horse and $50.00 for court costs, the Baron's temper flared. He demanded that Brooks show his credentials that allowed him to be a judge. Brooks responded by producing a deck of cards and declaring, "These are my credentials! Where are yours to be your own lawyer?"

Marent Trestle, highest wooden trestle in the world at that time.

O'Keefe raised his fists into the air. "These are mine!" he shouted and proceeded to strike Brooks right between the eyes. This started a brawl that cleared the house and was said to finally end in a draw. The jury was rounded up again and the judge, who had fled for his life, was found and brought back to finish the trial. The jury found the Baron guilty, but there was no sheriff to enforce the law and no one had the courage to confront the Baron to collect the fine, which he refused to pay.

The stories of the Baron caught the boys' imagination for quite awhile, but it seemed that they would never get to Daly's place in the Bitterroot Valley, and when they finally did they were sorely disappointed when they were told they had to stay close to the car while their father conducted his business, instead of being able to explore the ranch like they wanted. Two men came to meet them when they arrived, and after greeting Ovila, helped him haul his boxes into a building. Ovila was gone a long time, or at least the boys thought so. Bud wanted to go look at the famous horses but Rex shook his head. They didn't dare disobey their father. Eventually Bud fell asleep. When Ovila came back to the car his expression was pleased. The customer had been quite satisfied with the delivery and was generous with the payment, even including a fat tip for bringing the merchandise such a long way.

Ovila was in high spirits when they left Daly's and headed for Missoula again. He joked with the boys, singing and telling stories. To make up for the long wait and rather uneventful day the boys had spent, he took them to the fancy Florence Hotel to spend the night. He told them he was going to treat them to a steak dinner in the hotel's dining room after they washed up and combed their hair. Rex and Bud had never stayed in such a fancy place, let alone dine in one, and they were properly impressed. They couldn't wait till they got home and told the family about it! They combed their hair very carefully. After they were seated at the table, white linen napkins tucked under their chins, they waited as patiently as their rumbling stomachs allowed for the meal to be served. When the steaks arrived Bud's eyes lit at the sight of that lovely steak. "Wait," their papa told them and he showed them how the other gentlemen in the room were eating their steaks. He proceeded to pour Worcestershire sauce on the boys' steaks as well. Bud took a big bite, anticipating something truly wonderful. His eyes watered and his face fell into a grimace of disgust.

Florence Hotel.

"That stuff made my meat taste awful!" he protested loudly. The buzz of conversation paused as amused faces turned toward the disappointed little boy. Rex's cheeks turned pink when he tried a bite. He pretended he liked the flavor, trying to be very grown up, but later he confided to Bud that he didn't like it either. They both agreed that deer and elk steak was a whole lot better, much to Ovila's amusement. The next morning they headed home with nothing more eventful than a flat tire, and that was the end of the outlaw whiskey run that would forever be remembered by two young brothers as the time they tasted "that awful steak sauce."

POST CREEK RUSTLER

Frank Ashley rode up to the Ovila Cheff Ranch on Mollman Creek, and hailed Ovila as he swung down from his horse. Ovila came out of the horse corral closely followed by his second son, twelve-year-old Buddy.

Whenever Frank was around, Buddy wanted to be close by. Frank was a strong man, mostly Flathead Indian. People never thought of him as Indian or white, just as a good man. He could speak pretty good English, but was more comfortable speaking Salish. Frank and Isadore Sorrell, another Flathead Indian and friend of the family, showed Buddy and his older brother, Rex, how to trap and care for their furs. Frank was known to be an expert at trapping bears. He had shown Ovila and the boys how to trap grizzly bears, and in later years gave his bear traps to Buddy. (One of these traps is now in the Ninepipes Museum.)

The year before, Buddy had been riding a few miles south of the ranch when he heard the bellowing of a grizzly bear. He knew what it meant; Frank had a bear in his set. He rode his nervous and snorting horse closer until he could see the big bear. The way it was tearing things up, he thought he had better go get Frank before the bear broke loose. He loped his horse most of the three miles to Frank's place, and excitedly told Frank he had a very big grizzly in his set.

Frank grabbed his .30-30 Winchester, saddled his horse and a pack horse, then they headed back to the site where they'd trapped the bear. Frank reassured Buddy that the bear would still be caught when they got there. He explained to Buddy how he had carefully set the trap to catch the bear's front foot, and had made the drag just the right size to contain the bear, but not hold it fast. It would break loose if it was caught by a back foot, or held solid. They could hear the bear long before they got to him.

They tied their horses a good ways back and approached on foot to kill the bear. Frank handed the rifle to Buddy and said "Shoot him right under the chin." Intent and careful, Buddy did as he was told and the bear dropped. Buddy helped Frank skin him, then load the hide and the much-prized fat.

Listening now to Frank talk to his father, and the way Frank treated him as their equal, Buddy felt grown up and proud to be Frank's friend. Today Frank brought some serious news. He told Ovila, "My brother-in-law has a dozen or more of your yearling heifers locked up in his corral." He said Charley was a *"utus kaa soo apy,"* (a no good white man) who had threatened to kill him (Frank) on several occasions. Charley was lucky he never tried it, as Frank would have probably turned the tale on him.

Frank said they had better get their cows right away, since it was hard telling what Charley would do with them. Ovila wondered how the cows had gotten that far south, and said, "Buddy, get your horse and go bring those heifers home before Charley moves them out of the area. They will know the way home so you shouldn't have any trouble."

Buddy knew Charley lived over across Post Creek, close to Frank, about a five mile ride. He had only seen the man a few times and he didn't like him. He had heard talk of what a mean person Charley was, and how he didn't treat Frank's sister very good. Buddy was feeling a little uneasy going to his place. He wished Rex, his older, brother would have been home so he could have come along to help.

When he reached Charley's place he saw the heifers were still in the corral. He thought, "I won't go to the house, I will just open the gate and start them for home." He rode up to the gate and started to dismount when he heard a rifle hammer cocked, and a voice said, "If you get off your horse, you're dead, kid." Buddy turned in his saddle and blurted out, "I'm Ovila Cheff's boy. I came to get our cows." Charley said, "I know who you are, and these heifers belong to me now. You turn that horse around and get off my land. Now! Or I'll blow you right out of that saddle."

The look on Charley's face, not to mention his rifle leveled at his chest, told Buddy he meant what he said. If he made the wrong move, he would probably be dead. He turned his horse and rode away, expecting a bullet in the back any second. As soon as he was out of the line of fire he put the spurs to his horse and made a beeline for home.

The next morning Ovila started out on the twenty-mile trip to Polson to see the sheriff. Now that Lake Country was no longer in Missoula County, they had their own sheriff in the county seat at Polson. It seemed Charley had known what he was doing. He had run an ad in the Polson paper that he was claiming for feed cost, thirteen abandoned heifers with the brand bar V O on the left hip. He had filed the claim with the sheriff's office, and knew if no one claimed them in the allotted days, the cattle were legally his. He had put the ad in the Polson paper instead of the Ronan Pioneer, knowing Ovila would be less apt to see it It was also commonly known that Ovila and Marie Cheff could not speak or read English well. They didn't get or read any paper, and seldom went to town, so there was little chance they would know of the notice until it was too late.

Ovila wanted to go take the cattle back by force, but Marie and the sheriff convinced him if he killed Charley he would go to prison, or Charley would kill him. Either way, he would leave ten kids and a pregnant wife without a husband and father. Using the law, Charley was able to rustle the cattle legally.

Frank told Ovila, "Someday I'm going to have to kill him." But he never did. They both lived for many more years.

HECTOR MCCLEOD
By Josephine Chevre

As the town of Ronan came into view, four pairs of ears flickered back expectantly toward their driver. Even before Hector slapped the reins and let out the customary yell, the horses' muscles were bunching in anticipation of putting forth a burst of speed. They knew the routine and enjoyed it almost as much as the driver did. Hector let out a whoop as the team kicked up a cloud of dust, his weather-burned face split in a maniacal grin, and his trademark bandana streaming in the wind. Hector McCleod was a flamboyant cowboy with a booming voice and a big hat that matched his expansive personality. Whether on a saddle horse or with team and wagon, Hector always made his entrance into town fast and furious. On this particularly pleasant day in 1912 the dusty track that passed for the main street was wide open as Hector's team came thundering down it. Just as Hector prepared to make a noticeably grand stop, a small boy darted out into the street, then froze, big-eyed in terror right in the path of the oncoming team. Hector let out a stream of

Hector McCleod driving stage.

extraordinarily creative invectives, made all the more noticeable by his deep baritone as he struggled to bring the team and wagon to a halt. Which he did in a magnificent fashion, just narrowly missing the toddler, and effectively capturing the attention of every living soul on that particular street, including the dozing hound on the other side, who though an innocent bystander, was also the cause of the whole upset, being the object of interest that first caused the little boy to decide to cross over.

For once, Hector didn't notice how he'd impressed his unsuspecting audience. He rounded on the boy. "You get home, young Rex Cheff!" But young Rex burst into tears, so Hector relented, swung down from the wagon and picked the boy up in order to deliver him to his mother. Now Rex's mother was coming at a dead run herself, albeit somewhat hampered by her skirts, her attractive face mirroring a combination of emotions as Hector handed her child over to her. Hector wasn't entirely sure if the look she gave him was one of grateful relief or murderous intent, as he told her, "You should keep a picket rope on this kid, Marie." Marie, though lovely to look at, was no delicate violet, and might have been inspired to give Hector a piece of her mind, if it weren't for the somewhat apologetic look on his face. Hector, for his part, was somewhat relieved when she didn't scold him, for when Marie spoke, her pleasant, low-pitched voice revealed both her French Canadian background and the hard steel in her backbone. Marie shook her head in exasperation, frowned and then smiled faintly. She couldn't help but remember when the force of Hector's personality and his expert horsemanship had saved several lives including her own.

On that wintry day some of the residents of the new town of Ronan hired Hector McCleod and his sharp-shod team of which he was very proud, to pull a large bobsled they had rented from the livery, and take them out to Sloan's ferry and stage house for a dance. Hector, with his big voice, was also very popular as a square dance caller. Marie and her husband, Ovila, the fiddle player for the dance, were both in the sled, along with Pud Mains, the Roulliers, and the Gauthiers. Mr. and Mrs. A.M. Sterling and the Burlands also came along. The merry group crossed the Flathead River on the ice, and upon arrival, proceeded to dance and visit until dawn.

Marie Cheff.

During the night the weather changed as a chinook blew in. The group decided to leave, concerned about the rapidly melting snow and the river crossing. By the time they started across the river, the ice had water on it. As Hector drove the sled out toward the middle, there was a sound like a thunder clap and then another, and the ice began to break up. The women screamed, and the men, suddenly very sober, shouted to Hector.

"I brought you over here, and I'll get you back across!" Hector yelled above the noise as he cracked the whip over his fine team. The new blacksmith in town had sharp-shod the horses only a few days before the dance and the team clattered across the river running full out, the ice going down behind them as they pulled the sled across it.

Marie felt as though she were lost in a nightmare. In front of her, silhouetted against the paling sky, bellowing at the top of his lungs, Hector seemed like a madman driving a team of demon horses. But as he had promised he brought them across to safety. For a second they all sat in stunned silence, the labored breathing of the horses and the ice breaking up further along the river loud in their ears. Then the group broke out in sobs, relieved exclamations and prayerful thanks to God, while Hector expressed himself sincerely with his own brand of colorful expletives.

"*Mon Dieu!*" Marie whispered, whether at Hector's amazing vocabulary or the narrowly missed catastrophe, she herself wasn't entirely sure. Ovila put a comforting arm around her shoulders and handed Hector the whiskey flask with a look of wry humor. Hector slapped his leg and grinned. "Well, that was the best !#$&* damn time I've had in quite a spell!" he said.

And that, Marie thought as she carried young Rex, still sniffling, back to her porch, is a quote I will never forget!

NEW YEAR'S EVE 1926

The following short story gives us a brief look at how much work people used to go through to put a little fun in their hard working lives. They just took in stride what we would now think was way too much work for such a short-lived pleasure.

Ovila Cheff was busy getting the team harnessed, and giving them some extra feed since they would be in harness most of the evening and night. Ovila and Marie were going to a New Year's Eve dance, and these parties usually lasted until the wee hours in the morning. He pitched hay into the sleigh so everyone could burrow into it to keep warm if they wanted to, and the team could munch on it while they waited patiently for the return trip home. Marie was busy preparing food to bring for the pot-luck dinner that always accompanied these dances. Bernida, now fourteen years old, would rather have been going to the dance but she had agreed to stay with the younger kids. She and her sister Grace would have their own party. But they were just a little annoyed that their brother Buddy got to go with their folks. Buddy had been busy helping his dad with the chores, and at the age of twelve was feeling pretty grown up. He had insisted some of his friends would be there. Usually there were plenty of kids attending the dances with their parents. Brother Rex and Andy, both seventeen years old, already had left on horseback to go to a party of their friends. Andy Desetel lived with the Cheffs and was treated as one of their own.

Soon they were on their way, Marie and Ovila wrapped snuggly in a buffalo robe and Buddy in the hay, with Ovila's fiddle tucked in a safe corner. With the snappy team going at a mile-eating trot, it would take just over an hour to cover the nine miles to the Groslees' place, two miles southwest of Ronan. The Groslees had come to Montana from Ontario, Canada. They had a good-sized house with a big living room that was well suited for dancing. They did not have any children and always welcomed company. Upon arriving, Marie took her food into the house while Buddy helped his dad unhitch the team and tie them to the sleigh so they could eat on the hay in the sleigh box.

The place was full of people, but to Buddy's disappointment there were no other kids there. He danced the first dance with his mother, and his face lit as Evelyn Roullier came in. Evelyn was his good friend Sidney's sister and a cousin of Thurman Trosper. She had known the Cheff's would be there with Ovila playing and she hoped Buddy would be there to dance with her. Although she was barely eleven years old, Evelyn had walked by herself the two miles from town to get a chance to dance. Later Buddy recalled they had a real good time and danced every dance together. Evelyn and my mother, Adelle Rogers, became close friends and both were on the Ronan girls 1932-33 champion basketball team.

Some of the dance attendees Buddy could remember were the Nordbergs (he was the square dance caller), LaFlems, Dennisons, and Gauthiers.

When the dance was over in the early morning, Marie told Ovila they had to take Evelyn home as she could not walk home alone at this hour.

Although it made their trip home four miles longer Ovila readily agreed. Two other couples that had walked from Ronan happily accepted a ride into town also. The team never slowed down all the way, and Marie, Ovila and Buddy arrived home before daybreak, tired but happy. Bud (Buddy) Cheff Sr. was still dancing at ninety-five years of age.

THE SECRET
By Josephine Chevre

The main character in this story is my great-aunt Josephine, who recently passed from this world. The people and places are real and the two main events, the bee sting incident and the part about the coin really happened, but I don't know any details around the anecdotes, so the story around the events is reconstructed. I did not have the honor of knowing Aunt Josephine well, but I do remember standing in Bud and Adelle's kitchen at the guest ranch, right over by the ovens, listening to Aunt Jo telling me about blowing air into frog's bellies when she was young, and I made a place for that in telling the story. For those of you who are family and friends of Aunt Jo, I hope you will forgive the fiction and that this little cameo will stir real and dearly held memories of her for you.

Josephine's apple-cheeked little face poked itself around the corner of the barn where she had been hiding, back pressed tight against the logs as she listened to two of her brothers working out a secret plan. Jo loved secrets, especially if she knew what the secret was. The boys had found a secluded spot down on the Plassies' place near the beaver ponds where they could build a sweat lodge. Jo's nose itched. She wiggled it, but it just itched more. A carpenter ant stopped on its busy route, encountering Jo's dusty foot planted squarely across its path. After an initial exploration it continued on its way undeterred. Its tiny feet tickled her skin and Jo squirmed impatiently. Finally she could contain herself no longer and she burst from her hiding place, brown eyes gleaming, braids fairly snapping her face.

"AHAH!" she exclaimed triumphantly, pointing a chubby finger at the boys. "AaHa!" She put her hands on her hips the way Mama did when she'd had enough and stood expectantly. The two boys exchanged annoyed glances.

"Go away, Jo," Louie demanded. "This is boys' business."

Jo dug her feet deeper into the dust and frowned. Vila had an idea to distract her.

"Mama cat has new kittens in the barn, why don't you go find them? I'll bet they're all soft and fluffy," he added persuasively. Jo's lower lip quavered and she looked like she was getting ready to cry up a storm, so Vila hastily added, "I'll help you find them if you want."

"Jo's lip went out further and she stamped her bare foot, sending up a little cloud of dust, which wasn't quite the effect she wanted, so she crossed her arms and stuck out her chest (well, round little belly, really), squinting furiously at the boys.

"If you two don't let me in on this I'm gonna tell EVERYBODY!" She emphasized "everybody" with an expansive wave of her arms before crossing them again.

Vila and Louie looked helplessly aghast. Jo was the biggest little chatterbox this side of the Missions. If they told her about their secret plans, she would let it slip whether she meant to or not, and if they didn't tell her, she would tattle to the whole world and ruin their fun. Jo just naturally liked to share every little piece of information she came across. She was so free with information that her mother, Marie, was reluctant to let her visit the neighbors, because tiny Josephine was sure to air all the family's clean and dirty laundry, plus whatever she'd overheard about the rest of the valley. At five years old, Jo didn't think to discriminate about what to tell, she just enjoyed the funny looks that crossed the grown-up's faces when she reported the latest news about how a certain lady in town was said to have dumped a pail of sour milk on Mr. So and So's head; and according to her big brother Rex, the barn cat had three girl kittens and two boy kittens. She liked the grey one with the short tail and one white foot, but hadn't decided on a name yet. Mrs. Sterling had worn a really pretty dress to church last Sunday; and she was sure that butterflies ate mud, because they were always perched around mud puddles, and her favorites were the blue ones, although the yellow ones were nice too, and just as pretty as cowslips. The coyotes howled so loud last night that they woke her right up, and wouldn't you know it, in the morning her favorite sheep, Mrs. Mounton Noir's twin lambs, were missing! The bullfrog that she caught all by herself was this big, and did you know that if you blew air into a frog's tummy it would float down the creek like a boat?

The two boys looked at each other resignedly. Josephine felt a little smile slipping onto her face, so she tightened her lips and tried to appear stern and sad all at once. Louie gave her a shrewd look.

"Well, Jo, we might let you in on our secret, but you'll have to keep quiet about it."

Jo could contain herself no longer. Beaming, she hunkered down next to them.

"We'll show you after the chores are done, but right now you had better go up to the house. Grace and Bernida are calling for you. Remember, don't tell anyone."

Jo trotted off feeling very important. When she was out of earshot Louie leaned close to Vila and laid out a new plan to fool their little sister. They would take her to their old duck blind on the big pond on the Big Tom allotment and make a big deal of it, and let her tattle about it as she would, since they didn't use that spot much any more. She was a busy little bee and would soon forget about it when some new interest caught her attention.

The boys were true to their word and Jo was highly satisfied with the whole affair. She even managed to keep it a secret for a couple of days before she accidentally bragged to her big sister Grace that she knew where Louie and Vila had a hideout that nobody else knew about. Grace coolly asked her where this place was and Jo just naturally told her before she could stop herself. She felt guilty about having let the 'cat out of the bag.'

She wandered outside, and scuffed her shoes in the dusty yard despondently. She looked out toward the barnyard just in time to see Louie and Vila's backsides sneaking off through the pines toward the hawthorn thicket. Jo's eyes narrowed speculatively. That wasn't quite the way down to the big pond. Those boys were up to something again. Jo ran as fast as her short legs would carry her, until she reached the bushes the boys had disappeared into. She could hear them talking and snapping sticks now that they thought they were hidden in the thicket. The boys stopped at a gooseberry bush for a snack, which gave Jo time to catch up with them.

She snuck up behind them, jumped on an old log and took a deep breath to yell "AHAH!" when the log crumbled under her feet. Yellow jackets swarmed furiously out of their disturbed home and attacked the little girl. Jo felt like she was being hit over and over with a terrible thorny club. She screamed a shrill, high scream that brought Louie and Vila running. They carried her away from the log, knocking the angry bees off of her as they ran and ignoring their own stings. There were so many bees on her little body that the young boys were truly afraid for her. Jo stopped screaming and the boys paused, realizing they were dragging her. She had gone into shock and hung limply between them.

They carried her home to their mother, who set about treating her daughter with home remedies she had learned from her own mother and Old Tenum, the Flathead Medicine Man who had lived with them for many years. Eventually Jo recovered completely, and was extremely proud of her brothers for rescuing her, and she tagged along with them everywhere, much to their irritation.

It was a while before Josephine was healed up, though, and during that time Louie and Vila worried about how to keep Jo from talking about their secret. They had felt so sorry for her, all pitiful and puffed up in her bed, (even if she was a nosy little thing) that they had whispered the truth to her to cheer her up, promising to show her the sweat lodge and let her go in it once she was feeling better. But they knew Jo wouldn't be able to resist telling someone sooner or later.

The solution came from Jo herself, and her own irrepressible nature. Simple blackmail and a negotiated deal proved to be just the combination to keep Jo quiet.

As mentioned earlier, Miss Josephine was a busy little bee, and it didn't take too long into the recovery period for her to get a little bored. She tended to follow everyone in the house around and pester them, though not with her usual vim. She tired quickly and began to fuss, and would soon find herself tucked in the big bed in her parent's room. Jo particularly liked this, because when her mother was busy she could sneak about and poke into things.

This afternoon, Jo didn't feel that sleepy, but she pretended to nap when her mother came and went from the room. Peeking under her eyelashes, Jo noticed that her mother moved in a stealthy way. Her hand slipped into her apron pocket and then she placed something on the door frame above the door. Then Marie left, quietly closing the door behind her.

Jo was out of bed and over to the door in two shakes of a lamb's tail. She listened until she heard her mother's footsteps on the front porch. Quick as a wink, Jo dragged a chair over to the door and climbed on it. She reached for the door frame. Too high. Jo's eyes darted around the room. There. She could set that wooden box on the chair and she would be high enough to reach the frame.

Carefully balancing on top of the box, Jo stretched her arm to reach the frame. Her fingers patted the rough wood until they felt something cold and flat. Jo's heart skipped a beat. She grasped the object and looked at it with awe. It was a gold piece, stamped with the shape of an eagle. Jo was surprised at how heavy the coin was. She traced the engraving with her finger, then after giving it a kiss for luck, slid the coin back onto its hiding place. She put the box and the chair away and climbed back into bed to daydream about hidden treasure.

The next day Jo got tired and fretful a little more quickly than usual, and ended up in the big bed again. A bit of a breeze stirred the curtains at the open window as Jo dragged the chair over to the door. The gold piece was still there. Jo tried biting to see if it was real gold. She guessed it was. Jo started to slide the coin back onto the door frame when she heard a scuffle behind her. Panicked, she pushed the coin back against the wall. To her dismay she heard a thunking sound as the coin dropped through a crack between the wallboards.

"Busy Bee, what have you done?" Louie exclaimed as he hoisted Vila over the window jamb and started to crawl in himself.

"I didn't mean to, I was just looking at it!" Jo wailed, then began to cry in earnest, nearly toppling the box she was standing on. Vila lurched forward to steady her and help her down off the box.

Louie moved the box and climbed on the chair. After a moment he shook his head.

"We would have to tear the boards apart." He glanced at Josephine's tear-streaked face. "Mama and Papa are going to be very angry with you, Jo."

"Oh, please, please don't tell them, Louie, I'll be very good from now on!" Jo begged, her puffy face looking more pitiful by the minute. She looked beseechingly at Vila and then buried her head against his shoulder again, sobbing quietly.

The boys looked at each other. Louie winked and Vila winked back.

"You know Jo, we could make a pact," Vila suggested. Jo's head came up.

"What's a pact?"

"It's when everyone swears to keep a secret for each other, and if one breaks their promise the others will tell their secret. We won't let on about what happened to that gold coin, but you have to promise never ever say a word about our sweat lodge. If you do, we will tell Papa and Mama who lost the coin."

"And you will probably get a good switching," Louie added. Jo blanched. Her backside twitched at the mere thought. It still hurt from those bee stings.

"I swear!" she exclaimed without hesitation.

The boys put the chair and the box away and tucked Jo back into bed, then climbed out the window. They waved at her and she gave them a watery smile. At least they all had a secret to keep, she thought to herself. And guilty as she felt, she never could quite bring herself to confess to her mother. Instead she confessed to the priest before Sunday Mass (after all she had to tell someone), and was sent home to do a whole lot of Hail Mary's and some extra chores for her mother.

Marie never guessed what happened to the coin she had received in payment for washing and ironing laundry for Polly's Logging Company, but she probably wouldn't have been surprised to find out a busy little bee had something to do with it.

Buddy III prospecting on mountain ridge.

THE DIXON MINES
By Josephine Chevre

Light moves up along the canyon's narrow sides, scarcely warm, scarcely welcoming. Everything is spring wet, patches of snow glimmer in corners of ruined ground like the light that filters through the dirty white curtains that cover Velma's windows. Here and there mounds thick with brown needles huddle around the mine openings like old shawled women around a cradle.

She lives alone in a shack cluttered with years of poverty, junk stacked along grey papered walls in boxes, her dresser top crowded with black and white photographs of sons who visit only to borrow this month's government check. Outside, the flooding has nearly washed out the bridge and the creek is still high, full of silt and tailings, broken timbers slick with mildew.

She thinks of the boy from up the valley who knocked on her door last spring. She liked his eyes, the way they held the shapes of the canyon, the shadows and dappled light. Would she mind if he looked at her old cars, and yes, tea would be nice, thank you. He sat on the metal kitchen chair and sipped Lipton tea from a chipped cup the same yellow grey as her hair.

The light from the window shone gold and for a second she felt as clean as a bright coin in the glass on the sill. The sun was warm now, so she grasped her cane and his arm, and walked out into the clearing, past the dump and the fallen chicken coop to the rusted shells of cars grown over with rose thickets and gooseberry. The spareness of his frame and the width of his shoulders pleased her.

He comes back now and then, to show her bits of gold he's found, to drink her coffee and have a cookie from the box she keeps on hand for him. She worries when he disappears through the mouth of a tunnel that worms under the hills, wonders that he seems so light and clean even when he comes out covered with earth, pockets bulging with ore.

She feels too old to move from the kitchen table so she sinks back into her chair and closes her eyes. She dreams she has died, everything is spring wet and he is standing in the clearing, looking at the grey ashes of the trash pile. He bends down and picks up a copper penny, wipes it on his coat sleeve and holds it in his palm. It catches the watery light and glints red, a small dark flame.

**Author's note: My brother has a gentle gift of finding and revealing the magic in everyday life. When he was a young teen, he used to go down to the old Dixon mine shafts and explore the tunnels, looking for loose ore and panning it out at home. He discovered a very special friend while he was there, and he continued to visit her in her home until she died. One day he shared his secret friendship with me, and exposed me to the dangerous thrill of exploring the inky, dripping blackness inside the old mines. The treasure of experiencing the world through his eyes, its potential for beauty, its magic, ugliness and decay, the uncompromising reality of death, and the timelessness of human spirit I still carry in some back pocket of my mind. Every once in a while I pull it out and look at it, and see the dappled, green light of a wet spring in his eyes.

THE PASSING OF A LEGEND

Bud Cheff, a lifetime Mission Valley resident passed on to meet the Lord and join his beloved wife, Adelle, his daughter Viola, his parents Marie and Ovila Cheff, seven brothers: Leo, Rex, Chris, Louie, Vila, Jim, Ray, three sisters: Bernida, Grace, and Josephine, plus grandchildren: Corey, Billy, Amanda, and Cheri. He is survived by three brothers: Floyd, Herman, and Clarence. He is also survived by one daughter and five sons and their families: Bud Jr. and wife Laurie, Kenny, Buck and wife Cheryl, Mick and wife Karen, Dan (Happy), daughter Roxy and husband Don. He was blessed with thirty-three grandchildren, eighty-two great grandchildren, and eighteen great-great grandchildren.

Bud Vern Edmond Cheff Sr., 96 years old, died June 27th, 2011, at his home with his family. He was born April 2, 1915, southeast of Ronan on the Tehnum Finley place. He went to school at Ronan, and in 1933 married his childhood sweetheart, Adelle Rogers. They were sweethearts from the 5th grade on.

Bud took his first paying customers as a outfitter into the Bob Marshall Wilderness that year, starting a lifetime career as an outfitter and guide. He was honored in 2010 for being "the oldest living outfitter in Montana, and having the longest ongoing outfitting business in the state, from 1933 to 2011. It is still a flourishing family-owned business.

He has been invited to speak at a number of universities in the western states, including a convention of world-wide scientists held in Glacier National Park. Bud had a deep love for Montana and its wilderness areas. He was devoted to preserving the wildlife and land for future generations.

Bud Cheff Sr. in museum, standing by painting of him by Richard Sanders.

Bud's family had early roots in Montana, starting with a free trapper for David Thompson and the Northwest Fur Co. in 1810, to the settling of Frenchtown and Demersville in the Flathead. His parents came from

Ontario, Canada, in the late 1890's to join other family members already here.

Of French and Iroquois descent, Bud's family had close ties with the Flathead Indians. Bud went with them every year until 1933, on their hunting and gathering trips into the Mission Range and Bob Marshall area, under the leadership of Eneas Conko. Eneas and the old Indian hunters taught him well, as he had a vast knowledge of wildlife and the mountains.

Bud wrote two books, *Indian Trails and Grizzly Tales* and *The Woodsman and his Hatchet*. The magazine *Outdoor Life* did a series of stories about Bud and his hunting experiences. Starting as an ironworker on Kerr Dam, Bud also worked on Hungry Horse and Noxon Dams, the Frenchtown pulp mill, the Columbia Falls aluminum plant, and numerous bridges over the years. He was a top-notch cowboy and bronco buster, breaking hundreds of horses and mules in his lifetime.

Laurie and Bud Cheff Sr. at age 96.

Bud and Adelle were instrumental in starting the First Baptist Church in Ronan where their son Hap was a pastor. They were charter members and cofounders of the Ninepipes Museum of Early Montana. He was loved by the school children that toured the museum and received many thank you letters from them.

Bud was loved and admired by all that knew him, a testimony shown by close to one thousand friends that came to pay tribute at his funeral. He was a storehouse of Montana history, had a wonderful memory, and loved to share his knowledge with all that were interested. His hope was to leave this world a little better than he found it, and he prayed that he had not offended any of the wonderful people he had met and cherished in his long life. He will be sorely missed by all.

A REALLY BIG SOUL
By Josephine Chevre

Dear Grandpa, When you died, the wheel turned and we all felt it. Today, working in the yard, I noticed how the garden spiders have already completed their cycle this season, their hard work, their story of silk mysteriously gone from the flower beds. My thoughts web out, reaching for the fibers that connect us all together, the patterns that make up the tapestry of the Mission Valley, of Montana, of the continent and the world, of the human story that stands witness to the ever changing environment from which we've carved out our brief history.

It is an over-used metaphor, I know, but timeless as well, and it seems right while I am here in the garden, feeling time pull me ahead. This corner of the world has lost a bright thread in the pattern that has been woven across it for the past ninety-six years.

Dad's casket carried by grandson Bud III and great-grandson Micky III.

If each of us has a thread in the pattern, a color, a texture, a specific weave, then yours was surely bright red, Grandpa. Yours was a wide, solid bar of sturdy wool that ran across the fabric the way you ran down a mountain pass to catch two stray horses, the way you walked iron, carried your children, wept at your brother's funeral, spun your wife across the dance floor.

Dad's saddlehorse behind the wagon.

And as it wove itself into the whole design another band of color deepened the edges where the threads met, dark violet spinning out into

Adelle's lilac hues. Rich veins no miner could tap, all those shades of the human heart, yet one by one all of us, your children, grandchildren, all those who were connected by that heart, spin our own tiny threads out into the ever growing pattern, taking our places in the weaving of a design that keeps shifting just beyond human vision.

I read once that surgeons call a specific place within the heart muscle "the seat of the soul," a title bestowed with great respect and even awe, for when they reach that deep chamber, it feels as though they have touched the sacred. On the way home to your funeral, Grandpa, when we were driving toward the Missions, my husband Yo looked at me in quiet amazement and said, "Can you feel it? The whole valley feels empty. Your Grandpa must have filled it up, Jo. A really BIG SOUL just left this valley."

In the quiet moments, and the loud joyous ones, we miss you. We tell stories about your unbridled enthusiasm for life and your straightforward commitment to being finished with it, and then we pause, realizing all over again the richness of the human heart when it is open. This is our inheritance.

With love and gratitude, your granddaughter, Laurie Jo

MONTANA COWBOY HALL OF FAME CITATION
BUD CHEFF SR.

Vern Edmond Cheff Sr. (Bud) was born April 2, 1915, the fourth of fourteen children, on his parents' sheep and cattle ranch near Ronan, Montana, on the Flathead Indian Reservation. Bud was of French and Indian descent. He spoke only French and Indian until he started school, then he had to learn to speak English.

Bud married his school sweetheart on June 10th, 1933. Together they raised seven children, Viola Lietz (deceased), Bud Jr., Kenny, Buck, Mick, Roxena Sanders, and Happy. Bud died at home on his beloved ranch June 29, 2011, at the age of 96. He lived alone after losing his wife, Adelle, in 1999, taking care of himself until the last two weeks of his life.

Bud learned many tricks in breaking horses from his old Indian friends. His mentor was Eneas Conko, a full-blood Kalispel Indian who had ridden for the Buffalo Bill Wild West Show in his youth. He taught Bud many tricks in roping and horsemanship, as well as hunting and mountain lore. Bud in turn shared his wealth of knowledge with his sons and anyone who wanted to learn, and there were hundreds that did. He took great pleasure in teaching others, especially the youth. He loved sharing his life and history with the school tour groups that visited the Ninepipes Museum of Early Montana. He was still helping with the tours within a couple months before his death, and the kids loved him.

> **Montana Cowboy Hall of Fame**
> **2012 Inductee**
>
> This Award is presented to
>
> *Vern E. Cheff, Sr.*
> *'Bud'*
> For significant contribution
> to the Heritage and Culture
> of MONTANA
>
> DuWayne Wilson, President 2012

Bud had a special way with horses and cows. He could be riding through a herd of cows and point at a cow, and tell you, "She's out of old Crooked Horn, a good cow; always bring a calf in. And that one's grandma was the red line back cow. She raised some good calves." He might say, "See that filly, she must be out of that standard bred stud. You can bet she can run!" Or, "See how that horse picks its feet up? It will be a tough horse, but hard riding. It will beat you to death in a long day's ride." He was always looking, and noticed everything about the livestock.

Bud raised hundreds of horses in his lifetime. There were usually between 100 and 200 head on the ranch. In 2011 the count was about 180. He probably cut or castrated a thousand horse colts in his life, as he cut all of his own, and the neighbors had him cut theirs. In the early years when there weren't a lot of fences the horses could range over a big area and would often be mixed with other horses. Many of them were wild, unbranded, and there would often be a very undesirable stud with them. Bud always carried some loose salt and medicine in his saddlebags for doctoring the livestock if need be when out checking stock. A number of times he would rope these wild stallions and cut them, and turn them loose again. As a young man he and a couple of cowboy friends ran and caught wild horses in the Camas wild horse plains area. He also rode in the local rodeos. As a small boy he watched the great Nez Perce, Jackson Sundown, ride. Jackson's daughter was a neighbor and a friend of the family. Bud started breaking horses for pay at the age of 15, and broke many hundreds in his lifetime. This included not only saddle horses, but work teams and pack mules. He broke his last colt at the age of 93. He was still using teams for ranch work until the mid-1950's and hated to switch to a tractor. He always said it was the horse that won the West, they are wonderful animals.

You could say Bud spent his whole life on a horse. He started riding as a small child and was still riding at the age of 95. He is quoted in saying, "I wore out a lot of good horses in my life." Bud was a true Montana cowboy in every respect. He could not only ride or handle any kind of a horse and knew how to doctor a sick or injured cow, pull a calf, or dig a post hole. He had a special, calming way of handling both horses and cows; he could get them to do things that most people could not. His horse was taken care of, and the livestock all fed before he would think of his own needs.

Bud worked as an outfitter and guide all of his life, as well as owning a cattle and horse ranch. In 2010 he was honored by the Forest Service and the Montana Outfitters and Guides Association. They presented him with a plaque for being the oldest outfitter, and having the longest continuous operating outfitting business in Montana, from 1932 to the present. His son Mick and family continue to run the business and the ranch.

With the help of his wife Adelle, Bud wrote two books. The first book, *"Indian Trails and Grizzly Tales,"* was a book on his life, and how he benefitted, being part of both Indian and white cultures. He was invited to speak at a number of schools and universities about his life and the changing West. There have been countless newspaper and magazine stories written about him, including a four-month series in *Outdoor Life* magazine. He was a real Montana historical treasure. It was easy to see how much he was loved and respected when close to 1,000 people came to show their respects at his funeral. The last words he spoke were, "Open the gate and turn that last horse loose."

Chapter Three

STORIES FROM THE PAST

LOST GOLD MINE

Early one summer in about 1881 two miners went into the Mission Mountains afoot, leading three pack burros. Late that fall one of the two men came back out, with two burros. When asked where his partner was he said the partner had died from a injury and he had buried him there in the mountains. Then he said a grizzly bear killed one of the burros near their camp, so he decided to leave. He paid for his purchases at the Demers Mercantile in St. Ignatius with gold out of a large poke full of gold. Some of the store loafers saw this and decided the two miners had struck some rich diggings, and this one probably killed his partner for the gold.

Five of these men approached him, saying they represented the law, and made a citizen's arrest on the miner. They told him they were going to hang him for killing his partner unless he took them back to his camp, so they could determine if he had murdered the man or not. The party left horseback the next day with the miner in tow. It was slow going with no real trails. None of the group had been in this country before, except the miner who had only made the one trip in and out.

The party followed Indian trails when they could, and after several days of traveling, one of the pack horses was killed in a fall. Then they made the miner walk, and packed the horse he had been riding. The men thought he was having trouble finding his way back on purpose. The vigilantes told him if he was leading them on a wild goose chase he would be left for the bears. It was a lot more difficult traveling through the mountains with horses than it had been for the two men walking and leading the burros. The miner told them he was sure they would be there in two more days. The next day one of his captors, who had decided he really did not want to be part of this rough group, felt sorry for the miner. He discreetly told him as soon as they found his gold mine they were going to kill him, and say he was killed in a fight trying to escape. They didn't care a hoot if he had killed his partner. They just wanted the gold. The miner's boots were taken from him every night so he wouldn't try to leave. The weather was getting cold, frosting at night and a man couldn't get far in these rough mountains with bare, frozen feet.

That night the miner escaped, figuring he would rather die fighting the elements on bare feet than with a bullet in the chest. The vigilante group searched for him for several days, but gave up in a snowstorm and headed home before they were snowed in for the winter. The miner probably came out in what is now the Seeley Lake area, traveling up the Blackfoot Valley and over the mountains to Helena. He had gone for almost two weeks with no shoes, no gun or knife, and almost no food. He only had a little extra ration the good captor had given him the night he escaped, and he had no way of hunting or securing food. He might have tried to make foot coverings out of bark and moss but they would not have lasted very long. He had sure death behind him, and probable death in front of him. His only chance was to run into someone that would help him. This must not have happened as there is no record of it. His feet were in terrible shape, frozen and cut to ribbons when he was found just outside of Helena. No one knows just what route he took for sure. He was too far gone from exposure to talk when he was found, and he died a few days later.

This story was told to Dad by Eneas Conko and Phillip Pierre when he was a boy. Both men looked for the mine for many years. Dad and

Bud Sr., Bud Jr., son Jim, Bud III taking photo while searching for mine.

Bill Conko, Eneas's son helped Eneas look for the mine when they were boys. He would have them climb up certain mountains and look for old diggings, bringing him back rock samples. In later years, when I was a small boy, I listened with awe while Eneas and Phillip talked to Dad about this lost gold mine. Phillip thought it was in a different area than Eneas did, and he and his two wives, Mary Katherine and Clarice Paul, spent many summers looking for it, to no avail.

From left, Bud III, Bud IV, and Bud Sr. Bud Jr. taking photo while searching for mine.

Burro hoof with shoe.

When I was about fourteen years old, Eneas wanted Dad to take him in to look for the mine one more time. He said he was

Bud III and Bud Sr. panning for gold.

sure he knew where it was, as he had found some old axe marks and some burros feet with shoes still on them. He was sure the gold diggings would be right above this spot.

I was real excited but Dad said no. He told him, "You're too blind and those mountains are too rough for a man your age." Eneas said he knew in his mind where to go, and we could be his eyes. I insisted I could do all the climbing for them, as I was young and in good shape. I could do all the camp chores and take care of the horses while Dad took care of Eneas, but Dad said no, the trip would kill Eneas. I was really disappointed but knew in my heart Dad was right. Eneas looked so sad, and I think he would have been happy to die in the mountains he loved, with Dad at his side. Eneas died four years later and Dad joined him in 2011. They both left big footsteps to follow in their amazing lives, and I have tried to follow the best I could.

Bud Sr., Jim looking for mine.

Dad and I spent a lot of time through the years, looking for the gold mine. In later years my boys and daughter, as well as grandsons joined us looking. I am convinced the miner's gold came from the upper Blackfoot, not the Missions. Maybe it was gold they had with them from another source. We will probably never

Old diggings with shovel found in it.

know the truth, it's just another mystery of the Mission mountains that make them so special. Our treasure was the fun and companionship in looking for the mine, not finding the gold.

THE FIGHT BETWEEN SUM-A-KAA AND DAVE FINLEY

Author's note: The following story is a fictionalized version of real events, as they were told by Dave Finley to Ovila Cheff and his family, and later recorded by Bud Cheff Sr., who was nicknamed "Little Tehnum" as a small child. Tehnum Finley lived with Ovila's family until he died in 1925, and his brothers, August and Dave, visited quite often. The Finleys, the Cheffs and the Mollmans were all good friends. Louie Mollman would have been about 65 years of age at the time that Dave fought the grizzly bear, which was around 1895. Dave Finley was born in 1849 and died in 1927. He was Pend d'Oreille and Kootenai, with some Iroquois and French ancestry. He spoke a mixture of Indian and French, and a little English.

At the time of the story many French Canadian words had been borrowed and intermixed with the local Salish dialect, and vise-versa. Tehnum's name was originally a French expression- translating to "Little Man," which the French trappers called him when he was a child because he was always seen working alongside the grown men. Tet-le-me', the name the Indians called Ovila Cheff, meant "Little French Man," and referred to Ovila's short stature. It was originally derived from the Salish language.

"Ta-ska-suyapi" is apparently and older version of "Ta-ya-suwapi", meaning "no good white man." Ovila's children were commonly referred to as "Te-le-me's papooses" by the Indian families in the valley. They also used the term "squaw" to describe their women, and for authenticity's sake I have left in the words as the characters used them, although the spelling is sometimes an approximation.

Josephine Chevre

The old healer Tehnum Finley hailed his younger brother as Dave stepped up on Ovila's porch, moving with deliberate care. A strongly build man of medium height, Dave carried himself with a natural dignity. His movements had once melded power and grace, but the advancing years and old injuries stiffened his body. Today arthritis and the throbbing of old scars pulled his mind back in time, so that something about his face changed. Ovila's young children looked at him curiously. "Ho!" he told them, "I have a story for you." They crowded around him, their faces full of questions. His eyes became dark pools of stillness, and within the darkness something furious and violent stirred. The children watched him, fascinated and instinctively fearful. Dave's eyes lighted with grim humor. He knew how to tell a good story, and this one would make them shudder and cry out in their dreams.

"It happened a long time ago, before Tet-le-me's papooses were born. I had taken a white man hunting up Mollman Pass. He wanted to get a big mule deer buck, and if possible, a mountain goat. We left our horses by Mollman's cabin, and I visited with Louie and Philomene for a little while. I told Louie that I was not sure about guiding this man, something about him made me uneasy.

"The man had his rifle, but I had left mine behind so that I could carry out the game. I figured the hunter would be no help at all. We were climbing along the ridge where it falls away steep to the creek bottom when I heard Sum-a-kaa huff at us. That grizzly, he was a big one, and not happy to see us below him. I told the man, "Don't shoot him, he is right above us!" But the hunter, his face turned pale, then red like a berry. He pointed his gun and I yelled, 'Don't shoot!' He shot anyway, that ta-ska-suyape. He shot the bear and it came right down at us, bellering its war cry the whole way. We ran, and the hunter was ahead of me, running with the gun. Sum-a-kaa, he caught me so quick!"

"Dave's hand shot out and latched onto the britches of little Buddy, who was leaning against Old Tehnum's chair. Buddy's eyes got round as saucers and his sisters squealed. "Just like that, he had me!" Ovila leaned back, eyeing Dave expectantly, having already heard the story from Louie Mollman. His wife Marie gripped the back of his chair, her face riveted on Dave's.

"I grabbed my knife. Sum-a-kaa, he swatted me and my knife fell to the ground. I yelled to that no-good white man to help me, but he just kept on running with the gun. He left me for the bear to eat.

"Sum-a-kaa, he opened his big mouth and in the hot stink of his breath I smelled my own death." Dave twisted his face into a fierce grimace, opening his jaws wide, breath hissing, teeth bared to the young boy's face, then snapped them shut with an audible click. Nobody moved or spoke. Tehnum's amused chuckle danced soft-footed across the silence. Dave let go of the boy with a wink and continued his story. He was really enjoying himself now.

"All I could see were those big teeth and that big tongue. I knew he was going to bite off my face, so I stuck my hand right into Sum-a-kaa's mouth and grabbed his stinky tongue." Dave mimed grabbing onto the bear's tongue and squeezing. "I felt a terrible pain in my back. The last thing I remember is hanging onto Sum-a-kaa's big tongue." Dave's hands settled onto his thighs again. He was quiet for a moment, letting the scene play in the mind of his audience.

"When I woke up, Sum-a-kaa was gone. The hunter went back to our horses and rode off without telling anyone. Louie Mollman watched him go and thought it strange. He had heard the gunshot echo down the canyon earlier. When I did not return by the evening meal, Louie fetched my nephew, Moon Finley, to help him look for me. Louie knew we had gone up the old trail on the ridge, and lucky for me, we had not left it when we saw the bear. They found me unconscious, and bound up my wounds so I would not bleed to death. They brought me home. He glanced at Tehnum. My brother, he has strong medicine because I didn't die, but Sum-a-kaa, he got me good."

Dave stood up carefully. He removed his shirt, his face full of promise of something awful to come. The girls gripped each other. Chris and Louie both tried to climb on their father's lap at the same time, and Rex sucked in his breath. The old man had bite and claw marks over much of his body and both arms. The arm he had stuck into the bear's mouth was badly chewed and the bigger muscles of his back and shoulders had been torn loose, leaving him terribly wounded. The disfiguring scars were horrible to look at, but the children eventually could not resist touching them, and with a faint smile, Dave tolerated the curious little hands probing him. Some how, their enthusiasm and their awe soothed the throbbing pain that still held him in its grip after all these years, and relaxed the tenseness inside of him.

He had lain waiting for his wounds to heal, and had sworn to kill the *ta-ska-suyapi*. But word had spread of his promise of vengeance, and the white man had shown more common sense than he had courage, and immediately left the country. The old anger abated a bit as Dave reconsidered his battle wounds. He had been marked by a most fierce opponent, and both he and Sum-a-kaa had fought bravely. He wore his scars with the pride of a warrior, and told his story so that the dreams of young boys would strike fire in their hearts, as they had when he was a youth. Soon, a new century would begin, and somehow Dave guessed that both the time of the warrior/hunter and the grizzly would soon be over. He wondered how young men would prove themselves, where would they find personal courage and honor in a land of machines and crowded cities.

In his early days life touched the edge of death every day, and it had been easy and natural for a young man to prove his worth. He had hunted buffalo on the plains where the Blackfeet and the Crow were a constant danger. Even at seventy four years of age, Dave Finley felt a little uncomfortable with modern life, and he pitied the young men.

He began to tell Ovila about the last time he hunted buffalo, not to eat, but to capture.

The great herds had disappeared and, ironically, Canada and the U.S. were setting up preserves with the hopes of keeping the bison from complete extinction. After the famous buffalo roundup of the Pablo/Allard herd, Michel Pablo hired Dave and his brother, August, to hunt down the stragglers that had escaped, and bring them in. The whole herd, the largest in the world at that time, was to be sold to Canada, to go to the Alberta preserve. Dave and his brothers were the oldest and most experienced of the men, so Michel had asked for their help.

As was the Indian custom, they took their families and tipis with them on the hunt, only now they used wagons to carry the supplies. After the roundup there was one cow buffalo left that was determined not to be caught. August went up into the hills to try and chase her down to the river. He told the women and children to scare her toward the river where Dave was waiting if she came by the camp. The buffalo cow came charging down through the camp so impressively that the children all climbed trees, and the women hid in the wagons and let her go by. August rode down to his brother a short time later, disgust written all over his face. He said, "I have very damn soft Indians today. So damn soft I could poke a cattail through them! We are all soft, fat old squaws. We go to Ronan now and live in wood houses like white men." Dave had looked at his brother and suddenly felt obsolete. Their time was over, and their knowledge and skills were fast becoming unnecessary for survival.

Now Dave looked at the little boy who sat close to Tehnum. He followed the old man like a puppy, and everyone called him Little Tehnum. But the healer would leave this world before the boy was old enough to learn from him. The oldest boy, Rex, had the heart of a healer. Would he remember the medicine plants Old Tehnum had shown him? "The young ones will follow the roads and the old trails will fade from the land. They will forget even our stories," he thought. "But the earth will remember. The grandchildren will hear our voices on the wind, but they won't know what they hear."

THE DEER CHILD
By Josephine Chevre

The old woman sat in her favorite chair in the parlor, the one next to the piano. Her delicate hands were folded neatly across her lap, house dress and apron smoothed across her knees. A shy, delighted smile played across her mobile features as she faced the man seated across the room from her. In the eightieth decade of her life the irrepressible, childlike purity of her being seemed to illuminate her slender frame, belying the fact that she was of frail health, and that her long life had been filled with enough hardship and heartache to leach the joy out of someone with a less inherently good nature. The conversation had lulled, and in the tiny house the perennial quiet seemed exaggerated. In the kitchen the old refrigerator hummed and wheezed, and the clock over the oilcloth-draped table ticked along with relentless lack of imagination. But Louise's mind was running wild with quicksilver images of a younger life, brimming with recollections that this respectful man whose father she had played with as a child was pulling up with his questions. Like a magician pulling rabbits out of that cowboy hat he's holding, she thought with amusement. Tiny bubbles of joyful laughter rose up the curve of her spine. She remembered the first time she had met those boys, the one who would be her friend, and the one whom she would wed and bury before she had raised their children.

It was late summer, 1923, and she was just nine years old, and the world was unfolding before her wondering eyes. When the families met up to travel together into the mountains this time of year the fast changing world temporarily receded, and they relived the old ways that

Louise and Bud Jr.

had been their pattern for hundreds of years. The adults used the trips to teach their children what their parents and grandparents had taught them when they were small. The children would learn where and how to dig medicine roots, which areas were best for gathering pine nuts and picking berries, just as their parents had in earlier times. They would hunt and fish, and learn how to dry the meat properly and pack it for winter storage. Though she didn't give it much conscious thought, Louise felt the patterns of generations of ancestors, knew her moccasins stepped where her grandmothers had once stepped, and her digging stick prodded the same soil that women of her tribe had dug in long before her time.

Louise rode close to her stepmother, mimicking the woman's actions and chattering to her happily. She felt a twinge of sadness when she thought of her own mother, Margaret, a Spokane Indian who now lived near Worley, Idaho, close to her family. Margaret was on good terms with Pierre and his second wife, and Louise lived part of each year in each of the households.

The beauty of the morning surrounded Louise, and for a moment she was consumed with a passionate longing to share it with her mother. Voices called out and her stepmother's pleased exclamation brought Louise out of her melancholy thoughts. She looked up to see her friend, Agnes Chief Eagle, and her parents join the group. Soon the women and girls were all laughing and chatting together as they headed up the trail. Louise's father, Pierre Adams, a lean, handsome Salish man sat his horse straight-backed and proud. He led the band along the old trails that wound through the steep Mission Range, followed by several men, and then the women and children driving the pack horses. A couple of young men guarded the rear of the group. Compared to the lively women, the men were quiet, occasionally speaking a few words, and Pierre was studying the trail in front of him intently. He could see that horses had passed this way a few days earlier. He was certain that the tracks belonged to Eneas Conko's band. No one knew this part of the mountains better than Eneas, and he usually made a trip up here this time of year. Philip Pierre, a great hunter, was the only other person who knew the area that well, and he was with Conko's band now.

Louise.

Usually, Pierre Adam's band traveled through the Jocko into the Swan Range, but today Pierre asked the group if they would like to join Conko's band for a few days. Everyone agreed enthusiastically. Pierre had a good idea of where Conko would be camped, and told the others that they would meet up with his band the next day.

Bill and Buddy were best friends on all accounts, and both as full of mischief and fun as a couple of nine year olds on an adventure could be. This particular adventure was a trip with Bill's parents, Eneas and Sofia Conko, and other members of his band, into the Missions on a hunting and gathering trip. They were so busy playing and helping the adults that they didn't notice the second band riding toward their camp until the horses began whinnying at each other. Coming down the ridge in single file, Pierre's band made a colorful parade, the women in calico dresses and bright headscarves, shawls and blankets; the men with their big hats, braided hair and colorful neck scarves tied in front. The boys forgot their game and ran to greet the new arrivals. The air was thick with all the excitement of a rendezvous; horses nickering, dogs barking, women and children smiling and calling to each other, men laughing and exchanging high spirited banter as they mingled.

Louise and her mother, Margaret.

Once the initial greetings were over the women quickly helped each other set up camp while the men turned the horses into the meadow, putting hobbles on a few of the leaders to make sure they didn't stray. Buddy and Bill were set to work to help bring in firewood with the other children. Seeing them across the camp, Agnes grabbed Louise's hand and pulled her along as she ran toward the boys. Grinning, she stopped in front of Buddy and Bill, who suddenly became shy and awkward. Both boys were tongue-tied at the sight of Louise. She was just beautiful! Still grinning Agnes elbowed Louise and introduced her to the boys.

She knew they would be smitten with her shy, doe-eyed friend. Buddy, always friendly and generally unabashed, recovered first.

"It's nice to meet you, Louise," he said politely. Bill was still stunned. Buddy covered for his love-struck friend by making conversation. "We were just heading over toward those trees. There's a lot of good firewood in there. Do you girls want to come?" he said. Agnes flashed another big grin and said, "We'll race you!" Instantly, they were all off and running. The girls, having the advantage of surprise, took the lead. Louise loved to run. She surrendered to the excitement of the moment, pulling ahead of the others without noticing. She leapt a fallen tree as if she had springs on her feet and stopped in the trees as the others ran up panting. The boys tried not to show either their disappointment at coming in last or their admiration at the two pretty girls' athletic prowess. Soon they were all trudging back with armloads of firewood, shyness forgotten.

Louise, her dad, Pierre Adams, and her husband, Bill Conko.

That night the singing and dancing was especially joyful, and Philip Pierre filled the children's ears with his wonderful story telling, while Cecile Hewankorn, Sofia's daughter, and her husband Baptiste kept the group in stitches with their endless supply of jokes and sly humor. Cecile teased Bill and Buddy about their sudden willingness to help with camp chores when two new girls showed up, and soon all the children blushing and ducking their heads.

The morning was chilly and ghost trails of blue smoke from cooking fires hung over the camp, making two small boys' stomachs rumble as they hurriedly pulled on their clothes and moccasins, their skin prickling with goose bumps. They washed their faces and hands in the cold lake, noticing that some of the horses were gone from the meadow. Pierre Adams, Eneas and his oldest son, Leo, Philip Pierre, and Antoine Chief Eagle had already left to hunt some game to feed the camp. Bill saw a movement further along the edge of the lake. A fawn was grazing there, and for some reason, as he watched it, he thought of Louise.

Some of the women were going to hike to a good meadow for digging hausk, a valuable medicine root that they both used and sold or traded in the valley. Agnes and Louise went along to help, and Buddy and Bill walked with them as far as the meadow before veering off the trail to hunt for grouse with their .22 rifles. They walked in front of the women, knocking the dew off of the bushes along the trail with sticks so the women's long dresses wouldn't get so wet. This always earned Bill and Buddy Sofia's approval, and usually an extra hunk of dried meat for the always hungry boys to chew on. For several hours the girls were busy digging and cleaning hausk. The roots were small and covered with fine rootlets that had to be scraped off before they were dried. The plant had a celery like smell and strong celery like flavor, and was used both as a curative and preventative during the flu and cold season. Typically, the women would dole out small chunks of the dried root to the children daily to tuck behind their lip and slowly swallow the juices as it softened in their mouths. It was also used as a curative tea.

(In the 1960's Buddy would take some botanists up into the mountains to see this undocumented plant. The botanists were excited to identify the plant as an unknown subspecies in the parsley family and document it.)

Louise and Agnes each carried a share of the hausk back to camp with the other women and children. Bill and Buddy were waiting ahead of them on the trail, each with several grouse. They tried not to look as proud as they felt when Bill's older sister, whose name was also Agnes, smilingly praised their kill. The boys led the group back to camp, feeling quite manly.

Soon after they got back, the hunters returned with plenty of meat for the camp, and the women set to work butchering the meat and preparing a feast. Louise and Agnes helped their mothers flesh and stretch the hides for drying. Once the hides were sufficiently dry, they would be packed away to be tanned once they were back home. Then they joined the other women who were cooking the fresh meat for the night's feast, and cutting strips to smoke on the racks constructed over the drying fires. By the time the big August moon burst over the rim of the peak and shone down on a full and contented camp, the singing and drumming was well under way. The drumbeats, songs and bouts of laughter echoed back from the lonely canyon walls, as if the all the bands that had ever camped there were joining in from some other time.

The next day a couple of the women stayed in camp to finish drying the meat while the rest of the group headed toward Goat Foot Pass where large stands of limber pine grew along the high ridges on the way to Elk

Lake. By the time they reached a good stand of pine it was hot on the sunny ridge and the air was fragrant with the scent of pine sap. Men, women and children began knocking down cones and putting them into gunnysacks. Though gathering pine nuts was serious work the day had the air of a picnic, and all of them were enjoying themselves.

Louise and Agnes were thirsty and Bill's sister, who was twelve, suggested that she would show the younger children how to get to a spring that trickled out of the rocks not too far away. Several of the children in the group came along, following her along the ridge toward a big outcropping of rock. Bill exclaimed to Buddy that he remembered the rest of the way now, and the boys clambered ahead, with Louise and Agnes behind them like faithful shadows. They climbed around the rocks and reached the spring well ahead of the others, who were moving slowly to accommodate the little kids. After drinking their fill, the four decided to climb up to a nearby stand of pine to see if there was a good supply of cones that they could gather. When they had nearly reached the trees the ground flattened out so they picked up their pace. Without warning Bill stopped so suddenly that Buddy ran into him and Louise ran into Buddy. Agnes started to laugh, but Bill put his finger to his lips and pointed. Some other families had beat them to this gathering spot, only they had four legs and were covered with beautiful furry coats that gleamed in the sunlight.

Nine grizzlies were busy fattening up on the pine nuts. One sow had this year's cubs and kept them apart from the other grizzlies, who were all feeding together. None of the children had ever seen so many bears in one place at the same time, and they were awestruck. The bears, on the other hand, were unconcerned with the arrival of the two legged cubs. There were plenty of pine nuts for every one this season. The sow stood up on her hind legs, and her cubs stood up too, curious. She gave a short huff to warn the little humans to keep a reasonable distance, and then dropped down to continue her meal. The four children turned and moved cautiously back the way they had come, hearts hammering fast little drumbeats in their chests.

The next afternoon Buddy and Bill found some yew brush down in the bottom of the canyon, and proceeded to make themselves play bows and arrows. Later, they pretended to hunt deer in the little meadows along the side of the lake. Finished with their domestic chores Agnes and Louise wandered over to the boys to join the game. We will be the deer that you two are hunting!" Agnes announced, and proceeded to stomp her feet and snort like an alert doe warning her fawn of potential danger. The boys thought it would be a lot of fun to stalk the deer girls, so they helped them find small forked branches which the girls fastened to bands they had tied around their heads to be their antlers. Then the girls ran off, sneaking through the trees until the boys couldn't see them, but leaving 'deer tracks' for the boys to follow. Eventually they stopped and pretended to graze in a little meadow, every now and then raising their heads and scanning the woods for danger, flaring their nostrils as though they were scenting the air.

Before long they saw one of the boys sliding up behind a tree at the edge of the meadow. Agnes blew warningly and Louise heard the whistle of an arrow as it flew by them. Ambush! The girls bolted enthusiastically across the meadow for the safety of the trees, while the two boys ran from their hiding spots, shooting the crude arrows, which didn't fly very far after the fleeing deer girls. By the time they had found all their spent arrows the girls had disappeared, so the hunt continued.

This time the girls moved apart a little ways, each keeping close to cover and signaling to each other when they thought they saw or heard the hunters coming. Louise stayed in the shadowy edges of the glade, while Agnes, a little bolder, or a little more willing to be caught, gradually wandered further out in the open. There was still no sign of the two boys, which caused the girls to feel a bit nervous.

Louise felt a little strange. She took a few hesitant steps and found in front of her a narrow deer trail winding through the trees and downed timber. She spotted a few coarse hairs stuck in the split of a dead branch where a deer had grazed its side jumping a log. Louise carried a little medicine bag she had sewn, and now she plucked the hairs off of the log and put them in her bag, silently murmuring a prayer of thanks to the spirit of the deer. She imagined herself becoming the deer with its heightened senses. She felt her ears twitch at a slight sound.

Bill and Buddy had figured out about where the deer girls were hiding, and they decided that Buddy would sneak up toward the girls while Bill circled around the back of the glade, so if Buddy spooked the 'deer' they would run toward Bill and his arrows.

Bill slipped from tree to tree, careful not to step on a dry branch. He was doubling back toward where the girls were. He heard something ahead of him, then saw a flash of movement. He sneaked a little closer, and peeked around the trunk of a tree. Louise stood still, her slender legs poised to run, her dark eyes wide and curious as she looked toward his hiding spot. Louise stomped her moccasined foot on the ground. Bill's eyes widened as he followed the movement. He saw a sharp, black hoof stomp the needled ground! He looked up, confused. A young, spike buck looked back at him, then dipped its head, lowering its sharp prongs and blowing. Bill screwed his eyes shut tight and then opened them wide. Louise stood watching him, her large eyes reflecting the greening light that filtered into the glade. She danced to one side, the branches in her hair bobbing as Bill notched his bow and pulled it taut. He aimed and let the arrow fly straight toward the girl. The arrow seemed to falter, then fell harmlessly a few feet away from her. Bill's eyes had tracked his arrow, and now he glanced back at Louise as he notched another one. Only Louise was gone again and the young spike stood in her place. Bill shot his toy arrow and the deer bounded away, disappearing into the brush. The boy blinked and looked wildly around for Louise.

Buddy's voice softly hailed him as he caught up with his friend.

"I can't find those girls, have you seen them?" he whispered.

Bill shook his head, still staring at the spot the deer had stood. Buddy saw his arrows lying there and gave his friend a questioning look. They heard feminine giggles floating on the air behind them and whirled around. Signaling to each other, the boys sneaked back toward the edge of the glade, bows ready. Suddenly the bushes in front of them exploded and a small spike deer pounded off into the undergrowth. The boys looked at each other baffled, and kept moving forward. They heard giggling again, only this time it was off to the side, so they started to sneak that way. Then they heard whispers on the other side. With a burst of laughter the girls jumped up from their hiding spots and sprinted back to the meadows. They stopped to graze, and this time when the boys sneaked up on them, they allowed themselves to be "shot" by the hunters, and fell down to die dramatically, kicking at the hunters as they came to take their kill.

That night, lying side by side, Bill mused aloud to his friend, "When I grow up I'm going to make a dogwood whistle to call Louise to be my sweetheart, the way they did in the old days." Buddy turned toward his friend astonished, but found he had nothing to say. In her family's tipi Louise slept soundly with her little medicine pouch, and dreamed she was a doe bounding through sun dappled woods where a young hunter was waiting for her, only instead of a bow, he held a dogwood whistle.

Louise woke from her dream, her body stiff and chilled in the arm chair. Her friend had long since said his good byes, and her little house was quiet again, except for the indomitable ticking of the kitchen clock. Soon her daughter would stop by to check on her and make sure she had something for supper. Louise felt lonely for a second, then chuckled to herself, thinking she ought to give one of her grandsons, who seemed unlucky in love, that special dogwood whistle Bill had made to catch a deer girl all those years ago.

This tale is based on anecdotal accounts of the annual trips into the mountains the families in the story took. All of the characters were real people and are addressed by their correct names. Louise and Bill really did meet on this trip, play the hunting game with Buddy and Agnes, and really did get married.

THE PEND-D-OREILLE CAMP MEETS THE FAMOUS HARRY MORGAN.
Told to Bud Cheff Jr. by his father, Bud Sr.

In the late summer of 1924 a band of full blood Pend d' Oreille Indians left the Mission Valley on a hunting trip under the leadership of Eneas Conko. As was often the case, his friend, Ovila Cheff's son Buddy, was with them. Even though he was not a fullblood, he was considered and treated as one of them. Eneas's son Bill and Buddy were steadfast friends.

It was a colorful, and picturesque sight to see these riders starting into the mountains. Eneas and the men, with their big brim hats and bright colored silk neck scarves were in the lead. The women in their colorful dresses and head scarves laughed and joked as they followed the men.

Everyone in the party was wearing moccasins. Some of the women's horses had young colts, and they stayed close to their mothers. When this trip was over these colts would be experienced in mountain travel and make good future mountain horses. The boys brought up the rear, keeping the loose horses in check and thinking they were great warriors, acting as the rear guard. What an impressive sight this made; if only someone with a camera had been there.

The party traveled leisurely, digging roots and picking berries. Huckleberries and serviceberries were still ripe in the high country, and they hunted and fished enough to keep the camp supplied with meat. They would hunt in earnest just before they were ready to start home. They crossed the Mission Range, following the Jocko Canyon trail, then crossed the Clearwater River south of Seeley Lake. They continued over the low hills, following along the north side of the Blackfoot Valley and entered the South Fork of the Flathead, what is now called the Bob Marshall Wilderness.

The group stayed a number of days at the Danaher Meadows, a beautiful place to camp, with lush mountain meadows and the river winding through them. This was the headwaters of the Flathead River, with the many creeks converging to form the South Fork of the Flathead. The children had fun exploring the area and playing on the abandoned farm equipment left there. Buddy did not know it then, but his father, Ovila, had helped pack some of this equipment into the Danaher some fifteen years earlier. In 1898 Tom Danaher and A.P. McCrea each homesteaded 160 acres there. McCrea stayed only a couple of years, and Danaher sold out to the Missoula Hunt Club in 1907, which planned to make it into a horse ranch and hunting camp. Sheriff Jim Green and County Attorney Dwight Mason were key players in this venture, and Ovila was a good friend of theirs. Dwight Mason was elected mayor in 1935, and would become Missoula's longest-sitting mayor of that city, serving for ten years. But the weather proved to be too harsh in the Danaher and they gave up the venture after a few years, selling the property to the newly-formed U.S. Forest Service.

There was a lot of elk sign in the area but Eneas did not want his men to start hunting and drying the meat in earnest yet. The weather was still too warm and they were a long ways from home.

On the second day they were camped on the Danaher, one of the men rode into camp in a hurry. He said a *sue-aupy* (white man) riding a big white horse was approaching their camp. The women and children all quickly disappeared into the tipis, closing the door flaps. Sophie Conko gave Bill and Buddy the "don't talk" sign. They looked at each other, then slipped quietly to the tipi flap and peaked through, both unconsciously breathing hard. They watched as the big, tough-looking man rode up and dismounted from his impressive-looking horse. He had a rifle in the saddle boot and a pistol on his belt. The Indian men had scattered around, with their rifles leaning conveniently nearby.

Eneas was standing in front to meet the stranger. Before the man dismounted, he identified himself as Warden Harry Morgan. As of that moment not a single Indian in camp could speak or understand English, even though Buddy knew Whispering Charley and a couple of the others could speak English quite well – and he and Bill were learning it in school. Sophie kept the boys in the tipi so they would not slip up and say something in English. Another warden, Peyton, and the Swan Valley massacre was still fresh in the Indians' memories. Warden Peyton and a man named Rudolph had come to the Indian hunting camp. Rudolph waited at the edge of the timber while Peyton entered the camp. They killed the three men and a fifteen-year-old boy, then tried to kill the women. Clarice Paul, who was only sixteen and pregnant, grabbed her husband Camille's gun and killed the warden. Rudolph fled.

The tension was strong in camp this day, and everyone was careful not to make any hostile movement. Harry told the Indians they could not kill elk as the hunting season was not open yet. He talked, using sign language as he talked. He was well aware that some of them could understand English and they knew he knew, but this was how it was always done. Morgan's sharp eyes had noticed a couple of deer hides the women had been working on. He knew they had been killing such game as they needed to eat as they traveled, and he had no problem with it. This was their way of life. He felt keenly the poignancy of the fact that they knew their way of life was fading, even as they tried to follow the old traditions. The meeting ended on a friendly note, and Harry Morgan said his good byes and rode out, feeling as though he was riding away from something already lost to the past.

Eneas had heard of Warden Harry Morgan, and knew he had a reputation of being a good and honest, but no-nonsense warden. In fact, the harsh frontier life, coupled with a fine character, had shaped the warden into a man who was both well liked and widely respected.

Harry Morgan was the first baby born in the new town of Fort Benton on the Missouri River in 1863, when Montana was still a territory. His father was Captain John Morgan, stationed at Fort Benton. His mother died when he was very small and his father put him in the care of an Indian lady, since he was out in the field most of the time. His father was killed by the Blackfeet when the boy was only seven years old, and Harry ended up in Philipsburg, Montana, when he was ten years old. He was on his own at the young age of fifteen. Harry worked in the tough mining and logging camps and was deputy game warden from 1913 to 1947. He was widely sought for his knowledge of early Montana history until his death in 1957, at the age of ninety-four.

When Morgan was gone everyone relaxed, and with the tension gone, they were soon in good spirits again. Conko announced they would stay a few more days and let their horses fatten on the good grass here, then move on down the river.

The Indians took their time following the Flathead River down stream. They fished and hunted enough to keep fresh meat in camp. The boys helped fill the cooking pots with grouse and snowshoe rabbits. There was plenty of grass for the horses at most of the camp sites so they could stay there for several days if they wanted.

In the evening it was story telling time, and often drumming, singing, and dancing. Eneas would usually lead the men singing, and on some songs the women would join in with their high voices. This was a special thing to hear in the stillness of a wilderness night. The kids loved it, and without realizing it, were getting an education in history as well. At several camps on the trip a sweat lodge was erected so the men and boys could sweat, with the women and girls also taking a turn.

They continued down the river, camping at the mouth of Little Salmon Creek. The next day Eneas went up the canyon to check for elk. He found a lot of elk sign, and on returning to camp, he announced it was a good place to make their hunt. It had been nearly a month since they had left home, and they were almost out of flour, needed to make fry bread. It was time to start back. Buddy and Bill knew that school would be starting but they were not concerned about missing it.

The men built a sweat lodge on the bank of the river and all the hunters took a sweat bath to be clean for the coming hunt. At sunrise the next morning the boys followed Eneas to the river and watched as he repeated his morning ritual of unbraiding and washing his hair, then rebraiding it. He did this daily, summer and winter, without fail, even breaking the ice if necessary. Some of the others still followed this tradition as well. Eneas, who was widely respected for being a dead shot and a great hunter, led the hunters up the canyon. The boys wanted to go but were told no, as this was an important hunt, and only seasoned hunters could go. They were hunting for meat, not for sport, and they wanted to get as many elk as they could. Using sign language so he wouldn't spook the elk, Eneas directed the hunters to positions that would assure a good kill. The hunt went just as he had planned, and there was laughter and high spirits in camp that night.

The next morning the camp was moved close to the dead elk. It was no longer a time of leisure but one of work. Every one had a job to do. Drying racks were set up and the elk were skinned, boned, and cut into long strips to hang on the racks. The boys were busy bringing in alder and other wood that did not have pitch for the drying fires. Finding the right wood was not always an easy task, especially in the high mountain country, and some times they had to use snow brush. In three days of working day and night they had all the meat dried enough to get it home without any spoilage. The hides were also dried and made into packs.

Four days after the big kill, with every horse loaded, they were headed up over what is now Smith Creek Pass, a high mountain pass that is still dangerous for horses in bad weather. Once over the pass they dropped down into the Swan Valley, careful to avoid being seen by any white inhabitants as they rode across the valley. Then they crossed the Mission Range, going over North Crow Pass. After nearly six weeks of traveling through two mountain ranges, they were back home with a good supply of meat. Buddy was glad to be home and get a big, welcoming hug from his mom. Marie had started to worry a little as they had been gone longer than she had expected, and Buddy needed to be in school. She was relieved to have her mountain-loving son home, even though she knew Buddy had been in good hands, under the watchful care of Eneas and Sophia Conko. Buddy proudly presented her a parfleche full of dried elk meat, to which his brothers and sisters happily helped themselves!

Bud started outfitting at a young age, taking his first paying hunters in 1932. In 1936 Harry Morgan came to Bud's hunting camp to check his game kill. As soon as Bud saw him, he recognized Morgan as the man who had come to the Indian camp at the Danaher. Bud asked him if he remembered coming to that camp. Harry replied, "I sure do, how did you know about it?" Bud told him he was one of the boys peaking out the tipi flaps at him, and they had a good laugh as they talked about it. Harry had worked as a guide when he was younger, and told Bud about some of the early hunting trips he had guided. Bud liked Harry and could understand why he was so well respected by all who knew him. He always enjoyed meeting Harry on the trail or in camp, and was proud to have known such a remarkable man.

WINTER MEDICINE DANCE, 1924
Josephine Chevre

Young Bill Conko burst through the kitchen door, then stopped short so that his playmate, Buddy, in hot pursuit, bumped into him in the doorway. The two boys began to jostle and wrestle with each other, laughing and grunting, until a single word from Sofia ended the scuffle. *"Sk uy!* Is it true? Can Buddy really go to the Winter Medicine dance with us? For the whole time?" Bill asked his mother eagerly. Dressed as usual in the traditional style of long dress and beaded belt, with her *ciyalx qen* wrapped around her head holding her braids in place, Sofia always seemed solemn and dignified to Buddy, and he felt both shy and comfortable around her. Now he looked up at her with unabashed hopefulness. Unable to contain his own excitement, Bill hopped from one foot to the other. Sofia looked sideways at the two nine year olds. The chill fall air from the open doorway coiled around the boys' legs and pushed the warm smells of cooking food and wood smoke up toward the ceiling of the cabin. The fire crackled and popped inside the stove, and the wood floor squeaked under the impatient thump of Bill's moccasins. Finally, she gave a slight nod and the boys exploded back out the door, whooping and tumbling about, their bodies wreathed in the bright amber of late autumn sunlight.

Sofia chuckled and turned back to the cook stove after shutting the door. Buddy had been with them for a month already, hunting with them in the mountains, but Ovila and Marie Cheff had readily agreed to allow their son to attend the upcoming Medicine Dance Ceremony, recognizing the honor the Conkos were according him to witness such a prodigious event. In fact, Buddy had gone with them to the dance for one day and night the year before. The small boy knew how special it was that he was allowed to go, because only those considered "Full Bloods" generally attended, and Buddy was more French than Indian.

Because of his close ties to the head man, Eneas Conko and his family, and to the highly respected healer, Tenum Finley, who lived with Buddy's family until his death at age eighty-five, the young boy was known as "Little Tehnum" and was accepted among the Native people of the valley as the old man's adopted son. In later years Eneas Conko also referred to Buddy as his son, having lost four of his children to tragic events.

Although Tenum was not a medicine man in the shamanistic sense, he was a gifted healer with the use of plants, and held an honored position among the medicine men who were in charge of the medicine dance. The Pend 'd Oreille Winter Medicine Dance, like many other sacred Native ceremonies, had been outlawed by the government years earlier. Consequently, each winter the three to four day event was held with great secrecy at a hidden location, away from the populated areas where people might hear the drums. Anyone who attended was required to wear the old style traditional Native dress. Many of those who came to the winter dance were local, but some participants came from

Camas Prairie and other areas that were further away. The event was taken seriously. Alcohol was banned and all, including children, were expected to behave in a somber and respectful manner. Rambunctious as they were, Buddy and Bill understood there would be no horseplay on the Medicine Dance grounds.

Snowflakes drifted down and stuck on Sofia and Agnes's shawls, and the boys' coats. The children stuck their tongues out to catch the big flakes and laughed and blinked when they caught in their eyelashes. Ten-year-old Agnes looked like a smaller replica of her mother and had the same sweet face. Buddy stuck his tongue out further, crossed his eyes and waggled his mittens by his ears. Agnes giggled and made a face of her own. Not to be outdone, Bill puffed out his cheeks and pulled back his eyelids. John, one of the older boys, called to them from his horse that they were almost there, and the children forgot their game as they gazed at the busy scene ahead of them.

A flat meadow of about twenty acres sat just above a large creek. Families that had already arrived were setting up tipis and hobbling or staking their horses out to graze the tall grass. Children ran to and fro, playing or gathering firewood for their elders. Soon Eneas pulled up the sled as a pretty young woman walked toward them through the snow. It was Cecille, the oldest daughter, who had come earlier with her husband, Baptiste Hewankorn. Always sunny natured and full of sly humor, she greeted them with a broad grin and pointed to where their camp was set up.

Cecille Hewankorn.

The children climbed out of the sled, which was a wagon bed attached to runners, and ran ahead of the team as Eneas maneuvered the sled to a suitable spot near by. The women began to unload the sleigh while Eneas and his two elder sons unhitched the team and took care of their saddle horses. Their neighbors, Mr. & Mrs. Alex Beaverhead, and their son Pete Beaverhead and his wife Josephine were setting up their own camp near them, as were Antoine Chief Eagle, his wife and a young daughter, Agnes.

Born in 1874, Eneas was, at fifty, a handsome, impressive and highly respected man with the qualities of a natural leader. He wore his trademark big hat with a fancy shirt, vest, wool pants and winter moccasins. A big, colorful scarf wrapped around his neck and a blanket over his shoulder completed his attire. His oldest son Leo, slender framed and good looking, was dressed in much the same manner. All of the boys, including Buddy, were dressed similarly with leggings and breechcloths, but unlike Eneas, who still wore braids, their hair was cut short, as was required for school.

Soon Leo disappeared with a group of young men to get ready for dancing, and after awhile Eneas was sought out by the old warrior brothers, Louie and Charlie Mollman, to come to their fire. John, at age thirteen, an intelligent, athletic youth who would soon develop his father's proud stature and charismatic personality, went with the men. Buddy and Bill, awed by the two fierce old warriors, tagged behind, all ears, for surely some good story telling would soon be going on.

Inside the tipi, several old warriors from the Buffalo and Indian War days were seated around the fire. Little Buddy looked around the lodge. He knew the names of all the old warriors. There was Lassaw Redhorn, Old Patche, Little Martin, Antoine Finley, Thomas Coolshe, also known as 'Big Tom,' and Blind Michel. These old warriors and their wives had been born between the 1830's and 1850's and all had seen and survived many hardships during this tumultuous era. However, this time the men had gathered not to reminisce, but to discuss some of the details of the Medicine Dance Ceremony.

Eventually, Eneas and Whispering Charlie left the lodge and walked over to the east end of the meadow, where the dance was held. Again the boys followed quietly. Along the way, sixteen-year-old Joe Redhorn caught up with them and asked John to help the young men who had been selected to drag in logs with their horses for the medicine fires. John stalked off with him proudly, pleased to be invited to join the older youths. All such tasks, even wood gathering for the medicine fires were regarded with solemnity, and executed in a formal and honored manner.

The creek ran about twenty-five feet below the meadow, and along its north bank there was a level bench about five feet above the water. Three large sweat lodges had been constructed on this bench, and were already in use for healing the sick, who had been fasting and preparing themselves for the sweat lodge ceremony. The medicine men's tipis and the ceremony dance area were on the flat just above the sweat lodges. Eneas entered one of the tipis after instructing the boys to wait outside.

The boys scuffed their moccasins in the snow. It had stopped snowing and the temperature was dropping as the sky cleared, causing them to pull their blankets tighter around their shoulders as they wandered around the area. There were medicine poles set up, and the boys noted them excitedly, for some of the medicine men did impossible tricks on them. There were fire pits filled with hot rocks that some of the medicine men would walk barefoot on. Others would juggle the red hot rocks and roll them down their arms and legs. A little tingle of anticipation crawled up the back of his neck as Buddy remembered how he had watched one medicine man sing to the fire, and the fires seemed to listen. The flames shot up higher and higher in blue and red and green ribbons that stretched toward the night sky, until the whole fire exploded into an inferno of sparks. The spectators had leapt back in surprise, their faces and bodies weirdly illuminated, so that they seemed more spirit than human to the little boy.

Charley Kickinghorse.

The steady beat of the drums filtered through Buddy's consciousness, bringing him back to the present. People were beginning to walk toward the Medicine Lodges, called by the drums. Bill grinned at him and tipped his head toward the lodge his father had entered. The two boys hurried back to their post by the door, to stand quietly, hearts beating to the drums that echoed up the snow blanketed ridges and canyons beyond.

The door flap opened and the men emerged one by one. In spite of himself, Buddy's hair stood on end and his breath caught in his throat! Dressed and painted, the medicine men emanated power and were frightening to look at. They all wore something of their animal or bird spirit medicine. Some of these men were called Blue Jays, a secret society that held the Blue Jay Medicine, which was very mysterious and powerful. One had Grizzly Bear Medicine and wore a grizzly hide. He walked on all fours, talking bear talk, then stood with his paws turned in toward his chest, swinging his bead back and forth and huffing, "Xaw, Xaw!" The fearsome bear head swung toward them, and Bill and Buddy's little bodies went stiff, and their mouths became dry as if they had a mouthful of chokecherries. They backed away from the Medicine Lodge door to make room for the medicine men to pass.

Buddy could see some of the medicine men he knew. There was the head medicine man, Old Louie Hammer, Tenum Finley, Charlie Kickinghorse (also a healer with herbs). Charley had helped in the birth of Buddy's sister Bernida. Also Joseph Que-que-suh, among others he didn't recognize. There were also several younger medicine men who were born in the 1870's or 1880's. Buddy recognized Eneas Que-que-suh and Plassie Incashola, as well as Philip Pierre, who was a quite prominent medicine man known for his strong medicine, and one of the main organizers of the dance. His wives, Mary Catherine Mollman and Clara Paul, were busy making sure the needs of the medicine men were being taken care of and overseeing the preparations for the feast at the end of the dance.

Now that it had begun, the drumming, dancing and singing would

L to r standing, Antoine & Eneas Que-Que-Seh, Alex Beaverhead, Louie Hammer; sitting, Mitch Michel and Little Martin.

go on all day and late into the star-studded night. Periodically, some would rest and eat and drink and then start in again. In the early darkness of morning people would return to their beds to sleep for a few hours, until the activities resumed before noon, continuing three to four days and nights. The medicine men would take on the forms of their animal helper spirits and talk only in their animal language. They would take the sick into the sweat lodges to perform their healing medicine on them while they sweated. Buddy was fascinated by the medicine men and watched them healing the sick, although of course he was not allowed inside. He watched the Grizzly Bear Medicine Man crawl around and around the sweat lodge clockwise, grunting, growling, digging and rolling on the ground. Then the healer crawled back inside to administer his secret medicine. No one ever told what went on in the sweat lodge. It was considered dishonorable to the medicine spirits, and to speak of the experience casually would bring very bad luck or even death.

All aspects of the medicine dance ceremony were important. Roles and tasks were carried out with great care and seriousness so as not to offend the helping spirits. The fire tenders and helpers made sure there was plenty of firewood and kept the rocks hot and ready for use. The tenders also lit the ceremonial pipes when needed, and had hot coals ready for smudges. The rocks themselves were hard to find and had to be carefully selected, so they were gathered ahead of time. They had to be dry, round granite stones of a certain size so they wouldn't break when heated.

When the sick emerged from the sweat lodges they were submerged briefly in the icy water of a deep pool next to the sweat lodges. Sometimes an extremely ill person died during this process, but on this particular year there were no deaths.

The medicine dance ended with a feast and a final dance. The feast consisted of several kinds of roasted or boiled meat, dried fruit, and a special dish consisting of boiled bitterroot.

The people brought gifts to the medicine men in exchange for their services. The gifts were items that meant a lot to the sick person, such as beaded moccasins, leggings, necklaces, beads or beadwork, feathers, knives; anything that was of great value to the individual offering the gift. All of these gifts were then wrapped up and made into a large medicine bundle. A council of elders would select two worthy men to take this medicine bundle on a packhorse and hide it. It was up to the two men to decide where to hide the bundle so it would never be found.

It might be tied up in a tree somewhere. No one knew or wanted to know where the bundle was hidden, because all the sicknesses of the people the medicine men had treated were contained in the bundle along with the gifts. If anyone were to find the bundle and open it, bad luck would find that person and his or her family.

The feast and the hiding of the medicine bundle symbolized the end of the Pend 'd Oreille Winter Medicine Dance. Though their bellies were growling, Bill and Buddy were determined to try to get a glimpse of who had been selected to hide the bundle. They decided to stay where they could see the horses, knowing that three horses would be needed to carry the two men and the bundle.

The moon glowed above the peaks, an uncanny white face, ringed in rose and green hoops. There seemed to be shadows and shapes everywhere. The wind picked up and came whistling across the meadow, gathering drifts of snow off the ground and sending the shadows dancing and shifting. It reached the boys in a wailing gust, spinning snow in a whirling cloud around them, pulling their blankets off their shoulders and tossing them away. Shielding their faces, Buddy and Bill ran after their blankets, away from the horses. They heard bells and whispering voices in the swirling snow. They paused, glancing at each other in the semidarkness. Then both of them ran hard, grabbed up their blankets, and turned and made a beeline back to the beckoning fires.

The aroma of roasting meat caused their stomachs to rumble in protest, and the friends forgot about the eerie snow dance as they settled down to the serious business of filling their bellies. But in the years that followed, when the moon shown with that peculiar ringed brightness during the cold of a winter night in the Missions, each would turn his head to took up into the uncanny silence of the night sky, and remember.

MONTANA'S FIRST RECORDED MARRIAGE

Ross Cox, a fur trader working for John Jacob Astor's Pacific Fur Company that later became the Northwest Company, recorded this marriage in the year of 1813. The event took place at the mouth of the Missoula River, near what is now Paradise, Montana. The groom, Piere Michel, was a member of the trading party and was of French and Iroquois descent. The bride, Charolet, referred to as a Flathead, was an Upper Pend 'd Oreille or Kalispell. This event was taken from the book, *"Flathead Indian Nation"* by Major Peter Ronan, published in 1890. Eneas (Michel) Conko's own oral history of this was similar to Peter

Ronan's written story.
By Peter Ronan

"Mr. Cox speaks of the marriage, in the winter of 1813, of Piere Michel, the hunter, guide and interpreter of the expedition. As the descendants of the same Piere Michel are now among the very best Indians of the Flathead reservation, I shall give the account of the marriage as it is probably the earliest recorded in the annals of Montana. It appears Michel accompanied the Flatheads on two of their war campaigns and by his unerring aim and undaunted bravery won the affection of the whole tribe. He was the son of an Indian mother and a respectable Canadian. The war chief in particular paid great attention to his opinion, and consulted him in any difficult matter. Michel wanted a wife; and having succeeded in gaining the affection of a handsome girl about sixteen years of age and niece to the hereditary chief, he made a formal proposal for her. A council was thereupon called, at which her uncle presided, to take Michel's offer into consideration.

One young warrior loved her and had obtained a previous promise from her mother that she should be his. He, therefore, with all his relations, strongly opposed her union with Piere and urged his own claims which had been sanctioned by her mother. The war chief asked him if she had ever promised to become his wife; he replied in the negative. The chief then addressed the council, and particularly the lover, in favor of Michel's suit; pointing out the great service he had rendered the tribe by his bravery and dwelling strongly on the policy of uniting him more firmly to their interests by consenting to the proposed marriage, which he said would forever make him as one of their brothers. His influence predominated, and the unsuccessful rival immediately after shook hands with Michel and told the young woman, as he could not be her husband, he hoped she would always regard him as her brother. This she readily promised to do, and so ended the opposition.

The happy Piere presented a gun to her uncle, some cloth, calico, and ornaments to her female relative, and a pistol and handsome dagger to his friend. In the evening he proceeded to the chief's lodge, where a number of her friends had assembled to smoke. Here she received a lecture from the old man, her mother and a few other ancients on her duty as a wife and mother. They strongly exhorted her to be chaste, obedient, industrious and silent; and when absent with her husband among her tribes always to stay at home, and have no intercourse with strange Indians. She then retired with the old woman to an adjoining hut, where she underwent an ablution and bade adieu to her buckskin chemise, the place of which was supplied by one of gingham, to which was added a calico and green cloth petticoat and a gown of blue cloth. After this was over she was conducted back to her uncle's lodge, where she received further advice as to her future conduct. A procession was then formed by the two chiefs and several warriors carrying blazing torches of pitch pine, to escort the bride and her husband to the fort. They began singing war songs in praise of Michel's bravery, and of their triumph over the Blackfeet. The bride was surrounded by a group of young and old women, some of whom were rejoicing and others crying. The men moved on first in slow, solemn pace, still chanting their war song. The women followed at a short distance, and when the whole party arrived in front of the fort they formed a circle and commenced dancing and singing, which they kept up about twenty minutes. After this the calumet of peace went around once more, and when the smoke of the last whiffs had disappeared, Michel shook hands with his late rival, embraced the chiefs and conducted his bride to his room. Michel was the only person of the party to whom the Flatheads would give one of their women in marriage."

Eneas Conko's father, Michel.

This story is of great interest to me as the descendants of this marriage are very dear to our family. There are many photos in the museum of Eneas Michel (Conko) and his family. Eneas was the grandson of the French-Iroquois man, Piere Michel, talked about in the story above. Eneas's father, one of the sons of Piere, was called Michel. He had no

English first name, and I don't remember his Indian name. Michel died in 1886 when Eneas was only twelve years old. As a result, much of their family history was lost

.....AND THEN THERE WERE BOOTLEGGERS

The story below is based on events told to me by my father, Bud Cheff Sr. and put in story form by Josephine Chevre.

Author's note: *All the characters in this fictionalized account lived or worked in the Mission Valley in the early 1920's. This cameo is a composite of oral anecdotes, and is not meant to be an accurate account of the actual incident.*

Jack Curtis, the federal man, always carried a good sharp axe. He performed his duties as a Prohibition Officer with a certain relish, and this morning he felt particularly good because he just knew that today was going to be a satisfying one. Jack Curtis' nose twitched, trying to identify the scent of sour mash and wood smoke that might be lingering from the still that he was sure had been cooking somewhere in this swamp the night before. He rubbed his blood shot eyes with a grimy hand and stifled a yawn as he stepped on the trunk of a fallen alder. The rotted log gave way under the weight of his body and his left leg sank up to his thigh in black loam. The musky, pungent scent of crushed skunk cabbage assailed his nostrils. No longer smiling, Jack pulled himself out of the mud, cursing mildly under his breath. He had staked out the area all night, and nearly caught up with the bootleggers. Moonshiners usually worked in pairs and he hadn't counted on them having a third lookout man who would blow his cover. All the same, they couldn't have dismantled the still and he knew it was somewhere around one of these cedar groves, waiting for his discovery.

That was what the axe was for, payback for the lack of sleep and mud-soggy boots. He was not terribly disappointed in the bootleggers giving him the slip, he'd been on the trail of the Swamp Fox for years, and not quite pinning him down had become part of the cat and mouse game. His wiliest foe, the Swamp Fox, had earned Jack Curtis's grudging admiration and it would have taken the edge off his own occupation if he'd actually ended the Fox's career.

Jack Curtis emerged from the swamp smiling again. His clothes were splattered and reeked of whisky. Smashing the boiler and copper coils had helped the memory of the last botched job to fade to inconsequentiality. A bootlegger east of Pablo had been supplying old

Teh Num Finley with a large quantity of moonshine, and Te Num Finley in turn had been delivering it to the French Canadian who operated a pop and ice-cream stand at the Independence Day Celebration north of St. Ignatius. The Canadian was arrested on one occasion and being a good cook as well as pop and moonshine maker, was hired to cook for the duration of his mandatory visit in the Missoula County Jail. What Jack didn't know was that the sheriff and his deputies were also the Canadian's most regular customers, and good friends as well. It wasn't uncommon for a casual comment to drop into the cook's ears, and he, being on friendly terms with the Swamp Fox as well, would pass the tip on up the pipeline when a set-up was being planned.

The prohibition officer thought it was going to be an easy bust when he and his agents caught up with Teh Num Finley's spring wagon. He still didn't know how the old Indian has guessed they were waiting for him, but the wagon was empty, and the ten gallon keg of high priced, good quality whiskey was nowhere to be found. Jack had ranted and threatened, but the old man merely shrugged and grinning at him innocently, responded in Salish in a most pleasant and mild tone. Jack and his agents, known as the "dry squad" didn't know Salish. Backtracking along the path the spring wagon had taken, Jack pulled his horse up at the bank of a muddy stream. He looked up and down the stream. A horse would sink up to its belly in the muck. A whiskey keg would simply disappear. Jack whipped off his hat and swore in his well mannered way. He certainly would never find it, but he could take comfort in the thought that the bootleggers probably wouldn't either.

Jack Curtis crossed the street, heading to his office to make a report. A small boy carrying a box of shoes passed by him and climbed the steps into Scearce's Department Store. Jack frowned, trying to place the young face. "Ah. One of the French Canadian's brood." Jack watched the boy disappear into the store, something niggling at the back of his mind. He pulled at the niggling thread of thought, but it took him nowhere, so he shrugged and turned his face back toward his office and the business of writing up the report. The proprietor was in the storage room, and the boy stood alone in the store waiting to return the shoes as his father had instructed. He set the box on the wooden counter, and again heard a funny, swishing sound. Curiosity led his hand to untie the string and peek inside the box, and then he understood what kind of shoes his father had him return every so often on his way to school.

WAR SONG

It was a warm moonlit night when Bill Conko and Bud Cheff saddled their horses and swung into the saddle for their six mile ride home. They had ridden their horses to school as usual, unsaddled them, staking them out on good grass near the school. At noon hour they would water them, and stake them out again. If they weren't going right home after school, they would water them again and tie them up, ready to saddle when needed.

Bill and Bud had been friends all their lives as their parents only lived about a mile apart. Bill's father, Eneas was a Pend 'd Oreille Indian and his mother, Sofia was a Colville Indian. Bud's parents were both of French and Indian descent. The two boys had done everything together from hunting, fishing, digging roots, picking berries, and now playing basketball. Bill was a good ball player, fast and a dead shot. This night they were later than usual leaving for home. After ball practice they had been goofing off with Sidney Roullier, Kenny Burland, and some other buddies. It was after ten when they saddled up.

When the boys were younger and pretending to be great warriors they had made up their own war song. It was a great song and the two boys would sing it and dance, performing their war deeds in the dance. Eneas would drum for them and smile proudly at the boys as they danced around in earnest. On this night, as on numerous other nights, the boys sang their war song on the way home to break the monotony of the ride. The horses seemed to like the singing, too, as they stepped right out with their ears pricked forward, alert for the enemy. They crossed Crow Creek at the crossing, just below Old Louie and Elizabeth Hammer's place. Both were Pend 'd Oreille Indians. Louie was the son of Pascal, one of the old ones born in the 1840's. Pascal had hunted buffalo and fought both the Blackfeet and Crow tribes. This night when Louie heard the boys go by singing, he told Elizabeth, "Bud and Bill must have been in town drinking. They are out there singing again". A few days later Eneas came by Hammer's, and Louie told him "Your boys, Bill and Bud, come from town drunk. I hear them singing and giving their war cry. You should tell them whiskey is bad medicine." Eneas explained to him they were just having fun, not drinking. Old Louie was not fully convinced, but Elizabeth was, and laughed, thinking it was funny. "She said "Boys all the same. They want to be men."

As a boy I loved this song and learned to do a pretty good rendition of the war cry. Once when I was young and living a little on the wild side, I was in a bar in Rifle, Colorado. I drank my share of whiskey and, feeling good, I gave the war cry. A group of Ute Indians did not like it, and told me that was their Chief's special war cry, and not to give it again. I told them 'No, this is the Flathead war cry, and Flathead warriors were the best fighters of all!' and gave the war cry again. Probably lucky for me, they did not make me prove what kind of fighter I was."

In the late 1920's Louie Hammer and other old Pend 'd Oreille buffalo hunters that were still living had seen a great change in their life styles. Massaline Red Horn, Tehnum Finley, Charley and Louie Mollman, and old Patchee, all born from 1830 to 1840, witnessed the Hudson's Bay Company and the building of Fort Connah in 1845. In 1854 they saw the St. Ignatius Mission built, and the signing of the Hell Gate Treaty in 1855. They knew Major John Owen, Angus McDonald, Father DeSmet and his missionaries. These men were middle-aged in 1883 when the Northern Pacific Railroad came through Montana, and the great buffalo herds were no more. Many of the old ones could speak some French, which they learned from the trappers and the Jesuits.

It is a special thing for me to know that my grandfather and grandmother were friends with these old warriors, and my dad, as a boy was friends with them, spending time and learning from them. The old ones gave Dad the name *Tiet a lay m-e, Teh Num* (little man).

THE OLD WAGON TRAIL INCIDENT

It was a warm fall night in 1930 as Buddy, or Bud, as he liked to be called, left the town of Ronan for home. At fifteen years of age he thought himself quite grown up. He had stayed late after school so he could spend a little time with his dark-haired sweetheart, Adelle Rogers, and he was still feeling kind of dreamy as he mounted his horse. Bud was a natural born horseman who could ride anything with hair on it, and this night he was riding a spirited mare with a proudly held tail, a foal out of one of the famous Marcus Daly race horses. Babe was a top notch horse that only an experienced rider could handle. She was as hot-blooded as she was pretty, and had a tendency to buck.

As usual Bud cut through the woods on the old wagon trail, which made his daily trek home only about six miles. It was already dark, but Babe knew every step of the shortcut home. She would alternate walking and running at certain stretches of the trail, as regular as clockwork. Bud would sleep in the saddle on the slow stretches and wake up when she broke into a run. He had several horses that he rode to school and they all knew this routine.

When they came to the crossing at Crow Creek the sound of steel-shod hooves on the rocks at the creek's edge woke Bud up. He was thirsty so he stopped the mare and dismounted, fumbling around to get a drink in the inky dark. He was standing on the lower side of the creek bank, and without bothering to turn Babe around, he started to remount from the low side. He couldn't reach the saddle horn, but being young and agile, he stuck his foot in the stirrup and jumped to catch the saddlehorn all in one motion. In the dark he missed the saddlehorn and fell back wards, losing his grip on the reins and spooking the mare. She bolted with Bud's foot hung up in the stirrup, dragging him through the boulder strewn creek, and ran toward home. In her wild panic, Babe dragged the young man about a quarter of a mile. Just before Bud lost consciousness he managed to grab hold of the horse's tail and raise himself up a little. He twisted his body around desperately, trying to free his foot. Stars exploded in his head.

Bud woke up from darkness to find he was still in darkness. His whole body was racked with pain and he couldn't remember where he was. He pulled himself up and started limping down the trail. He was halfway back to the creek before he realized what had happened and that he was walking in the wrong direction. He turned around and made his way painfully toward home. When he reached the lower gate Babe was waiting there. He found a stump and managed to climb back on the mare and ride the rest of the way home.

Incredibly, in spite of being kicked repeatedly and dragged for nearly a quarter of a mile, the terribly battered fifteen year old suffered no broken bones! If he hadn't caught hold of Babe's tail he would never have been able to ride to school again on the old wagon trail.

THE BLACKSMITH'S DAUGHTER
By Josephine Chevre

Amelia Rose slowly dried a dinner plate, eyes dreamy and soft as a Jersey calf. Her sister leaned close and whispered something in Amelia's ear, then jumped away giggling as Amelia swatted at her with a dish towel. But Amelia was not really annoyed, and her lips curved in a secret smile as she put the plate on the shelf.

John Lewtz, who had been eyeing his daughters from his favorite chair, frowned and rattled his paper in annoyance. Amelia was mooning about again. Could it be the thought of that young rascal, Ancelet

Martin, that brought a smile to her face? He'd spied the two of them together outside the mercantile, his daughter's head demurely tipped as the young man leaned in toward her, to all appearances engaging her in a most ardent conversation. Lewtz's jaw tightened and he shifted his large frame, the chair suddenly less comfortable. That night, as they readied for bed, John complained loudly to his wife that young Martin was no good and the boy was certainly mistaken if he thought John would allow such a rascal to court any of his daughters!

Lovella shushed him with a look and then said quietly, "John, the girl is smitten, and young Martin is equally taken with her. Forbidding her from seeing him now would only serve to draw them closer. And you know Amelia is just as stubborn and headstrong as you are." John grunted and turned over in bed. He'd just have to nip this romance in the bud!

Resolute with his decision the next morning, John was troubled with one looming problem. He was powerfully fond of his womenfolk, and knew that if he caused his pretty Amelia grief he'd not hear the end of it for many a long night. He'd think on it, he decided. Surely an opportunity would present itself.

Anaclet (Buck) Martin and sisters Valli and Rose.

Soon after the young Martin approached him and respectfully asked if he might accompany Amelia to a dance. John gave his consent through gritted teeth, and was all the more aggravated to see Amelia positively radiant at the news.

The next morning his neighbor came over to help him slaughter a pig. Once the unpleasant chore was done, John glanced at the head of the pig lying in the barnyard muck. A devious idea formed in his mind. In a few days that pig head would start to stink, and in a few days the offending young man would be arriving to take his own sweet daughter to the dance. Amelia was lovely and Ancelet was dapper and darkly handsome. It was not surprising that they were attracted to each other.

But what if each could be convinced the other was less attractive than they'd first appeared?

A grin spread across John's face. He bade his puzzled neighbor a jovial goodbye, then went about the rest of the day in the best of spirits and remained amiable all week. His daughters, in an effort not to upset the delicate balance of their father's unexpectedly agreeable demeanor, enthusiastically set about pleasing him, plumping the pillows on his chair, rubbing his feet at the end of the day, and showering him with kisses until he started to feel guilty about what he was about to do. Lovella merely looked at him suspiciously.

Finally, the eventful evening arrived with a cooling breeze that carried the scent of mountain pine and ripe summer hay from the fields. Ancelet pulled up in a one-horse light spring wagon, suitably nervous and quite handsomely turned out. John greeted the young man cordially and then quietly exited amidst the feminine flurry as Lovella invited Ancelet in to wait until Amelia made her appearance. John spoke soothingly to young Martin's horse while he reflected that Amelia was indeed as beautiful as her mother had been when he's met her all those years ago. He felt a twinge of remorse for tricking his daughter. Then he thought of her marrying young Martin and the twinge went away. He fetched the now ripe pig's head and quickly hid it under the robe-covered wagon seat. Then he slipped back into the house unnoticed as the girls fluttered about the bemused Buck Martin, whose eyes, incidentally, were permanently affixed on Amelia's lovely person.

The young couple started out under the rising orb of a bright moon, both utterly aware of how close they were to each other on that spring wagon seat. Soon they became aware of something else quite close, a nasty odor that seemed to emanate from the person next to them. Amelia wrinkled her nose distastefully. He seemed so clean and handsome, but up close Buck smelled horrid! She could have sworn he was freshly bathed, but then why would he smell so awful, Amelia wondered. Perhaps he had some terrible affliction that caused the odor, she thought, and for a moment felt sympathetic toward him. Then a shift in the breeze brought the unsavory scent back to her nostrils and all she could think about was how she was going to endure a dance in his arms.

Meanwhile, Ancelet's hopeful anticipation of a wonderful evening in the fair Amelia's company was rapidly deflating. He didn't even dare try to imagine what could cause the budding Amelia Rose to waft such a noticeable fragrance. Well, "reek" was more like it. The two edged further apart until Amelia was nearly falling off the wagon seat. Buck's mare stumbled and he seized upon the opportunity to stop the wagon and check her feet. Anything, he thought, to get further away from Amelia!

"I think she's coming up lame," he lied.

"Oh, perhaps we should go back then," Amelia replied, trying not to sound overly hopeful. Ancelet agreed, and soon the two had pulled up in the Lewtz's drive once again, neither seeming to notice that the mare hadn't come up lame after all. John, crusty old trickster that he was, had heard the wagon returning and was waiting in the shadows as Ancelet dutifully escorted Amelia to the door. He quietly removed the stinking pig head from under the wagon seat, and young Martin drove away, relieved that the awful stench had remained behind with Amelia. From then on Amelia never looked at Ancelet Martin, except to throw him a pitying glance now and then, and it wasn't until many years later, long after both Amelia and Buck had found other loves, that John confessed to his wife how he had spoiled the blossoming romance by means of a rotten pig's head.

Author's Note: by Bud Cheff Jr.

Ancelet (Buck) Martin was the third son of Gaspard and Malvina Martin, early settlers in the Valley. They were my great-great aunt and uncle. The town of Martin City was named for them, and was part of one of their homesteads. Mel Ruder, editor of the Hungry Horse News asked Grandma Martin (as she was called) while interviewing her in 1947 what she thought of Martin City, famous for having a dozen bars and only one grocery store. Grandma replied, "I watched Demersville, Columbia Falls, Kalispell, and Whitefish all start the same way. They straightened out in a few years, and Martin City will too." Aunt Vina was a lively sweet pioneer lady and made a big impression on me. She was born in 1869 and died in 1956 at Martin City.

This was a true story. Amelia was the oldest daughter of Lovella and John W. Lewtz. John was born in 1864 and lived a very colorful life. As a young man he worked as a drover on cattle drives. One of many jobs he held was cutting ties for the new railroad coming into Montana. He stood at the Custer battle site the year after the battle was fought. He experienced the bustle and excitement of the new cattle and mining town. He said he even got to dance with Calamity Jane. John married Lovella Mary Swingly in 1897 in Cascade City, Montana. He moved his family to Columbia Falls in 1902 where he had a blacksmith shop and a homestead north of town. During probation years he ran a still at the homestead. He only sold to a few special clients, one a prominent person from Glacier Park. As a boy I spent many happy hours at this homestead with his grandson, Allen Hamilton, my lifelong friend. We even fired up the old still and made some moonshine.

ANGELINE BY THE LAKE
By Josephine Chevre

Author's note: This is a fictionalized account of real events, as told by Mary Dupuis of Evaro. The story is seen from the eyes of Mary Dupuis, when she was very young. I wish to thank Mary for so graciously sharing these stories with me and giving me permission to shape the story for the paper.

Angeline Louise was tired and cold, and her rump was sore from long days of riding. She sniffed and rubbed her cold, little nose miserably. She felt her father shift in the saddle, his voice a soft rumble in her ear as he pointed into the distance. Angeline felt a little dance of excitement inside of her. Spirals of smoke from cooking fires sent out their welcome into the crisp, blue of a late autumn sky. She imagined the sheltering warmth of a lodge, and her mouth watered. Surely, they would soon be eating a good, hot meal! As they approached the encampment, dogs came rushing forward, barking their warnings, and people began to emerge from their lodges to greet the visitors. The friendly band was Pend d' Oreille, and had set up their winter camp in the Jocko Valley. In 1854 the Jocko had not yet seen the coming of white settlers, although a few years later, in 1856, an Indian agency would be built. Angeline was three years old.

Baptiste Eneas lifted his tiny daughter to the ground. Her moccasined feet felt wooden as she stood on the frozen ground, watching her father converse with some of the men from the camp. Suddenly overwhelmed by the noisy bustle of activity, Angeline forgot her numb feet and ran to hide behind her stepmother, Mary, who smiled at her reassuringly. Soon they were unloading the horses and setting up their own teepee.

Angeline blinked sleepily, her belly round and contentedly full. Her stepmother was chatting quietly with two women, and her brother, only a few years older than she, played with another boy near the fire. He yawned widely, his eyes heavy lidded. Angeline yawned too, her young limbs relaxing and her head lolling to the side as she gave in to slumber. Baptiste looked at this daughter and his wife, and at his young nephew, whom he had taken as his own son, and listened with unease as his host tried to persuade him to winter his family with their band. Baptiste was moving his family to the great lake north of the Jocko, lured by the stories of good grass and mild weather along its shore. An Iroquois, Baptiste had acquired skill in farming and building from the Canadian Missions.

Although the lower Flathead Valley was unsettled, it was part of the busy fur trade route, and there was need for a ferry to be built at the foot of the lake where the great body of water drained into the Flathead River. But the Blackfeet and the Gros Ventre, as well as the Assiniboine, frequently raided the area in winter, looking to take horses and captives. Because of the relentless raids there were no camps wintering up there. Already ice was closing over the Jocko River and the cottonwoods along its bank creaked under a new blanket of snow. Worried about the safety of his family, Baptiste agreed to stay with the Pend d'Oreille until spring.

The ice on the Jocko River had receded, and her banks were swollen with rushing snow melt when Baptiste and his family continued their journey north. They enjoyed the mild weather as they traveled through the Mission Valley, its many ponds and potholes noisy with waterfowl returning for the summer season. They crossed the spring-flooded stream that would later be known as Post Creek and climbed the greening slope of a glacial moraine toward the trading post where they planned to spend the night. Fort Connah stood alone against the fierce rise of the Mission Peaks behind it, squarely facing the open valley and the hills to the west, small and somewhat incongruous with such a wild, splendid landscape. A storage shed, a corral, and a cabin used for trading, as well as several tepees were clustered around it. Fort Connah was a supply post for other Hudson's Bay Trading Posts, and it provided a continuous supply of buffalo tongues, pemmican and dried meat. An imposing Scotsman named Angus McDonald ran the successful operation.

As the family approached the post, children and dogs popped out from everywhere. They dismounted amid the commotion, and Angeline's father stepped forward to meet the tall Scotsman. Angus wore a thick, black beard and his searching gaze was intense as it glanced over Angeline and her brother. She squirmed behind her brother, Issac, staring at the unusual stranger. Angus winked and Angeline ducked her head, breathless! He began speaking to her father in French. A mixed blood boy of about six, already tall for his age and carrying the same intense gaze as his father, circled around her brother, sizing him up. Abruptly, he introduced himself as Duncan, and began to name his siblings as he pointed them out. Before long the children were trotting along with him, happily exploring the Post.

Angeline wandered over to her mother, who was chatting shyly with Angus's wife, a woman of Nez Perce, Iroquois and French descent. "My daughter is a good helper," Mary told the woman. "Already she helps me set up the camp!" Both women smiled at her and she beamed proudly, then began to pull at a parfleche, trying to drag it over to Mary. She grunted and fell backward on her bottom. The women hid their laughter. Angeline kicked at the parfleche, lost her balance and sat on her bottom again. She gave a disgruntled snort, then announced she would find some firewood, and marched off on her errand. An older girl, Christina McDonald, grinned at the women and followed after Angeline, offering to help so Angeline wouldn't know she was keeping an eye on her.

The next day Baptiste led his family away from Fort Connah, his horses laden with supplies, toward the lake, which was still a good eighteen miles away. The children chewed happily on the buffalo pemmican that Angus had given each of them as they were leaving. It was late afternoon when they finally looked down on the vast expanse of water spreading across the whole end of the valley, shimmering around rocky, tree-cloaked islands. White thunderheads boiled up in a sky that was impossibly blue, moving fast on a high wind, skimming the snow-locked peaks that bordered the east shore of the big lake, and piling up along the foothills in the west. They stood on the crest of a hill, last year's bunchgrass bleached by winter, still standing as high as the horses' bellies.

The trail along the ridge marked what would in later years become the old highway into the town of Polson. But for now there was only the sweep of grass, water and mountain. Angeline looked at the waves capping on the lake, and at the sea of grass rippling and swaying in the wind. Loose strands of her hair blew about her face, and the horses manes and tails streamed out. She looked down. The fringes on her buckskin dress danced a joyful pattern. "Father, she said with wonder. "Everything is in motion!"

Mary bit into a yellow plum. It tasted of honeyed sweetness and the heat laden days of late summer, and the juice ran down her chin in a most satisfying way. Steadying herself on a lichen-covered branch, she reached for another plum, spying through the dusty leaves her grandmother's faded cotton dress as the old woman wended her way through the orchard, pausing now and then to examine the fruit on a particular tree. Though she no longer lived at the crossing where her father and stepmother had planted these orchards, she still came to harvest the fruit and visit the aging trees. A stone building now stood where her family's cabin had once been. Angeline's practiced eye took note of an apple tree whose branches would soon be unable to bear the weight of its wealth of fruit. She reset the stakes supporting one of the branches and tied them off, then resumed her measured walk through the grove. She knew her granddaughter would be in the yellow plum, and eventually she stood in its shade, enjoying the coolness and the drunken hum of hornets and wasps feasting on the splitting fruit that littered the ground. Mary slid to the ground, the pockets of her pinafore bulging with soft bumps. She emptied them into the bucket and grinned at her grandmother. The two of them sat down, carefully avoiding bees, and squashed plums to sample the contents of the bucket. The lower Flathead River coursed by them, teal blue in the bright sun, its watery song teasing them with the promise of cool relief from the hot summer afternoon.

Angeline pointed toward the bridge spanning the river. Once, she told Mary, her father's ferry had made countless crossings on that very spot. One year, she remembered, the river had been full of Pend d' Oreille and Kootenai horses crossing as the bands headed for the Missoula Valley for the council for the signing of the Hellgate Treaty in the year of 1855. Governor Isaac J. Stevens had called upon Chief Alexander of the Pend d' Oreille, Chief Michel of the Kootenais and Chief Victor of the Salish to join the treaty council, which would set the tenets for the new reservation and the confederation of tribes.

The movement of the bands signaled the beginning of reservation life for these groups, but that held little meaning for young Angeline. She was caught up in the excitement of having so many people around her, and overjoyed to find brief playmates among the small groups that stopped along the bank of the river for the night. Some of the bands stopped at the new mission at Snielemen, which had been the winter camp of the Upper Pend d' Oreille. With one other priest and two brothers, Father Hoecken started what would later be known as the St. Ignatius Mission the year before the Hellgate Treaty Council met. Before that year had passed, more than one thousand Indian people had settled near the Mission.

All of these changes kept Angeline's father busy, and his fledging business profited from the shift in population. But as yet, there was still no settlement on the south end of the big lake, and most days Angeline's sole companion in play was her brother. Issac was patient with Angeline, letting her trot along with him on his own small adventures. Quiet and thoughtful by nature, his serious eyes often seemed to be troubled, as if he had a glimpse into some unknown future. Still very young himself, Issac dogged his adoptive father's footsteps, striving to follow Baptiste's instruction and help him in his daily work. Baptiste was kindly toward his children, and as likely to laugh at their antics as he was to frown, so they were often tumbling about him like rambunctious puppies. He was pleased whenever Issac gave over to a bout of childish pleasure, the boy's somber face usually marked the tragedy of his young life.

Mary jumped up and darted after the stray puppy that trotted past, nose bound to some irresistible scent that he followed in the grass. For an instant Angeline saw herself in Mary's sturdy form, giving chase to her brother, who teasingly stayed just a few steps ahead of her. An old sadness came upon her as she watched her granddaughter return, puppy in arm, a ready smile spreading across her open face, her eyes, as always, bright with the spirit of adventure. Settling the wiggling puppy on her lap, Mary noticed the expression on Angeline's face and looked up at her questioningly.

The slope to the south of them was the color of a dun horse, the grass heads ripened in the dry heat. Angeline thought of how green the slope had been on a certain spring day so long ago. They had been living at the ferry crossing for almost three years. After cutting timber and building a cabin, her father had built a raft and strung rope across the span of the river. Later he replaced it with strong cable. One day he came home with two milk cows, and it became Angeline and Issac's job to bring the cows in for morning and evening milking. Since no one else was there, the livestock had the whole expanse of land along the south shore of the lake to graze. When the two children set out riding double on the grey mare, the late slanting rays of sunlight gave a soft golden glow to the air, intensifying the green of new grass sprouting under the bleached stalks of bunchgrass which still stood tall after the winter snow. The cow tracks led them father along the slope out of sight of the cabin, back into the little swales where feed was good. Angeline's bare feet pressed against the mare's warm sides behind Issac's, as they climbed over a small rise. Both of them were at home on the bare back of a horse, and Angeline, like her brother, was already a skilled and fearless rider.

They could hear the cowbells just ahead of them, and the smell of fresh manure lingered in the cooling air. The grey mare snorted, suddenly skittish, and Angeline felt Issac's body tense. A strange sort of stillness seemed to settle over him that made her heart begin to thump in her chest and her breath catch in her throat. Issac stopped the mare and slid silently to the ground. His eyes met hers, steady and purposeful in his young face, but something in them filled her with dread, and she felt tears welling up, without knowing why.

His voice was as soft as the underfur of the little rabbit they had caught the day before.

Angeline felt the taut line that stretched beneath the softness, and it held her fast.

"I'm going to slap the horse hard on the rump. I want you to ride, ride as fast as you can home, and no matter what, don't stop or look back." Now his voice seemed like stone, but his dark eyes were the little rabbit's as it froze when her hands closed around it. Angeline could not speak, and even as she nodded her head, he had turned the horse. The mare lunged forward, responding both the sting of his quirt and to his strangled yell, and the little girl clung to her back as they raced toward home.

Angeline looked back. She saw the warriors rise out of the clumps of grass, saw her brother standing proud and fierce and terribly small with his knife in his hand, then the mare leapt down a gully and when they had scrambled up the other side, she could see nothing behind her.

As Baptiste tied up his horse, Angus McDonald stepped out of the Post and strode over to him, his face serious. He greeted Baptiste, then wasted no time telling him the news he had received from the Pend d' Oreille that had settled near the Mission. A war party of Crows had been spotted in the mountains. Several parties of Pend d' Oreille and Salish were out looking for them. They reported that signs indicated the Crow were on foot and were headed north toward the lake. Angus was concerned for Baptiste and his family, who were isolated and unprotected on the lake shore. Baptiste immediately untied his horse, but Angus bade him wait, and shortly they would send a party of warriors with him. Darkness was just setting in when they reached the ferry landing, but Angeline's and her mother's faces told the men that they had arrived too late, and in the darkness the raiding party slipped away undetected.

"Did they ever find your brother?" Mary asked her grandmother.

Angeline shook her head. "No, but I believe the Crow took him home and raised him as their own, because they did that, back then. I'm sure of it," the old woman added. "When the railroad was put in to Missoula, I was a grown woman with my own children. Some Crow came into Missoula on the train, asking if anyone knew of Angeline who lived at the foot of the lake. I never did find out who was asking about me, but I think it was Issac, or someone who knew him and was trying to get a message to me." Angeline fell silent, memories crowding her mind in a continuous stream. Then her face cleared and she smiled at Mary. "Let's go down to the rapids and catch some fish for supper," Mary grinned happily. She loved to watch her grandmother fish, though Angeline would make her sit back on the bank away from the treacherous rocks while she fished the rapids. Something about fishing seemed to make her grandmother younger and more spry.

Angeline Michel holding grandaughter Mary (Davis) Dupuis.

The roar of the rapids filled Mary's ears as she sat in her customary spot, a safe distance from the roiling water. The setting sun threw out a shifting mix of salmon and gold, bright as a tanager's wing onto the frothy surface. Her grandmother's form was slowly becoming a charcoal smudge against light and water. Mary slapped at a mosquito on her bare arm. A pair of nighthawks swooped and dived, molten stars under their wings. She looked up again. Light and shadows seemed to shift, and she squinted at the rock Angeline sat on. Mary craned her neck forward, her eyes widening in surprise. The figure of her grandmother seemed to have diminished to that of a small child. A shadow slipped across the rock, lithe and supple as a young boy, and stood next to the little girl. Mary shaded her eyes against the brilliance of the sunset. The little girl that was and was not her grandmother looked up. The shadow boy squatted down next to her and his hand reached out for her willow pole as he helped the girl cast out her line.

Mary's mouth opened to form a soundless "Ohhh!" The sun sank behind the hills, shooting out crimson streaks into the deepening sky. A fish flashed on the end of Angeline's line, netted by the last orange rays of the sunset, and she drew it in. Mary watched the little girl stand up on the rock, only it wasn't the little girl, it was her grandmother again. Her grandmother climbed carefully down the rock, but the shadow boy did not move. Instead he seemed to diffuse into the settling twilight, and when Mary blinked instinctively and looked again, the rock was empty of any form but its own. Mary clambered over to her grandmother, who took her hand in her own, cool, old person's hand.

Mary stared hard at her grandmother in the gathering darkness, and her grandmother stared back. Then Angeline's face split into a mischievous grin and she waggled her catch in front of Mary's face. The old woman laughed, fully and heartily, and Mary's eyes rounded again. Her grandmother gave her a knowing look, eyes crinkled in merriment, and she tweaked Mary's nose.

"Some good fishing tonight, hmm, Granddaughter?"

Mary nodded and grinned back.

Chapter Four

BEAR STORIES

THE SHEEP KILLER

I have always considered dogs and horses to be highly intelligent, the other animals to a lesser degree. Some of them, such as sheep can be a little on the dumb side. Cows… well they are kind of like my grandson Austin said, "The only thing dumber than a cow is its calf." This is mostly true, but God gave them what they need, and some times they amaze me with their thinking. One example happened about forty years ago when we were raising sheep, as well as cattle.

There was an extra big four- to five-hundred-pound black bear killing the sheep. He was trap wise, and people wise. This bear had been giving Dad a lot of trouble the year before at the guest ranch. Dad set a trap for him, and caught him but the bear got away and moved over to our ranch. For two years he harassed us, and I had had no luck trapping him or killing him. I spent some long cold nights waiting for him to come, but he always seemed to know I was there. Then, when I finally had him in my sights, I messed up my chance to kill him.

I woke up one night to the sound of sheep dying. I grabbed my 12 gauge shotgun, a flashlight, and, dressed in my birthday suit and my boots, I ran to the barn where the sheep were penned up for the night. The bear was in the middle of the sheep, and stood up when I put the light on him. I shot at his head and chest, but he had a dead sheep in his arm, which took most of the shot and saved him. The bullet broke or badly injured his left foreleg, and he headed through the sheep to the hole he had made in the fence when he broke in.

I raced around the pen to intercept him and tried to shoot him in the head as he came out, but there was only a click when I pulled the trigger. I thought I had two shells in the gun, but there was only one. That big bear seemed to lead a charmed life; he had broke loose from Dad's trap the year before, and now was saved by a dead sheep. He killed seven of them that night.

The bear was gone for about three weeks, and then came back, killing again. Early one morning I heard boards breaking. When I got to the pen he had killed two sheep, but I got there before he could carry them off. Later that morning my two boys, Jim and Buddy, were helping me repair the pen. We had dragged the dead sheep about sixty feet from the pen so we could pick them up with the truck later. We were busy working on the pen when we noticed one of the dead sheep was gone. That old bear had come out of the woods and taken that sheep without any of us seeing or hearing him. I think my boys probably learned a cuss word or two right then. That bear killed thirty-three sheep, two calves and a yearling steer of ours that we knew of.

 The sheep got so they were afraid to leave the corral to graze unless I was with them. None of them wanted to get too far from me, but after a while they would get so busy eating that they would forget. Sometimes for fun, I would hide. In a little while one of them would notice I was gone, and start blatting in alarm. Then they would all come running, looking for me. When they found me they would settle down and start eating again. They were intelligent enough to know that they were safe from the bear if I was with them.

 A few years ago we were keeping a small herd of about forty Longhorns and their calves in the big pasture around our house, separated from the main herd of Angus. I had a smaller pasture of about sixty acres on the south side of the creek that I would save until mid-summer. One morning before leaving I went over to open the gate to this pasture. The cows saw me and knew what I was about to do, and came stampeding through as soon as the gate was open. When they were all in I closed the gate and went back to the house. A while later I went out to the pickup to leave and noticed one of my favorite Longhorn cows standing at the gate bawling. I thought she must have left her calf in the big pasture so I went back and opened the gate. I thought it odd that, instead of coming out the gate, she ran back across the creek. I left the gate open so she could come through, then I left. When I got back home that afternoon, as soon as I got out of the truck the cow came back to the gate and started bawling again. I knew something was going on so I went over to the cow. As soon as I got to her she turned and trotted back across the creek. I followed her through the trees, and she took me right to her calf. Its head was caught between two birch trees that had grown across each other, forming a narrow 'v'. The calf's head was caught in it, with its hind feet just barely touching the ground. It must have been pushed up into the notch as the cows stampeded through there. I got the calf out with the cow's encouragement. It was not injured, but hungry and right away started nursing its mom. As soon as it was done, she took her baby and went off to join the herd. She was smart enough to know she needed me to help her and she never gave up until she got me there.

A GRIZZLY IN THE TRAP

The big black sheep-killing bear would not go into a bear set normally used to trap a bear. I tried to outsmart him by making a different kind of set. He was wise to it, but a young grizzly was not. I awoke on a Sunday morning to a bear bellowing. I went down to the trap to find I had a two-year old grizzly instead of the black. I did not want to kill an innocent grizzly but I didn't not know how I was going to get the grizzly out of the trap. I hurried back to the house and called Dad, but they had already left for church, so I called his church to get his advice and help, but no one answered the phone.

Laurie took Josie and drove into town to the church. She and Jo went in to the service as quietly as possible and whispered to Dad and Mom what had happened. Dad got up and motioned for my brothers, Mick and Buck, to come out in the hall where he whispered the story to them. They in turn went back and whispered to their wives that they were leaving and why.

By this time everyone in the church had given up trying to pretend they were listening to the sermon, and poor Pastor Sjoblem's service was in shambles. Dad called our vet, Doc Read, and told him he needed some medicine real quick. Doc said to meet him at the clinic.

When Dad, Laurie and Jo got to the clinic there were some other people there also. Dad said he needed something to put an animal to sleep. Doc said "What kind of animal?"

Dad did not want tell him in front of the other people, so he said "A real big, mean dog! Doc looked at Dad as if he was crazy, and said "A big mean dog?"

Dad said, "A really, really big dog!" Doc looked dumbfounded, and finally in desperation, Dad pulled Doc outside and told him what kind of a "dog" he needed to put to sleep. Laurie and Jo were trying to keep from laughing; they said Dad was so funny trying to talk to Doc in sign language. Doc got the serum as well as antibiotics and medications for any possible injury to the bear.

It didn't take long for them to accomplish this and drive the eight miles back to our place. Meanwhile, the bear was tearing things up, and while being toggled to a drag pole had been able to travel a couple hundred yards. The mother bear was there but stayed back quite a ways, she and her cub would be going on their separate ways shortly so she was not as aggressive then as she would have been if it was a young cub. Dad had a syringe of sleeping serum, but we didn't have any way to give it to the bear.

My brothers laughingly said to me, "You caught it, now you get in there and give it a shot." We ended up getting some lariats and ropes to tie the bear with. We roped him and with a good deal of effort we got him tied and stretched out. Now we didn't need to put him to sleep to take the trap off, but we gave him a shot anyway. We figured he was going to be one mad grizzly when we turned him loose. We thought it would be a lot less stressful for the bear and us to take the rope off while he was sleeping. Dad gave him a shot and he went right to sleep. We took the trap and ropes off, doctored his leg where it was skinned up, and gave him a shot of antibiotic.

Sleeping bear.

Before we finished we could hear voices and laughter in the distance. Coming through the woods was about half the Cheff clan. They had come to witness the process. The kids were all wanting to pet the sleeping grizzly, but we knew he needed some breathing room. Buck let out a big growl that sent the kids scurrying back to their moms. The bear woke up pretty fast and after it got its balance back it loped off to the woods. It was a real circus, but all ended well.

Dad with bear trap.

The big black bear that was the start of it was shot and killed by someone else that fall as it crossed the road a couple miles below the ranch.

A BLOND GRIZZLY

In the summer of 2004 I was leaving the house on my way to Ninepipes and had just crossed the creek when I saw a bear come out of the woods up ahead, about forty yards off the road. I thought it was a blond black bear. I had seen blond blacks before but not on the ranch. Then as I drove by it, I realized it was a grizzly.

I had never seen anything like it before, so I stopped and backed my rig up to get a better look, and the grizzly stopped and stared at me. It was small and looked young, maybe two or three years old, weighing less than two hundred pounds. All four feet and the legs about half way up were dark brown. The face might have had a little brown around the eyes also, I can't remember for sure, but all the rest of it was pretty light blond.

I could not believe it was a grizzly, but it was. It had the hump and grizzly face, plus I could plainly see the long front claws on its right foot as it stepped over a log. I have seen light brown grizzlies, and some with so much silver guard hair that they looked white, but never one this color. I have never seen this bear again or heard of anyone else seeing it. That was one more of the hundreds of times I wished I had a camera with me.

OBSERVATIONS OF RANCH BEARS

There is not much bear activity on the ranch right now, but there have been some grizzlies down in the valley, some just a mile from the museum. I have heard of three different bears that were killed, with just the claws taken. What a waste!

Laurie and I were privileged to watch some amazing sights of the grizzly bears again this spring. I am happy to say that Shadow was here. I had a good view of him several times; he was in fine shape and sooo big. Before he showed up, I thought he might have been killed. I was told the Fish and Wildlife people had accidentally killed a big grizzly a couple miles north of us.

This year we have watched a big sow with three yearling cubs; a small sow with two new cubs; two other adult grizzlies with collars and ear tags; and two beautiful two-years-old. They also had been here last spring with their mother. One is dark with a silver blanket and one is real light brown with a lot of silver. They spent quite a bit of time in the area, and I worry for their future if they get too used to people.

We watched the mule chasing two grizzlies, and a few days later the longhorn cows chased the same bears out of the meadow several times. The bears wanted to cross the meadow. They would get about a third of the way through when the cows would see them and run them back into the trees. On the third try the bears made it across.

We did not see as many black bears as usual, fewer than a dozen different ones. Throughout the years we have lost some livestock to predators. The biggest losses come from dogs and coyotes, with black bears next, and every once in a while, grizzlies or mountain lions. This spring we lost an Angus calf to a bear. My son Buddy had some of his best Angus cows and calves with a special bull in a pasture by his house when the bear came late at night. A calf was killed, and from the looks of the bite marks it was a big bear. The Fish & Wildlife biologist said it was a grizzly. I thought it might have been a big black bear that had been causing problems in the area. My son's dog ran the bear off before it could eat on the calf, which was good, because once they start killing and eating livestock, there is no stopping them. The fact the bear did not go up a tree as black bears usually do when a dog is after them did point to a grizzly as the culprit.

I looked out the window last evening and there were four grizzlies walking up the field to the house. They followed the yard fence towards the barn, and the apple trees that grow behind it, not stopping at any of the trees by the house. Laurie and I took a camera we had just bought, but did not know how to use, and went out to the barn. We watched the bears from the barn loft window until dark. They were beautiful bears, fat with their long winter hair.

Our pictures did not turn out, but it was fun watching them take turns shaking the apples out of the trees. Two of them got into a fight, and Laurie got to see and hear them bellowing up close.

One of the bears climbed up into one of the apple trees. He went up just like a person would, with his legs spread and each foot on a limb, climbing the tree one limb at a time. Two of the bears were busy eating the apples the climber knocked down. The fourth bear was sitting on his rump a short distance out from the tree with one arm raised, as if he was showing the bear in the tree where the most apples were. It's a good thing to remember – the grizzly bear can climb some trees if there are enough branches. I saw one big grizzly chasing a black bear go thirty feet up a tree that had no lower limbs, before falling back down.

Summer is gone and fall is here, a beautiful time of year in western Montana. The bears are in a feeding frenzy, fattening up for the long winter. This year, 2005, there have been very few grizzlies at the ranch. In the south meadow behind the barn there are half-dozen wild apple trees scattered around, one with early sweet yellow apples. It is the first tree on the ranch the bears hit in late summer.

I was changing sprinkler pipes one morning in the meadow about six weeks ago, and I saw where a big grizzly had been feasting on the early apple tree. It was easy to see the bear had been having a fun night. I wish I could have watched him as he ate apples, then played in the sprinklers, and then grazed a bit. He didn't break any sprinkler heads, but some were laid over. The tracks were plain to see in the soft, wet new grass. His big feet and long stride made me hope it was Shadow. I have not seen him for a year.

It was another poor berry crop this year and the black bears have been making a nuisance of themselves around the valley. We had one at the museum last week, entertaining everyone but me. I had to clean up after him. In another incident, a big male black bear got into the beekeepers hives on our place. There was an electric fence around them, but the bear went through it and destroyed a lot of hives and supers full of honey.

Summer 2006. It's been a warm spring and summer so far in western Montana, with the snow fast disappearing on the peaks. We had a couple good rains this spring and the cows are in grass heaven. This lush growth of grass and brush could mean trouble later this summer in the fire season unless we get some late rains.

There has been less bear sign this year than ever before. We have watched three different black bears and two grizzlies on the ranch so far this year. Laurie and I did have the pleasure of watching a bear we named Shadow walking up the road one morning, a few weeks ago. He acted like the road was put there just for him, The Grand King. I think he's still growing, and he is a very big, powerful looking bear. I love to watch these big bears move, they seem to almost float along in their rolling gait as if they are light as a feather, instead of five to one thousand pounds of muscle, moving silently along with some definite destination in mind.

Spring, 2008, has been slow coming this year; windy and cold with almost no precipitation. The winter was the same with little snow below five thousand feet elevation, but it looks like there's a lot higher up, above six thousand feet. It was an easy winter for the elk and deer, but tough on the mountain goats. The grizzlies will probably not find as many winter kills to feed on this spring, at least in our area. The winter-killed animals are the grizzlies survival food after they come out of hibernation, until the first new grass and plants start growing. I think they will find slim pickings in many areas where the wolves and coyotes have already cleaned up the kills. I always thought it sad that the old and weak wildlife and domestic animals struggle through the long winter and then come March, they give up and die, with spring just around the corner.

On March 28th the old grizzly "Shadow" showed up. This spring was the same as before; his first stop was the big, creosoted corner posts where he rubs and bites them. It seems he really likes that creosote! He plays and rolls around, kind of like a cat with catnip.

A lot of grizzlies have been killed in the last few years, some by accident, but many of them poached. Last fall one was shot a few miles south of us, at Post Creek. Whoever poached the bear took only the claws, leaving the carcass behind. I would hate to see these bears killed. They came by the house last week and put on a show for my daughter and son-in-law, who were here on a visit from the Seattle area. The grizzly bear spring in the cedar grove, or as our kids called it, the Magic Forest, was well used this year. A cool bubble bath probably felt awful good on the hot 90 to a 100-degree days. This spring never freezes over, even in below zero weather, and there are always air bubbles rising.

BEAR ROMANCE

We had an unexpected grizzly show the second week of July. I was looking out the window one afternoon when I saw two grizzlies come out of the woods and cross the road into the meadow below the house. One was a big, pretty sow with a lot of silver-colored hair, and the other was a smaller, homely male. I thought breeding season was over but I guess not. They wrestled and played around for about fifteen minutes, then she let him mount her.

While they embraced two more bears crossed the road into the meadow. One was a big silver male, the other was smaller. The big bear ran up to the lovers and drove the smaller male off. The smaller bear came right back, but stayed a respectable distance from the big fellow.

The big male then started romancing the female. They wrestled, rolled on the ground, then stood up, biting and mauling each other, all the time coming closer to the house so we had a good view of them. Looking through the spotting scope I could see right into their huge mouths as they opened them wide, mouthing each other. I guess you would call it "grizzly kissing." They went all over the meadow, then moved into the area to the north where they played until dark. The other two bears did some mock fighting, but mostly just sat or laid and watched. None of the bears seemed to be in a aggressive mood. In the past I noticed and have been surprised when several males were after the same sow grizzly, and there were no big battles.

FALL, 2008

We were able to watch some beautiful bears along with many species of birds and animals of western Montana this past year. Living a mile and a half off the county road has its rewards for us. We counted over a hundred deer coming in close to our house last spring. It is quite a sight to see new fawns racing around the field playing tag with the wild turkeys, or a couple of bull elk in velvet following some strutting turkey gobblers around, wondering what in the heck they were doing. For me there is no better way to rejuvenate my spirit and faith than spending time with nature, even though Mother Nature almost sent me to the happy hunting grounds this winter. I was sawing a wind fallen tree when it barber-chaired, and the butt hit me in the head. Laurie took me to the hospital were they sewed me up. I have a little vision loss in the left eye, and headaches, but I am thankful that's all.

It's peaceful on our ranch now that the bears are sleeping. They stayed out later than usual this year. There were a couple of black bears

Deer and wild turkeys in our yard.

I thought were never going to go to bed. We finally went almost two weeks without seeing any bears, and Laurie asked me if I thought they were all denned up. I said, "Yes, I think they are. We can start putting the garbage out on the carport again next week." I had just sat down in my chair, and looked over at Laurie standing at the kitchen sink. I said, "Laurie, someone wants to help with the dishes. Look out the window." There was a brown bear standing up, looking at her with his nose pressed against the window. I guess he decided he wanted to move in with us for the winter. It took me three days to convince him he was not welcome around the house.

SPRING 2010

Laurie and I have been blessed this spring with a generous supply of wildlife to view from our home. The wood ducks, my favorites, come here to nest in the giant aspens and cottonwoods every spring. It is not unusual to see ten pair of the beautiful little ducks scampering around the yard getting slugs, or perched resting on the dock rails.

We have watched six grizzly at one time in the meadow, and have seen eleven different grizzlies this spring, including Shadow. We saw him in full daylight twice, and a half dozen times in the evening shadow. In contrast we have only seen two black bears so far. All the grizzlies looked to be in good shape, but two of my nephews saw one right behind the museum that was in real poor shape. The grizzlies go out on the open prairie to get the voles when they are plentiful. The vole or meadow mouse is a large fat mouse, a lot like an arctic lemming. Often the arctic snowy owls migrate to our valley to feast on the voles. Two great horned owls spent the winter roosting in a big willow tree next to the museum. From the looks of their scat under the tree they consumed a lot of voles during the winter.

We watched a big grizzly sow and her two yearling cubs several times. This is a bear we have watched for a number of years. She and her cubs had a chance encounter with Shadow while grazing in the meadow in front of the house. At first all three bears, mother and cubs stood up watching as Shadow approached. When he got close the mother got in front of the cubs and took a defensive position, turning a little sideways to the danger. Shadow gave them a little more room as he went by, never stopping but going on about his business.

This particular sow's udder was very large and all the teats looked like they were full of milk. I have never known a sow to nurse her yearling cubs so I asked Dad if he knew of this, and he said he didn't. I called Charles Jonkel, a friend of the museum and of our family. Chuck is a world renowned expert on bears, and I figured he would know if anybody would. He said he had known of a black bear nursing yearlings but not a grizzly. He thought possibly the cubs had nursed and stimulated her milk production during hibernation, or maybe she had new cubs and they had died. Sows normally don't have cubs two years in a row, but anything is possible. At any rate she was a beautiful bear and fun to watch.

FALL 2010

There has been very little bear activity this year, maybe because of the heavy logging going on around us. The hot dry weather might also be a factor but whatever the reason there aren't as many bears around as usual. We have one medium-sized grizzly bear around almost every day, feasting on the apples and plums. Laurie and I watched him from the barn loft last night until it was too dark to see. He was fat and beautiful.

There was also a grizzly sow with two cubs in the plum bushes behind the garden last week. They spent several days gorging on plumbs and tearing the bushes down. I don't know which bear is the worst to destroy fruit trees, the grizzly or the black bear. The grizzly reaches up and tears the limbs off, and the black climbs up and breaks them with his weight.

The deer are starting into the rut. I watched two bucks fighting in front of the house this week. A fawn came up to see what the fuss was all about, and one of the bucks chased it off, then came back and resumed the battle. They kept at it for about fifteen minutes before they moved off into the woods. The wildlife here on the ranch sure help us relax after a stressful day.

JOSIE AND HER CUBS

The winter came with a bang in mid-November one year, catching many of us not quite ready, including some grizzly bears. We had the pleasure of watching a sow we call Josie and her two cubs, all fat and beautiful with their long winter silver-tipped coats. We had seen this grizzly family a couple of time earlier this year. Laurie and I had a lot of fun watching them, especially the cubs. They were sure full of energy, chasing each other, wrestling, and running around jumping and bucking like a couple of spring calves. Every once in awhile they would attack

Josie and cubs.

Mom, and she would look at them with tolerance and pride like any loving mother would do. Then one hit her in the face and she looked like she was saying, "Watch it, young man, or I'll whap you one!"

One day three coyotes came out into the field near them and the two cubs took after the coyotes, running them back into the woods. A little while later the coyotes came out again, and the cubs chased them again. I think the coyotes thought it was a game, and maybe it was. All the while this was going on the mom was just sitting there in the snow, watching. She would hold one of her hind paws in her two front paws like she was trying to warm it, then do the same with other hind paw. She spent a lot of time just sitting, looking off into space. I think she was daydreaming of her nice warm den and a long nap. With a foot of snow and the temperature close to zero, she finally had enough, and left for her den on Nov. 27.

We have not seen any sign of Shadow this fall. There have been several reports of a big grizzly killed this past summer in western Montana that might have been him. I sure hope it wasn't him.

SPRING 2011

The mamma grizzly we call Josie and her two cubs, now yearlings, showed up here March 17th. I think they denned here on the ranch as it was so late and cold when they left last fall, November 27th being the last day we saw them. They were the first bears here this spring. We

Josie and cubs in mock battle.

usually see the male bears first.

    Josie sure is a good mamma; she is always wrestling and playing with her rambunctious cubs. She will let them take her down and maul her. I watched her gently take one cub's head in her mouth and hardly ruffle a hair. At one point all three of them were laying on their backs in the snow with all four feet in the air. I don't know what they were doing, just having fun I guess. The snow is almost gone in the woods but there is still about ten inches in the meadows and that's where they like to play, in the snow. Josie was walking along when she must have felt frisky as she jumped up and around a little, then sat down in the snow, grabbed both hind feet with her front feet and fell backwards onto her back. Then the two cubs pounced on her. Another time we were watching them play tag and having mock battles. While the yearling girl cub was racing around, she turned a complete summersault on purpose, then did another one. I have never seen a bear do this before.

    A few weeks before the bears came out we had some way below

Two cubs in mock battle.

zero weather, and one night some wild turkeys froze to death on their roost – and the carcasses then fell to the ground. Turkeys like to roost in the bare cottonwood trees where they have no protection. It has been such a long cold winter with the deep snow, and I think the turkeys were in poor condition, which contributed to their deaths. The first day the bears showed up the cubs found a couple of the dead turkeys. They spent a good thirty minutes playing "Keep Away" with them. One would run with a turkey in his mouth, then he would throw it, and they would both scramble to get it. They had turkey feathers scattered all over the place. Josie often initiates the playing and mock battles. I think she is training them for future encounters. Watching how gentle she is with them, and how much fun they have, you tend to forget how big, powerful, and dangerous these bears can be.

There has been no sign of Shadow this spring, he is usually the first one here. We will miss him, but he has left us with some special memories. Another favorite was Becky, who was here every year for over twenty years, before Shadow.

MY FIRST ENCOUNTER WITH BECKY

Late one afternoon in the first part of June, 1974, a neighbor called to tell me some of my cows were in his pasture. A close friend, Hugh Adams, and his wife Marlene had come to visit and spend the night with us. Hughie was a big handsome ironworker and had been a world champion contest logger twice. We had gone to school, worked iron and hunted together through all our years. Hughie loves the outdoors and joined me in a lot of adventures, including catching mountain lions alive.

There is a heavily timbered swamp between our ranch and the neighbor's so I decided to walk instead of riding a horse, as it would be over three miles to go around horseback. The cows can get through the swamp in one place, but a horse cannot. Hughie, my thirteen-year-old son, Jim, and I got to the neighbor's field just before dark, but there were no cows. They had evidently headed back home, taking the long way around. We started back, and when we came to the swamp, Jim said he knew a good way to get through, and he would be the guide.

The sun was going down as we started into the swamp. We were about one-third of the way through, in open, wet ground with scattered trees when a big bear stood up, about thirty yards in front of us. The bear was in heavy timber, and it was getting dark and shadowy in the trees, so we could not see it clearly. In the shadows it looked black, and at first I thought it was the bear that had been killing our sheep and calves all spring. He was a real big bear, close to five hundred pounds, and had a crippled front leg. Over the years he had killed twenty sheep, two small calves and a yearling. I sure wanted to kill him, but he was 'trap wise' and had outsmarted me on every turn. He seemed to have a charmed life.

As my eyes adjusted to the darker shadows where the bear stood, I could see that it was about a four hundred pound grizzly. Then I saw two small cubs standing behind her. Her hair was standing up, and she was popping her teeth. I told Hughie and Jim, "She's on the fight! We'd better get up a tree." There was a tamarack (larch) tree about fourteen inches in diameter, with no limbs, right beside Hughie, and a big, bushy spruce tree just behind Jim, just across a small stream. I was standing a little in front of them and there were no more trees close by. Hughie started up the tamarack, and Jim jumped across the stream and went up the spruce. I think when Jim jumped across the stream to reach the tree, it triggered the bear to charge. She started to bellow and came at us. I turned to run and stepped into the bog, up to my knees. The bear was there in a instant, coming directly at me. Hughie and Jim were climbing, but not yet out of her reach. However, she had her sights set on me as I was on the ground.

Hugh Adams catching cutthroat.

I have raised hounds all my life and learned it's the big voice of the hound that puts bears and lions on the run, not the dog itself. In desperation, I turned and faced the bear just as she reached me and started bellowing like a hound, right in her face. I do a pretty good hound impersonation, and I think I surprised her. Anyway, she stopped, turned in one motion and ran back to her cubs. She acted like she was going to leave, so Hughie and Jim came down from their trees, and Jim jumped back across the creek. When he jumped, the bear let out another bellow and charged again.

Jim jumped back over the creek, and went up the same tree, while Hughie shinnied up his limbless tamarack. I turned and stepped into the same bog again. The baying seemed to work the first time, so I turned to face the bear and started baying again. The bear stopped about fifteen feet short of me this time, and with a woof she seemed to say, "Stay back from my babies." She turned and ran to her cubs, moving them back into the woods.

Tagging Becky, 1977.

When she turned back the second time I realized she was just bluffing, and didn't really want to attack me if she didn't have to. Hughie saw and heard me baying like a hound on the bear's first charge and this time he started barking too. He did not see that the grizzly had turned back and he was thirty feet up that limbless tree, still climbing in big jumps, and barking every jump. It was the funniest thing I had ever seen. Jim was wearing a T-shirt, and had some nasty scratches from the rough spruce tree, and Hugh had some too. I was fine, except for being wet and muddy. What a great video this would have made. We must have looked like the three Stooges; Becky was probably laughing at those crazy humans.

I had seen this bear the year before but had not gotten acquainted, and she had not, then, been named. I believe it was the next year that

Chris Servheen caught her and named her Becky. Chris was doing his doctorate on grizzlies in the Missions, and they were trapping bears on my dad's ranch and on ours. We have had a lot of grizzlies on the ranch throughout the years. I have seen as many as eleven different grizzlies in one day, nine of them adults and two of them two-year-olds. Becky was special. She and her cubs were here every year, and every third year she would have new babies. Late one fall I watched her and her two yearlings cubs dig their winter den. Her strength and stamina were amazing, she really made the snow and rocks fly.

After 1990 we never saw her again. We saw her two-year-old cubs, but not her. In the seventeen years we shared the ranch with Becky she never gave us any kind of a problem. She and her cubs did give us a lot of pleasure. Every spring we were always watching for her.

MY SECOND ENCOUNTER WITH BECKY

My second encounter with Becky was a little humorous, as was the first one. This also would have made a good video. I was home when two young men came to the door and wanted to use the phone. They were working for Chris Servheen on the grizzly study he was doing on our ranch and had a yearling grizzly in their snare. The mom grizzly wouldn't let them get close enough to shoot the bear with their tranquilizer gun to put it to sleep so they could do their work on it. They tried to call Chris to see what to do, but could not reach him. They were pretty shook up because the mom bear had charged them; she ran them back into their truck, and they had no way to turn the cub loose. I told them I would take the hounds down and keep the mother back while they did their work on the cub.

I got three of my hounds and the 12 gauge shotgun for my wife, Laurie, as she was going to be the back-up guard. The bear trap was about four hundred yards below our house, by the north creek. The mamma bear was Becky, and she was not about to leave her cub. It took a while, but I finally got her back far enough for them to tranquilize the cub. They got back into their truck and waited for the bear to go to sleep.

When she was out, they brought their equipment and started working on her. Becky would only go so far away, about fifty yards, and the hounds kept her at bay there. Laurie was standing guard with her shotgun, between the men and Becky during the whole procedure on the cub. Gus was a big tan-colored hound with a loud voice. He was one-half Black and Tan, and one-half Bloodhound. In my eyes he was a beautiful hound dog with his long ears, sad eyes and loose skin-wrinkled face. Gus left the other two hounds and circled back to check on the sleeping yearling cub. When an animal's dead, the hounds have no more interest in them. Gus came up behind the two fellows working on the cub, unbeknownst to them. When he smelled the bear he realized it was not dead, and let loose a big bawling roar a few feet behind the men, scaring them out of their wits. One guy was squatted down, holding a metal tool box with pliers, ear tags, tattoo gun, medicines, syringes, and what-not in it. The men yelled, and the one with the tool box fell over backwards, throwing the tool box and its contents over his head.

This was really funny to see, but not for the two guys, of course. They didn't think it was funny at all! It was hard for me to contain my mirth as I caught Gus and took him back to the other hounds and Becky. All this time Laurie was steadfastly guarding the two guys. They finished their work with the cub, which was quite extensive. They determined the sex, weighed it, tattooed it, tagged and collared it, took blood samples and other samples. Then they named it Laurie, in honor of the brave young woman who stood shotgun for them. When the cub started to wake up the men got back in their truck, I pulled the hounds back, and Becky reclaimed her cub.

Grizzly named Becky.

Laurie, the cub, was around for quite a few years and ultimately brought her own cubs to the ranch. An interesting note is that a few years after she was tagged, our kids watched from our window as she played with a huge old male grizzly name Bud. The bear was named after my dad who assisted in his tagging. The kids tried to take a picture of them, but couldn't get the camera to work.

Eagle Tree.

BEAR SCARE AT THE EAGLE TREE

A few days after a windstorm I was checking the fence below the house. There always seems to be at least one tree on the fences after a windstorm. There were no downed trees on this fence that day, but as I was close to the eagle nest tree on our property, I thought I would go to it and check on the young eagles. The nest is in a big cottonwood tree with heavy timber and brush around it. This area is one of the bears' favorite daytime resting areas, with numerous bear nests under some of the big spruce trees.

I was almost to the eagle tree when I thought I faintly heard the snuffing of a bear. I stopped and listened, but did not hear anything. Then I heard a rustling high in a tree a ways in front of me. The trees were too thick-limbed to look up through them, but I thought one of the parent eagles had lit in the tree to check on who was coming close to its nest tree. I started on, but only took a few steps when I heard a bear woof, and saw the brush moving ahead. I stopped short, and slowly started backing up. I realized that I might be in bad trouble. The noise I heard up in the tree was probably bear cubs sent up for safety by their mom when she smelled me coming. I'd had a close call with a grizzly sow and her cubs many years ago, just a few hundred yards from the spot where I was now.

I could see the light brown color of the bear as it moved towards me, but I could not tell for sure if it was a grizzly. Both a grizzly and a black bear will send their cubs up a tree, and often the black bear will go up with them. I was hoping this was a brown colored black bear, but it looked more like the color of a grizzly. I was backing up all the time, not wanting to turn my back to it, and trying not to make a lot of commotion, all the time talking to the bear. It is surprising how many of the wild and tame animals on the ranch know my voice and will calm down when I talk to them. I was watching for a club of some kind and picked up a stout chunk of tree about six feet long and three inches in diameter. The bear was still coming towards me, at about the same speed I was retreating. It seemed to be stalking me. I had been stalked by a bear before, and it is not a good feeling.

I had a long club, but there was no room to swing it in the brush and trees. I backed into a little opening where there was room enough to swing my club and stopped to make a stand. I might bluff a black bear, *but a grizzly* – that would be a long shot. When I stopped again, this mamma bear stopped also. She was still in the brush where I could just barely see her. I glanced around to see if there was a tree nearby that I could climb easily, knowing I was getting too old to quickly scramble up a tree. When I looked back, the bear was not there. I did not know if it was circling around me or had left. I waited, listening, and then I could hear the cubs coming down from their tree. I guess the mamma bear had decided I was not a threat to her babies. She had just made sure I was leaving, and lucky for me she was not in an aggressive mood.

I made a circle in the opposite direction and continued on to the eagle nest tree. There seemed to be only one young eagle in it and it was almost fully-grown. It perched on the edge of the nest, giving me the once over. There had been two young eagles in the nest, the other one might have been down in the nest where I could not see it. When the mother eagle came back, the eaglet probably told her, "That man was here checking on us today."

I had given the bears plenty of time to leave the area, so I was not concerned about meeting them on my way back.

ROCKS AND BEARS

Looking back through my life it seems I had a thing for rocking black bears. It always seemed like the natural thing to do when a bear was getting into mischief – just pick up a rock and chase it off. I have rocked dozens of bears through the years and a few stand out in my memory. On one occasion I was simply walking to our barn and there was a medium size black bear standing up, pushing on the chicken pen. I picked up a hardball size rock. I hollered at the bear and threw the rock as it turned towards me. The rock hit the bear in the left front leg, just above the paw. It must have really hurt as the bear sat down and started to bawl, holding his left leg in his right paw. He sat there, rocking back and forth crying for quite a while before he got up and left. I felt like a real meany, but maybe it kept him away from chicken houses and from being killed himself some day.

On another occasion I was out for a morning run in early spring. I always loved to run and ran everywhere I went. At this time in my life I was spending a lot of time in the Missoula office, with the boys and our hired man doing most of the ranch work. I would take a mile or two run around the ranch early in the morning before I left for Missoula. A cow had died during the winter, and I thought I would check and see if any bears had found her yet. I came running around some trees and was startled to find a big brown-black bear on the cow.

I recognized this bear as one I had seen before, fighting with a black one just as big. They were both close to four hundred pound bears. They fought hard for quite awhile, then the brown got the better of the black. The black broke away and started running across the meadow towards the house, with the brown in pursuit. All the while they were fighting, there was a coyote sitting nearby watching them. When the black bear ran, the coyote joined the brown chasing the black. He was yapping and nipping at the black like a cow dog. They disappeared into the woods. It was a special thing to see.

On this particular day I guess the brown bear thought I was there to take the cow away from him, as he was instantly on the fight. I started backing up and scooped up a coconut size rock as I moved. The bear kept coming and I knew I could not get away from him. When he made a run at me I let out a beller and charged him. I hit him in the rib cage with the rock, and the adrenalin must have been flowing as I hit him hard enough that I heard the air go out of him. That took the fight out of him and he retreated back to the cow carcass. I backed away and headed for the house. I thought, here I have championed grizzly bears all my life and I just about got ate up by a lowly black bear. I was a little embarrassed to tell any one a black bear had scared the dickens out of me.

The rock throwing at this bear probably saved my life, but at another time it nearly cost me my life.

SHADOW

I have mentioned a big grizzly bear we called Shadow. We named him that because although he is often around, we seldom see him. He is quite shy and only comes out in the open at dusk, so we would usually only see a shadow. He is a big brown grizzly with the silver guard hairs, not as pretty as the dark grizzlies with the silver chests and silver down their backs, and shoulders, but still a striking bear. His face looked wise and self assured, not aggressive or mean like some bears seem to look. He has been around our place for about twelve years and has made his winter den on the ranch three or four times.

I have only seen him in full daylight about a dozen times in all these years. One spring a while back I watched him biting and rubbing on the creosote at the bottom of a power pole. He spent a good ten minutes there. He would bite and rub on the pole, then jump around and roll in the snow, then do it again, acting like he was having a great time. Often I would see his tracks where he would follow along the fences, biting the treated bottom of the posts. He seems to have a thing for post treat, and I don't know if he likes it or hates it. Since I had written often in our museum newsletters about Shadow, so many people have asked about the big grizzly that I decided to relate my first and second close encounters with him.

When I first met Shadow I had not seen him before, although he had probably seen and smelled me plenty of times. He sure made a life-long impression on me that day. I was working in my shop, which is close to the creek. There is a dike across the creek with a small pond backed up behind it. My sweathouse is by the pond so I can jump in it when I take my sweat bath. Just across the pond I had a grain feeder for the wild turkeys. I heard a racket at the feeder and I went out to investigate. There had been a brown black bear at the feeder a few days before, and sure enough I could see the brown hair of the bear through the bushes at the feeder.

I thought, "I will put some fear into this bear!" So, I picked up a softball size rock and walked out on the dike. I hollered and threw the rock at the brown spot moving in the bushes. I hit dead center in the brown, but instead of a brown bear high-tailing it out of there, a big grizzly came boiling out of the bushes right at me. I have been blessed with fast reflexes but compared to a charging bear they were mighty slow. My mind was trying to think of a way out, I knew it was useless to try to run; he would be on me before I got off the dike. I thought, "My only chance is to jump out into the water."

I was just bunching my muscles to jump and the bear was there! He stopped about four feet from me, close enough to hit me with his huge paw if he'd wanted to. We stared each other eye-to-eye for a couple of long seconds that seemed like minutes to me. Then he wheeled around and loped off while I stood frozen in my tracks, wondering why he had spared me. Except for the surprised grunt when the rock hit him, he had not uttered a sound during the whole encounter. He was so fast he had gotten to me before I could even jump.

I forgot what I had been doing in the shop and headed for the house, still in shock. As I walked, my mind replayed everything, and I thought, "That was a <u>big</u> bear! He was looking me in the eye while standing on all four feet." I like to think when he got to me he realized what and who I was, and stopped short of hitting me. I do know wild and tame animals identify you by your smell and the sound of your voice. I always talk to them, especially horses. It seemed when we were face to face he was telling me, "Sorry for scaring you, but don't ever hit me with a rock again or you're dead."

We never saw him close to the buildings again, at least not in the daylight. I emptied the wild turkey feeder as the turkeys were getting well established and did not need help from me anymore, and I did not want to entice the bears to a free meal.

ANOTHER SHADOW STORY

My second close encounter with Shadow was in late spring a couple of years after our first meeting. I was just about to get into the pickup parked at the house when I heard a fawn deer bleating in the woods across the meadow. When a fawn gets hurt or caught by a predator it makes an extremely loud bleating, so pitiful, it makes your hair stand up.

This fawn bleated for a long time before it stopped, so I was pretty sure a coyote had gotten it. If it had been a bear, it would have died quickly, but a coyote will start eating its prey before it's dead.

One spring several years before this day, while checking fences I spotted a new fawn washed up against some logs and debris in the middle of Crow Creek. It was high water time and the fawn must have been washed down while trying to cross with its mother. I took my boots off and waded out to rescue the fawn. When I got to it and started to pick it up, it commenced blatting. My ear drums were almost broken by the time I got it to shore.

I was just back to my boots when a coyote came charging at me. I don't consider a coyote to be a very scary animal, but when one comes at you with its teeth barred and death in its eyes, it gives you a different picture. This coyote wanted that fawn, and I was in its way. The fawn was blatting for all it was worth and the coyote was jumping at it. I was kicking at the coyote, but kicking a coyote barefooted wasn't easy. I finally got a good kick in and knocked him to the water's edge. This took the steam out of him, and he quit the fight and left. I got my boots back on and carried the fawn upstream where I turned it loose, hoping its mom would find it before the coyote did.

Back to Shadow. The coyotes had been taking a heavy toll on the wild turkeys and had killed all of our tame geese and both our house cats. I thought, "Maybe I can reduce the coyote population a little." I had a .22 rifle in the pickup, which I grabbed and headed across the meadow. I came to the fence and crawled through. Walking slowly, I went down the fence line towards where I thought the noise had come from. When I was almost there a coyote came zipping out of the thick trees and ran alongside the fence, but he was too fast for me and I couldn't get a shot. I took a few more steps, and two more coyotes came zipping out. They were only in sight a couple of seconds and, again, I couldn't get a shot

I walked on down to where the coyotes had come out of the thick foliage. The trees along here were spruce and white fir with thick limbs that extended clear to the ground. I thought I heard a noise under a bushy white fir so I pulled a heavy limb back and peered in. I was shocked to be looking at the big rear end of a grizzly, the same one that had scared the dickens out me a few years earlier. I could have reached out and goosed him, but that thought never crossed my mind then. My only thought was "I'm dead." You don't walk up on a grizzly eating his breakfast and expect to live to tell about it. I slowly let the branch go back into place and started backing away, knowing my life was hanging on a thread.

A .22 rifle is not the best gun to use on grizzlies. It would take a perfect shot or a miracle to stop a bear with it. I walked up the fence line a ways as quietly as I could, then crawled back though the fence, took a much needed deep breath and hurried to the house. The bear had to know I was there, but had given no indication of it. Walking to the house I thought, "Either that bear likes me or the Lord is saving me from myself." I could hear the bear crunching the fawn's bones.

When I got to the house I told Laurie, "Come out and listen to this." You could hear him plainly from the house. When Laurie heard the bones crunching she said, "That sounds just awful! Nature can be so cruel!"

When I'd heard the fawn bleating, Shadow had evidently heard it too. He must have gotten to the fawn just before I did and ran the coyotes off.

I had a few more meetings with Shadow but none so life-threatening as that one. But I did have another chance encounter with him a few years ago that was kind of special to me.

A CHANCE MEETING WITH SHADOW

A couple of years ago I wanted to check a gate to be sure it was closed. The gate was about a mile from the house but it was across the lower swamp area and, as it was more than three miles to drive around to it, I decided to walk as the exercise would do me good. It was early May, the dry time of year for the swamp, and I could get across it without getting too wet. I made it across okay as I knew where I could or could not get through without bogging down. A horse couldn't get through any where and they have enough sense not to try. But once in a great while a cow will make it through, and there are probably a few in there that didn't make it back out.

On this day I came through the open slough grass area on the far side of the swamp and into the timber. Just a short ways in, on higher ground, there is a old wagon road, now just a wide trail. I was going to follow it to the gate. Just as I started to step out onto the trail I saw a big grizzly coming down it, towards me.

I didn't have time to go back as he was almost to me. There was a big spruce tree with no lower limbs right behind me so I stepped behind it, holding as still as possible, being careful not to touch it and make a noise. The only thing I moved was my eyes as I watched him walk by. His head was down, swinging from side to side with his rolling gait. It was, sure enough, Shadow, and he looked like he didn't have a care in the world. I finally remembered I needed to breathe, and filled my lungs as quietly as I could. He never missed a step, just kept steadily on his way. When he was about seventy five yards past me I stepped back into the trail to go in the direction he had just come from.

When I stepped out, he stopped and half-way turned around, and looked at me. We both stood staring at each other. He seemed to say, "Hi Bud, I knew you were behind that tree." He turned and went on his way with his lazy swinging gait, and I went on my way. We both had business to attend to.

OUR RANCH AND BEARS

You might wonder why there are so many bears on the ranch. We are at the western base of the Mission Mountains, which have always had a good grizzly population. In the spring they come down into the valley to clean up winter kill carcasses and graze on the new grass.

Our ranch is a favorite place for them as we have two timbered swamp areas for them to hole up in safely during the day. There are numerous springs with good grass and especially dandelions, which they love. We see them grazing on them, just like a cow. In the late summer and fall there is usually a lot of fruit, with chokecherries, sarvisberries, thorn berries, and wild apples throughout the ranch.

One day in 1973 we watched thirteen different grizzlies. This was the most we had ever seen in a day, but in 1998 we watched eleven grizzlies, all adults or sub adults, and five black bears at the same time. The blacks were grazing in the north meadow and the grizzlies were in the two meadows below the house. At one point eight of the grizzlies left, walking single file, going north on our road. In the meantime two grizzlies came up into the north meadow where they encountered a black bear and chased it up a tree. They went into the woods and in about a half hour came back out. A short time later here came the eight grizzlies back down the road, all still in single file. What a special day this was for us – but I didn't get much work done.

A number of times throughout the years I have heard grizzly bears bellowing on the ranch. Although I could not always see them I assumed a female was fighting a male that was harassing her cubs, or maybe two males had a dispute. It is a little unsettling to hear them, knowing how powerful and dangerous they are when they are mad. A few years ago I was in the yard when I heard what sounded like two grizzlies bellowing to the northeast of the house. As I listened, I glanced down the meadow below the house just as Shadow came loping out of the woods. He came toward the house, crossed the creek, and went across the north meadow, running all the way, and then disappeared into the woods. The bellowing had been going on a long time, but it quit shortly after Shadow was out of sight. About thirty minutes later he came walking back. I guess he straightened out the trouble. It would sure have been fun to see what all had happened.

Laurie and I are blessed to live in a place where we can witness so many of God's wonders. In the spring, from our living room window we can watch the newborn baby mountain goats playing on the peaks above us, wondering how they keep from falling. Every spring we witness the rebirth of all nature. Plants, trees, and wild creatures are busy doing their job of making sure their species lives on. We get to see many of these wonders first hand, from the otters playing in the creek to the arrival of a momma grizzly with her new cubs.

One of the special treats for me is listening to the eagles, chirping and trilling as they settle down for the night in their roost trees below the house. Living a mile and a half off the county road makes us a little isolated from the rest of the world. I think the wildlife feel comfortable and safe here with us, as we are with them, but when a strange vehicle comes in they make a hasty retreat. Once in awhile a bear, usually a black bear or a mountain lion, will help themselves to a meal that they didn't pay for but these occurrences are rare. The only disadvantage of living a mile and a half off the road is, as we age, it gets harder to keep our road maintained and plowed in the winter. But we both love it, and would not change a thing.

SO LONG SHADOW

This week a six-hundred-pound, old male grizzly was killed by the Fish, Wildlife and Parks game warden in the Swan Valley, just over the divide from the ranch. In July of 2010 this bear had been caught and tagged by the Tribal bear managers here on the reservation, close to our ranch. It was released on the reservation, but left the valley and traveled over the Mission Range to the Swan Valley where he lost his collar. He broke into a number of outbuildings in the Swan Valley that fall and was killed in the interest of public safety. They said he weighed 600 pounds, was more than twenty years old and some of his teeth were worn down to his gums. The age, size, and history of this old bear makes me think it had to be my friend, Shadow. The spring of 2010 was the last time we'd seen him, and if he weighed 600 pounds in his old age, he would probably have weighed over 700 pounds in his prime, which is what I guessed Shadow weighed.

In all the years he spent here he never caused us any problems, but he left us with some good memories. He made his winter den here on the ranch four times that I knew of. It was always a treat on a sunny, warm winter day to see his tracks where he came out of his den and checked things out, going back to his den to continue his snooze. One sunny winter afternoon, a couple of days after he had been out I wanted to know just where his den was. I followed his tracks back to where he went into a heavy-timbered area of the swamp. This was where I thought his den was so I made a big circle around it to see if the tracks came out the other side. They did not, so I went on home, knowing exactly where he was sleeping. The next day I saw that he had come out of his den and followed my tracks around where I had made the circle, and up to the edge of the meadow. Then he then went back to his den. I guess he was wondering what I was doing around his den.

The next year he denned within a hundred feet of the same spot. In my mind I can see that big bear rolling and playing in the snow, and, in the summer, running through the sprinklers in the meadow, never breaking a sprinkler head. A couple of times he scared the dickens out me, but it was always my fault, and, being a gentleman, he gave me another chance. So long, Shadow, thanks for the memories.

In one of my museum newsletters some years ago, I mentioned Frank Linderman, a great Montana author and historian. Frank's granddaughter, Sarah Hatfield, brought my attention to the book, *Big Ginny*, written by Frank Linderman and illustrated by Elizabeth Lochrie. It is a great book for both children and adults. Scarface, the old bear in the story made me think of Shadow in his old age.

FEBRUARY 2012

Our winter started out with a bang in late 2011 but kind of fizzled out, although we did get twenty-one inches of snow two weeks ago. We had a little grizzly activity here late that fall. I ran into a big grizzly on October 17th when I was going to check a bee tree. The next day he raided the last apple tree with apples on it, near the house. On November 5th, when I thought the grizzlies had all denned up, we had two big males around for a couple of days. Both were big beautiful bears, one bigger than the other. I think one of them would have weighed 600 pounds or more. They kept some distance between them, but did not seem aggressive towards each other. They did a lot of rolling in the snow, and spent some time at the creek. They did not have any ear tags which I like, they seem more natural without tags in their ears. I measured the big one's tracks and his front foot was twelve inches from claws to heel, and eight and one half inches wide.

The big grizzly I mentioned above has been around for a week this spring. We first saw him April 7th, 2012. He is dark with silver guard hair and looks as wide as he is tall. He was a beautiful bear with a huge pretty face, not as tall as Shadow but of a more chunky build. The bear was also quite shy, which is good. Then one morning I saw a big old male coyote that I know walking beside the bear. The coyote looked like a little toy poodle walking beside the grizzly.

Late in the spring of 2012 Laurie, Jo and I were watching a pair of two-year-old cubs out of our front window. Both cubs had tags in each ear and a radio collar around their necks. They must have been in trouble the year before, and their mom probably had been killed. They were a little thin and scruffy looking and appeared to be just fresh out of hibernation. The two were grazing on the new grass by the pond in front of the house. The smaller one was laying down resting on its front legs, eating. It would eat all it could reach, then scoot forward to fresh grass, not bothering to get up. After a while the bigger one started down the meadow and the smaller one jumped up and followed.

I was watching them through a scope and as I moved it, I spotted a big male grizzly, the first one that had been here earlier this spring. He was behind a big tree in the edge of the forest, watching the cubs coming towards him. He stood up and watched them for a minute, then dropped down and stood behind the tree again with just his head sticking around. I told Laurie and Jo, "Those cubs are walking into trouble." The big bear remained perfectly still. When the cubs got close they started by the spot where the big one was hiding. They must have smelled or heard him as they both stood up, looking at him. Then they turned, dropped on all fours and went running north down our road. The big bear came out on the road and watched them until they were out of sight. After they were gone, he went back into the woods, probably chuckling, "I sure scared those kids."

The two kids came by again a few days later. They had gained some weight and their hair looked better. I figured they must be getting enough to eat.

The two-year-olds going into the swamp north of our house.

Early this past winter I watched the little band of mountain goats above us through the scope. They were in deep fresh snow, in the lower area. I watched one climbing up a forty foot cliff. When he was right at the top, he slipped and went over backwards. He did a complete flip over, landing on his side on the snowy slope below. He got to his feet and just stood there a long time. After a while he started back up, and made it that time! This was only the third time in my life I have seen a mountain goat fall. I have a lot of admiration for them; they are amazing animals.

A LION BY THE TAIL

In the late 1960's I was iron working on the construction of a new phosphate mill near Hall, Montana. My good friend, Hugh Adams was also working there. You may remember that I wrote about Hugh in the story about my first encounter with Becky. At this time in my life if I had any free time, I was running my hounds. Hugh was with me whenever he could be. We had a lot of fun and treed plenty of cats, both lion and bobcat. We weren't killing them, just treeing them and letting them go.

There were a lot of cats in the hills back of Philipsburg at that time. We treed a number of lions in that area that winter. One lion is still vivid in my mind as one of the prettiest sights I had ever seen. The hounds had treed it in a big-limbed pine tree in a snow-covered meadow. In all my years of lion hunting I never fail to get a thrill at seeing one of those beautiful cats looking down at me from a tree. This lion was a big male, laying full length on a large limb, just out of reach of the hounds. It was a beautiful sunny day, and the lion was looking down at the hounds as if to say, "Come up and get me, boys." Hugh and I were both wishing we had a camera with us.

A few weeks later we treed another lion in that area, a young one, just newly on its own. I had the ropes and steel cable needed to catch one alive so we decided to catch this one and take it home. To do this, one person would climb the tree that the lion was in, or a tree close to it if there was one. I had a twenty-foot piece of braided wire cable made like a lasso with a rope tied to the end. The lion couldn't chew the cable off, which it could do if you used a plain rope. We would cut a stout, long but slender pole and fasten the cable loop to it in such a way it would come loose easily. One person climbed up to the lion, put the loop over its head and under one leg. If you put it just around the neck you would choke the lion to death. It was not hard to do if you knew how. You held the loop just out of reach of the lion, and when it reached out at you, you slipped the loop over the leg and around the neck, and you had it.

The lion I had by the tail.

Hughie wanted to climb the tree and put the loop on the lion, as he had never done it before. So up he went, in the same tree as the cat. The cat had moved up pretty high. The tree had a lot of limbs and Hughie had a little trouble getting the noose on the lion. He finally got it in place and, standing on the ground, I pulled it snug with the rope. Hughie got the pole loose and dropped it to the ground. When he started down the cat jumped out of the tree. I had tied the hounds back out of the way so they wouldn't be trying to fight the lion when we were tying it up. I didn't want them or the lion to get hurt.

When the lion hit the ground, one hound, Blue, lunged at it and

Mick and live lion by the tail.

broke his tether rope. I caught ahold of Blue's collar as he charged into the lion. I'm not sure what all happened next as everything was going so fast and furious, but I ended up with a hound in one hand and a lion by the tail in the other hand. I was swinging them around in a circle trying to keep them apart, and the lion away from myself. All the time I was hollering for Hughie to hurry up and get down and help me.

When he reached the ground we got things back in control, and secured the lion. I was pretty winded, I had about used up my strength up by the time Hughie made it down and saved me.

We were standing there recuperating when I noticed a twinkle in Hugh's eye. Now he is a serious, no nonsense kind of guy, not prone to get tickled easily. I thought how funny I must have looked with a hound in one hand and a lion by the tail. He couldn't hold his mirth back any longer and we both had a good laugh.

Hugh walked on over the Great Divide a number of years ago, he was one tough guy and a great buddy. We shared a lot of exciting things together.

Another incident comes to mind that some of my brothers thought was funny, but for me, not so much. I am not sure, as it's been so many years ago, but I think my younger brothers Buck, Mick, and Nels were there. Nels Jensen was not a blood brother but the family considered him one. I guess we must have been bored and needed some excitement. A medium-size black bear had gone up a tree a short ways above the barn. We had caught and tied up lions and bobcats, but never a bear before and thought it might be fun. We got the pack with the climbing spurs, tie ropes and cable, and went up to the treed bear. I was the oldest and you might say the dumbest, but I would like to think the bravest. I would be the one to climb up the tree with the bear and put the cable on it. The bear was up quite a ways, and went even higher as I climbed. When I got up close she did not seem a bit happy to see me. She was growling and snorting something fierce. When I tried to get the cable on her, she emptied her bladder on me. She must have drank a lot of water that day as she really soaked me. That took all the fun out of it and I came down the tree in a hurry, to the laughter of the boys below.

Bud Jr. with a big male lion.

Years later I was hunting in the Bob Marshall wilderness with my good friend, Allan Hamilton, and his son Mark. We were sitting down taking a breather on a steep mountainside. I don't recall the conversation but I remember Allan telling Mark, "You know the movie *Crocodile Dundee?*" He pointed at me and said, "He has nothing on Buddy." A couple years later in Chicago he, his wife Phyllis, and Laurie and I were having dinner in a fancy hotel and restaurant he owned. He introduced me to the manager as Montana's Crocodile Dundee. I took it as a compliment then, but sometimes I wonder.

KATIE AND THE GRIZZLY

A few years ago while visiting a dear elderly friend, Mrs. Joe Hamilton, I noticed two deer hides stretched on the wall of her husband's shed. Josephine said Joe had tacked them up there many years ago and was always going to tan them, but never got around to it.

Joe was gone now, but I asked her if I could have them and maybe finish the job for him.

One of the hides was just too brittle to use, but the other one I thought I could salvage. I put it in the creek by the barn to soften it. On the third day it was finally soft enough to stretch. Late that afternoon I went to the creek to get the hide and it was gone. I could see the fresh tracks of a grizzly bear in the mud. I followed the wet tracks from the bear and the dripping hide for about a hundred yards to where the bear had dropped it, but not before leaving teeth marks all over it. I cleaned the hide up and tanned it anyway, using brains in the old Indian way of tanning.

When I was finished, I gave the hide to Mrs. Hamilton to give to Hoke, her and Joe's son and my lifelong friend who lived in Chicago. Joe would have been proud of the grizzly bite holes in the hide, as grizzlies were very dear to him.

Before I had gone to take this hide out of the creek, I had just finished skinning and fleshing a huge buffalo skull and had left it a short distance from the barn. I finished stretching the deer hide and went back to get the buffalo head, but that was gone! Just then I heard the sound of a bear going through the fence about two hundred and fifty feet from me, but I couldn't see him because trees and brush blocked the view. I hollered and took off, running after him. I was thinking, "If I can get him to drop it quick enough, maybe he won't ruin it." He ran into the heavy timber and as I started in, I stopped, thinking "I should go back to the house and get a gun." But I decided that by the time I did that, it would be too late to save the head.

So I picked up a stout club to make a lot of noise with, and went charging after the bear. I didn't go very far when I came upon him, laying down with the head in his front paws, chewing on the skull. He jumped up, dropped the head, and took off. I retrieved the head, but he had pretty much ruined it. All that was left were the horns and the skull down to the eye sockets.

That following Saturday my mother and father and my young niece, Katie, were having dinner with Laurie and me. I looked out the window, and there was this same grizzly coming across the field, heading for the barn. I had seen him by the chicken house the day before, and thought, "He's getting too tame and brave, and is going to cause some real trouble one of these days." He was a fair sized bear, probably about four hundred and fifty pounds. I grabbed the 12 gauge shotgun and hurried outside to the barn. I didn't notice that Katie was right behind me, and Dad was coming behind her. The bear was already at the chicken house, and when we came around the corner he stood on his hind legs and looked at us. He was too close to shoot without seriously injuring him, and that was not my intent.

It was a good thing I didn't need to shoot, as Katie squealed and grabbed my left arm for protection. I hollered at the bear, thinking when he got out far enough away I'd pepper his behind just to let him know that it wasn't all that much fun to hang around people and buildings. He turned and ran, but took a quick turn to the left, back towards the house. I was not able to shoot with Katie still holding on to me. As we came around the shop the grizzly was there, and again he stood up and looked at us. Then he dropped down and ran towards the heavy woods. I waited until the last minute before I shot, I wanted to be sure I didn't injure him, just scare him. He never came back around the buildings after that day.

While we were walking back to the house, Dad remarked how beautiful and dangerous these bears are and that he hoped this one would avoid people from now on. Katie, still holding my hand said, "Uncle Bud! This is the most exciting day I ever had!"

Chapter Five

COWBOYS AND LONGHORNS

THE LONGHORNS....
Anyone who has read my ramblings in the past can tell I am a little partial to the Longhorn breed of cattle. We only have a small herd of Longhorns now, as it is more profitable to raise Angus cows. My younger son, Buddy III, and I keep the Longhorns because we like them and they are fun to watch and easy to keep. Unlike the Angus, we very seldom have a Longhorn crawl through a fence.

We have had a few Longhorn bulls that would jump a fence and had one that went on a rampage, tearing up a lot of fences. When he came to one in his way he would rip the barbed wire off the posts with his horns and walk through. Needless to say, he was sold as soon as we could capture him. It was quite a job to get him roped and dragged out of the thorn thickets where he hid out, and then force sixteen hundred pounds of fiery-eyed horn and muscle into a trailer. He was not the norm, as most are easy to handle if you take them slow and know how they think. And they do think; in my opinion they are quite intelligent.

Buddy IV on cattle drive.

I get a lot of joy watching them from my front window. We keep most of them through the summer in a large pasture at my house. They will be grazing along peacefully, or all laying down for a nap when the lead cow will stand up with her head and tail raised. Then they will all stand up. She seems to say, "Are you ready?"and then takes off at a run with all the

179

cows and calves running behind her. They will run to a different meadow, then go back to grazing or maybe lay down again. They just like to run. The Longhorn steers we kept at the Ninepipes Museum Exhibit Area would run the eight miles home when we brought them back in the fall.

We used to own a ranch that joined the National Bison Range at Moiese, Montana. We ran several hundred Longhorns then, as well as that many beef cows. We trailed the cows sixteen miles out to Buffalo Flats in the fall and back to the home ranch in the spring. We had to have a couple of riders in the lead to hold back the Longhorns, as they wanted to run the whole way. This fast pace was too hard on the beef cows. Their tongues would be hanging out in the first couple of miles. We finally had to stop driving them as there were too many houses and unfenced lawns to try and keep the cattle off.

Bud Jr. with nephew Buck Jr. moving cows.

LONGHORNS AND BEARS

This spring one of our old Longhorn cows died. She was laying at the edge of the woods and the next morning a grizzly found her. Two of the big steers saw the bear and ran over to the cow. They started bellowing and ran the bear back into the woods. The other Longhorns heard the commotion and they all ran down to the steers. Some of them, in their hurry, left their calves behind, but soon realized it and ran back to them. They must have told the calves. "There's danger so you stay with me." and all the calves stayed close to their moms. When the bear moved, you could tell where he was because the cows would face that direction as he moved back and forth. The bear knew better than to get too close to those long horns. Some of the steers weigh two thousand pounds, and have a seven-foot spread to their horns. After about a half-hour, the cows started to drift away feeding, but there were always three or four there, standing guard over the dead cow. They seemed to take

Longhorns in the meadow.

turns at guard duty. They kept this up for more than three hours; then the bear gave up and left. The cows finally realized the old cow was dead, and paid no more attention to her.

A few days ago I saw a Longhorn cow running across the meadow with the rest of the herd strung out behind her. In a minute they were out of sight and I could not see what they were chasing. I figured they must have been after a bear so I got into the truck to leave for the museum. Before I got to the bottom of field, they came back. It was not a bear

Good Boy, twenty-year-old steer.

they were chasing, but two cow elk.

When cows are laying down resting, you will always see one standing guard. After the calves are three or four weeks old the cows will leave them with a couple of babysitter cows while they are off feeding. The baby sitters will not leave the calves until the mothers return.

Grandson Austin.

Grandson, Buddy IV.

My son, Bud III, and his two sons, Buddy IV and Austin, and I were moving the Longhorn herd to the south pasture. I was riding lead, with my son Buddy, and Buddy IV flanking, while Austin rode drag to keep the calves coming. I noticed the lead cow and several others stop, with their heads up, staring into the woods. Then they turned and ran back to their calves. As I watched, I saw what had upset them. It was two good-sized black bears. Black bears will get the calves and those mommas were making sure they were close to their calves to protect them. A few weeks later, driving down the road in the pickup, I saw four Longhorn cows standing under a pine tree, looking up. I stopped to see what they were doing. They had a big brown bear up the tree. It came out of the tree and as soon as it hit the ground the cows were after it. They treed it again…and then let it go, and treed it a third time. Three of the cows lost interest and headed back to the herd, but one cow still had the bear treed when I left.

I have watched cows chase bears before, but not tree them. I never get tired of watching the wonders of nature. And I'll bet you that by now you have noticed I kind of favor Longhorn cows and grizzly bears.

OLD BLUE

Much of Montana's early history and the romance of the colorful cowboys was the result of these hardy cattle. The early trail herds with the lead steer out in front would have been a sight to behold. In the Ninepipes Museum of Early Montana we have a bronze by Ray Dan

Herd Boss.

Sleeping Bear of the most famous of the lead steers, Old Blue. Blue was born on the Nueces River near the Texas coast in 1870. When he was a three-year-old, Blue, along with fifteen hundred other brush cattle was rounded up and trailed to New Mexico. The herd was sold to John Chisum, who noted what a special steer he was. When Blue was five years old he was sold to Charles Goodnight who was trailing a herd of 5,000 cattle to Colorado.

Every morning Blue would take his assumed position as the leader of the herd. He was powerful and smart, understood every signal from the point riders and would guide the herd accordingly. It was said he was worth a dozen riders in managing the herd. Blue was not sold to the Army in Colorado with the rest of the herd, but was taken back to Texas to lead another herd. He had proved himself to be too valuable to be sold for beef. He survived an Indian attack and had a arrow removed from his rump, but this did not slow him down. Back in Texas he was fitted with a shiny new bell and bell strap. They said when he heard the chime of the bell he marched out proud as he could be. He would not bed down with the herd, but after they were bedded down he would sneak back to camp and there he could bum treats from the cowboys and the cook. Blue would not run with the herd in a stampede. He would stand and start bawling, which had a calming effect on the herd. When fording the many rivers he would wade right in and swim across, giving the herd the confidence to follow. In his sixteen years of leading trail herds he covered many thousands of miles, and never got sore-footed. They said his hooves were as hard as steel. Blue died from old age in 1890 at the age of twenty, and earned his place as part of our western history.

In 1989, when Montana celebrated its one hundred years of statehood, the main event was a cattle drive from Roundup, Montana, to Billings. There were 2,500 head of cattle gathered from all over the state, and even a few Longhorn steers brought up from Texas. I had ten head of our big Longhorn steers in the drive, and was pleased to see at the end of the first day's drive three of my steers were in the lead.

THE COWBOYS
Dedicated to the Cowboys of the West

From 1880 to 1910, after the fur trade waned and the mining peaked in the West, big cattle ranches and the cowboys were the dominant figures on the northwest plains.

Through the years you have heard some writers and historians try to discredit the western cowboys. These naysayers were wrong; those young men were all or more than they were pictured to be. Raised as I was, I had a taste of the hard life that the early cowboys led; the long days and nights in the saddle, and I hold them in very high esteem.

I have taken quotes from two of Montana's famous pioneers, Granville Stuart and Charlie Russell. Granville Stuart was one of the first cattle kings and knew these cowboys well.

Buddy IV and his dad, Buddy III – cowboys.

In his journal Granville Stuart wrote that "Cowpunchers were strictly honest, they were chivalrous, held women in high esteem, and were always gentlemen in their presence lighting fast with a gun and the best shots I ever saw. Others were fancy with a rope, and others could ride any horse that could be saddled. The best were the men who did all these things reasonably well. A cattle herd was perfectly safe in their care, every man would sacrifice his life for the herd." Granville stated: "It was a pleasing sight to see a herd strung out on the trail. The horse herd and the white covered chuck wagon in the lead, followed by a mass of sleek cattle a half mile long; the sun flashing on their horns, and on the silver conchos, bridles, spurs, and pearl handle six shooters of the cow punchers. The brilliant handkerchiefs about their necks furnished the needed touch of color to the picture."

Charley Russell was one of these early-day Montana cowboys. His paintings of them will live on forever and his stories are as good as his art. If you have not read his book, *"Trails Plowed Under,"* you will surely enjoy it.

Cowboys in the rain, Bud Jr. and son Jim.

The following excerpt was taken from this book:

"Speaking of cowpunchers, it was sure amusin to read some of them stories about cowpunchin. You'd think a puncher growed horns and was haired over. It puts me in mind of the eastern girl that asks her mother: Ma, says she, 'Do cowboys eat grass?' 'No, Dear,' says the old lady, 'They'r part human.' I don't know but the old gal had em sized up right."

The puncher was rigged, starting at the top, with a good hat, not one of the floppy kind. The top cover he wore was made to protect his face from the weather, maybe to hold it on he wore a buckskin string under his chin. Round his neck a big silk handkerchief, tied loose; an' in the drag of a trail herd it was drawn over his face to the eyes, hold-up fashion for protection from the dust. Coat, vest an shirt would suit his own taste. His pants might be plaid wool, sometimes foxed or reinforced with buckskin, and over these were chaps or leggins. His feet was covered with good high-heeled boots, finished off with steel spurs of Spanish pattern. His weapon's usually a forty five colt six gun.

"Cowpunchers were might particular about their rig, an in all the camps you'd find a fashion leader. From a cowpuncher's idea, these fellers were sure good to look at. I tell you right now, there ain't no prettier sight for my eyes than one of those long backed cowpunchers, sitting up on a high-forked full-stamped saddle with a live hoss between his legs. Of course a good many of these fancy men were more ornamental than useful, but one of the best cowhands I ever knew belonged to this class. When the sun hits him with all this silver on, he blazes up like some big piece of jewelry. You could see him for miles when he was riding the high country. He's the fanciest cow dog I ever see, and don't think he don't savvy the cow. He knows what she says to her calf."

The following story is also from *"Trails Plowed Under"*:

"Old Bedrock Jim tells me on time about him and his pardner. They're prospecting in the Big Horns. One morning they're out of meat. They ain't gone far till they jump an elk. It's a bull. Bedrock gets the first shot – that's all he needs. The bull goes to his knees and rolls over. They both walk up, laying their guns agin a log. The bull's laying with his head under him. Bedrock notices the blood on the bull's neck and thinks his neck's broke, but when he grabs a horn and starts to straighten him out to stick him, the bull gets up. And he ain't friendly and goes to war with Bedrock and his pardner. He's between the hunters and their guns. There's nothing to do but give the bull the fight.

"Bedrock makes a scrub pine that's agin a rock ledge. This tree won't hold two, so his pardner finds a hole under the ledge. It's late in the winter; there's plenty of snow and the wind's in the north. There ain't much comfort up this jack pine. When Bedrock looks around he notices that Jack Williams (that's his pardner's name) keeps coming out of the hole. Then the bull will charge them. Jack goes back but he don't stay long. The bull ain't only creased, and he's mighty nasty. His hair's all turned the wrong way and the way he rattles his horns agin the rocks around that hole tells he ain't jokin'. But Bedrock can't savvy why, when the bull steps back, Jack comes out of the hole.

"Bedrock's getting cold and plumb out of patience, and he finally hollers down from his perch. 'If you'd stay in that hold, you damn fool, that bull would leave and give us a chance to get away'.

"Jack is taking his turn outside. The bull charges. Jack ducks in as the bull scrapes his horns on the rocks. The bull backs away, shaking his head. This time when Jack shows, he yells up to Bedrock, 'Stay in the hole, hell! There's a bear in the hole.'

It's near dark when they get away. Bedrock gets on a lower limb and flags the bull with his coat. He's taking a long chance. The footing he's got, if he ever slips, it's good-bye. As I said before, the bull ain't joshing, but he holds the bull till Jack gets his gun, and when he does he sure kills him. He empties his Henry into him and not a ball goes by."

As a boy I was lucky enough to have known two of these old cowboys. They both had made several trips north from Texas with trail herds. Tom Cottrol lived with his wife on a little ranch out of Ronan. Tom would saddle his horse every day, and ride out to bring in the milk cow for his wife to milk. He rode his horse even if the cow was only a hundred yards out in the field. He said he was never going to milk, or "drive no damn cow on foot" as long as he could fork a horse. He had many stories of the his cowboy days. I was amazed when he showed us how he could shoot his old .45 colt. He threw a can out in the road, drew his gun firing, and made the can bounce up the road, hitting it with every shot. It was mighty fancy shooting for a man in his eighties.

The other old cowboy I knew only as "Old Jay". He looked like he had just stepped out of a Zane Grey book, hawked face, tall and slim with a straight back from a lifetime in the saddle. He had gone to work for the Park Service in Glacier National Park as a cowboy when the big cattle ranges ended. The Park Service furnished him with a log cabin to live out his days. He knew Charley Russell when Charley had lived in the Park and he was a treasure chest of stories.

I was at his cabin one time when I was fourteen years old. He had his war chest open and was getting dressed in his going-to-town clothes. He had his plaid wool gabardine pants and shirt, and bright red bandana on, also his good boots and hat. Still in the trunk were his gun belt and .45 Colt, his chaps, rawhide rope, spurs and other horse items. How I wish I had his picture and his old cowboy outfit now! They were just starting to film the movie "Cattle Queen" at East Glacier on the park's eastern edge, starring Ronald Reagan. Jay was going to see if they needed a real cowboy in the movie. He must have been close to ninety then, but still a striking figure. I think the movie firm thought he was too old.

These two old cowboys were the last of an era. But it's good to know that there are still cowboys today that can "ride for the brand": Never put your foot in the stirrup to mount your horse without holding a tight rein.

BILLY SCHALL, A MONTANA COWBOY

Brothers Rubin and Ed Schall were early pioneer ranchers in the Jocko Valley. Rubin's son and only child, Bob, became famous for his buffalo herd and rodeo productions. His son, Bob Jr., made a name for himself as one of Montana's top all-around cowboys. Ed Schall had a number of children, including Billy, born in 1926. All made their own mark in this world. They were honest-to-goodness real cowboys and cowgirls. It would take a good hand to keep up to any of the Schall girls.

Billy was a Montana living legend and my hero when I was a young boy, wanting to be a bronc rider. He was a top all-around cowboy, riding all over the U.S. Billy rode saddle bronc, bareback, bulls and bull-dogging. To see him step off a bucking horse when the whistle blew was like watching a work of art. You would think he was just stepping off an old, gentle saddle horse, he made it look so easy. He

Billy Schall on famous saddle bronc, Snake, 1956.

looked just like what you would think a Montana cowboy should look like, lean, dark complexion, handsome with a ready smile.

Billy rode in the championship at Madison Square Garden in 1953, and won the bull-dogging event at Boston a few days later. He was always in the money at whatever rodeo he went to. Unlike many of the rodeo riders today, he was a real working cowboy. There was no part of the ranch work or wild critters he could not handle. If you met a lanky cowboy in town wearing moccasins and walking a little lame, you were looking at Billy Schall.

He was always ready and willing to help the young cowboys get started "rodeo'in". I was raised with horses, and being a pretty stout kid it took a rank horse to buck me off. I found out rodeo riding was not the same. There were regulation saddles and rules to follow. Billy showed me how to take the correct rein on my first saddle bronc. After watching me ride a couple of bareback horses, he said, "Buddy, what hand do you rein a saddlehorse with?" I told him, "My left hand." He said, "Why are you riding with your right hand?" I answered, "My right hand and arm are stronger." He said, "You have been riding all your life left-handed with your right as the balance arm. You are riding with your strength, not your skill. Try it left-handed. I ride left-handed myself." The next horse I rode left-handed, and it made a big difference. It was also easier to get hold of the pickup horse when the whistle blew, and Bob Schall spurred in to pick me off.

Billy could ride about anything with hair on it, but he sure looked pretty on the top of a saddle bronc. His biggest win in life was when he roped and married his former classmate and sweetheart, the lovely Betty Mae Wemple. They were married in August of 1948 and raised a family in the Jocko Valley. Billy died in 1995. Betty still lives near Arlee and is a member and supporter of the Ninepipes Museum of Early Montana.

The poem below was written about Billy by Robert H. Retallick. He met Billy only twice, but thought enough of him to write the following:

Billy rode in Madison Square Garden, the year was 1953;
It was the only time he went back East, it was all he needed to see.
He's been married now for almost 50 years and I see his life still has that shine.
Spent is honeymoon in the stables with his bride and some Cherry wine.
Old Billy says there ain't many like him no more
And I agree, I've seen a cowboy once before.
And 'Old Billy' says times a comin' for a change,
Ya better stay out boy, stay out, stay out of the rain.
His walks a little crooked; bucked too many times;
But the horses they don't know it as he rides the fence lines.
His rides are getting shorter as the fences they move in;
But an outlaw in a saddle you can never keep him in.

I can hear the longhorns callin' as they're waiting to be fed;
I can hear again those words that are runnin' through my head.
I sit and feel the breezes that are comin' from on high'
An find myself rejoicing there's no fences in the sky.
Written by Robert H. Retallick

Chapter Six

UNWRITTEN INDIAN STORIES

THE BEE TREE

This story is about Mary Catherine Mollman and of a huge old pine bee tree that was near Mary's house. Mary Catherine was our neighbor when I was young. She was born about 1866 and of the age group that were the last of the old traditional full bloods on our reservation. As a girl she participated in buffalo hunts in the Three Forks area. Her mother was a Pend d'Orielle and her father, Louie Mollman, was half Pend d'Oreille and half Iroquois. Louie and his brother Charley were the tribe's bow makers, and it was said Louie could shoot an arrow clear through a buffalo. My two uncles, Louie and Vila, (Charles), were named for these two old warriors.

My sister Ola and I would follow Dad and his team plowing, and pick the camas roots that were turned up. We took the camas to Mary Catherine and she would return the favor by making moccasins, gloves and jerky for us. Dad gave her elk and deer meat, and hides to tan whenever he could.

A number of years ago loggers cut this big bee tree down and left it, as it was no good for lumber. My family was quite sad to see the old tree cut, and paid homage to it. Counting the rings that I could read, the tree was close to four hundred years old. My younger son, Buddy, saved a piece of the old honeycomb and it is now in the Ninepipes Museum of Early Montana.

MARY CATHERINE'S PLACE
By Josephine Chevre

When she was a young woman she heard the sound and followed it as it hovered and darted about her ears like a bright green hummingbird, until she stood under a yellow pine. It was an old one, the bark was clawed where the honeyeaters had tried to gouge a way inside. She leaned on the tree and felt the deep trembling in its dying core.

She closed her eyes, let the ancient song pulse through her blood until her heart felt full and pregnant, and her braids seemed to pour over her shoulders in rivulets of dark honey.

She never spoke of the place a little way back of her cabin. She went there to listen, to learn the hollow music, once to bury her stillborn. She rested at its foot, an old woman, after her husband's other wife died, and after he died, she walked there one last time, slowly in worn-out buckskin moccasins, feeling shriveled and dry as the empty seed pods of hollyhocks in the garden. She wanted to hear the bees' medicine song again, to feel their voices swarm inside her ears. She leaned against scaled bark and didn't need to breathe.

The pine dropped cones another forty seasons while its rotting core swelled into a swarming tower, a body of honey. In early winter loggers sawed its knotted trunk and left without noticing the faint hum of fanning wings, and then the silence. The stump was as wide as a pickup bed, and held three hundred years of decayed pith, generations of bees and their treasure, and the bears not even down from the mountains to gorge on the honey. In April, among slash and yellow dog-tooth violets, mice and surviving bees move bits of honeycomb from Mary Catherine's place. The trees, the cabin, even the hollyhocks are gone, and somewhere further up the mountain, the humming builds into song.

ENEAS CONKO
Eneas Michel Conko
Born 1874 - Died 1954
Upper Pend d'Oreille & Iroquois Indian.

I am often asked, "Who is this Eneas Conko? We see a lot of pictures with the name Conko and your newsletters (for the Ninepipes Museum of Early Montana) often reference the name." The Fall 2007 issue, #31, included a story about his grandfather, taken from Major Peter Ronan's book.

Eneas Michel (Conko) dropped the name Michel and took the name of Conko when he was still in his teens. Most people simply called him Conko. He was a tribal leader but not a chief although his uncle, his father's older brother, was Chief Plenty Grizzly Bear, the Head Chief of the Pend d'Oreille. Conko's older cousin, John Peter Michel, became Chief when his father, Plenty Grizzly Bear, died. Blind Michel, who was Conko's second cousin, was the last Pend d'Oreille chief. Eneas was very handsome and strong, much to the delight of the girls, and the envy of the boys. This led to his name change when some of his jealous male cousins tried to kill him. The attack on him was almost fatal, and it took him a long time to recover. He had a big scar on his head where he was struck with a war club. For the rest of his life he combed and braided his hair in a way to hide his scar. He said he would never again be a Michel.

As a boy he witnessed the last of the annual buffalo hunts in the Three Forks area of west-central Montana. In later years he guided historians to the hunting and camping areas. Eneas' father, Michel, died when Eneas was thirteen years old. Shortly after his father's death Eneas and his friend Phillip Pierre were allowed to join, as horse tenders, the last known horse stealing raid by the Pend d'Orielles into the Blackfeet country. This was a great honor for the two boys.

Eneas Conko in tipi, getting ready for the dance.

As a teenager Eneas got a job on a cattle ranch where he learned to be an excellent roper and bronc rider. He lived in the bunkhouse with the cowboys, and they taught him how to write his name, the ABC's, and to speak some English. He already knew a little French that he had learned from his dad. When he was about nineteen, his mother died, and Eneas took his younger brother, Camile, whom he dearly loved, and joined the Buffalo Bill Wild West Show. This was about 1893. In the show they danced and took part in the mock battles. Eneas also performed as a roper. He could catch a horse by the head, by the two front feet or by all four feet, wherever he wanted, every time he threw the rope. The old cowboys had taught him well. He was also a dead shot with a rifle. At the end of the season, Eneas told Camile, I am tired of always having to fall off my horse in the fighting. So, in the last show, instead of falling off, he jerked the soldier off his horse, and quit the show. Camile died a year or two after they left the Buffalo Bill Show.

Eneas was in his early twenties the first time he was sent to

Washington, D.C. The big hand-tinted photo of him in the museum was taken on this trip. He was such a striking figure, he was sent just for show, but ended up being the main spokesman for improving conditions on the Reservation. He was sent again in later years, and was there for three months.

Conko was noted for his skill in hunting and raising fast horses. One of his best studs came from the famous Copper King, Marcus Daly's race horse string. I am proud that we have preserved this famous blood line, and it is still flowing in our own horses today. I like to think Conko is smiling when he looks down from heaven, and watches the off-spring of his fleet-footed horses racing across the same meadow his once did.

Eneas Conko in Washington D.C.

Laurie and I built our home right next to Conko's log cabin, and we use the same garden spot he used. I can still feel his big strong hand holding my small hand as he led me out to the strawberry patch. This was my first memory of him, and I felt safe holding his hand. He loved my father and thought of him as a son, and my father loved him in return. He was a grandfather figure to me, and it was very special when he came to visit us, or when I got to go with Dad to visit him and his family. I remember Eneas drumming and singing at the jump dances. He had a very good and special voice.

Sophia, his wife, and Eneas had the heartbreak of losing their daughter, Agnes, when she was shot and killed at the young age of eleven years, and all three of their sons, Leo, John and Bill died as young men.

Eneas was very wise, and a great orator. When he was old and blind, he gave a speech on the importance of young people becoming educated so they could manage their own affairs in the fast changing world. He was speaking in Salish with his granddaughter, Jeanette, translating. He said, "It is hard for the old full bloods to understand the new ways, so the young must learn." He said, "I will be okay. Even though I have lost three sons, I still have one son, Bud Cheff, to help me." There was always a sadness in his eyes for the loss of his children. I am sure he and Sophia look down with pride at their many grand and great-grandchildren today. I like to think he sometimes smiles at me and my effort to preserve the past. Many of the newsletter stories were taken from events that Conko told to Dad and the family.

Jeanette Conko, lifelong friend to me and my sister Ola.

TRADITIONAL MEDICINE CEREMONIES

A few years back, I was invited by George Kickingwoman and his family to participate in the Holy Smoke Ceremony at Browning, on the Blackfeet Reservation. It was a real honor for me to be invited. I brought five buffalo tongues for the berry soup. The ceremony started at 8 p.m., and finished at 5:30 a.m. George Kickingwoman, the head holy man, presided over the ceremony.

At ninety-two years and just recovering from a car wreck after hitting a horse, he was still one very tough man. Even after spending the day directing the ceremony preparations, then running the ceremony all night, he was still chipper when I bid him goodbye the next morning. George was most fortunate to have some very competent daughters and grandchildren to help him, and to carry on these special traditions. I have been pleased to accept his invitation to other ceremonies including the opening of the thunder bundle. George and his wife Molly were wonderful people and were a storehouse of traditional Blackfeet history.

I have been very fortunate to have also been invited to the Fort Peck Northern Sioux Sundance, where I was presented the ceremonial pipe. It was a special thing to participate in this.

George Kicking Woman pointing to painting of himself.

I was also invited to a Flathead Winter Medicine ceremony by the Conko family, which was extra special to me, knowing my father had gone with the Conko family to the winter medicine encampment some sixty-five years before.

The instance that is the most dear to me, though, was at Eneas

Dad and his brother Vila at the sweat lodge.

Pierre Adams headdress.

Eugene Conko's funeral four years ago. He was a grandson of the old Eneas Conko in the stories. During the wake I thought how beautiful the eagle feather headdress looked on the casket. I recognized the headdress, as Louise (Eneas's mother) had showed it to me in the past. It had belonged to her father, Pierre Adams, and she held it very dear. After the wake the casket was carried from the longhouse to the Mission for the mass service. After mass it was taken out into the street for a military service. All this time I was thinking what a special thing to have Eneas's grandfather's headdress on his coffin. I was standing on the church steps with others, where we could see better. At the close of the ceremony they called my name and asked if I would come out in front. When I did, the Conko family presented me with the headdress. I was stunned to think they would give me such a special gift. I was having a hard time keeping the tears back as I knew what an important heirloom this was to the family. I get a lump in my throat just writing about it.

THE BRAVEST OF THE BRAVE

Joseph Que-Que-Sah was born about 1850 and died in 1938 at the age of eighty-eight. He was said to be without fear of man or beast, and was considered the best horse thief in the Pend d'Oreille Tribe. Joseph was a big, strong, ruggedly handsome man. His strength, honesty, and love of life showed in his face; there was a twinkle in his eye, and he could find humor in almost anything. It was also said he always had a smile on his face, even when in battle.

The Pend d'Oreille Tribe was noted for having the best horses in the Northwest and the warriors were known for their excellent horsemanship. Joseph could ride anything with hair on it, and no one loved a good horse more than he did.

By the time Joseph was about twenty years old he was already a seasoned and

Group with Joseph Que-Que-Suh in center, holding up war club.

highly respected warrior. He and two companions were planning a horse stealing raid into the Nez Perce country. The Pend d'Oreille and Salish were allies of the Nez Perce, but that didn't mean they wouldn't steal horses from each other if they could. Some years earlier the Nez Perce had stolen a fine mare from the Flatheads, and a stud colt from this mare was believed to be the best buffalo runner and the fastest horse in the country. This famous stallion was coveted by all the northern Plains tribes.

Joseph was determined to get this horse. He had some good mares he wanted to breed to it, and he wanted to race and run buffalo with it.

Of course the fun and prestige of stealing such a prize was more than he could resist.

It was probably in the year of 1869 that the three started out on their long journey from the Mission Valley to the Bitterroot, and then over the Lolo Trail into the Nez Perce country. This would have been eight years before the Nez Perce War, when Chiefs White Bird, Looking Glass, and Joseph, with their people and hundreds of horses made their famous flight north over this same trail.

When on the buffalo hunts east of the mountains the Nez Perce and Flatheads, (both the upper Pend d'Orielle and Bitterroot Salish were called Flatheads by whites and some other tribes) often camped close to each other for mutual protection from the Blackfeet, Sioux, and other hostile tribes. There was a lot of intermarriage, trade, and socializing between the two. There was also a lot of competition between them, especially in horses and horse racing. At times there were strong disagreements between the two tribes, but not to the point of going to war with each other.

The horse raiders knew who owned the great stud horse, and about where their village would be set up this time of the year. They were riding good horses on this raid, for if they traveled on foot, (the usual way to travel on a raid) and were seen, they would be recognized as a war party. Riding boldly over the trail in daylight, they were given little notice. After locating the right village and the famous horse, they found that he was always on a picket during the day, and tied up at the owner's tipi at night.

The three raiders back-trailed to a secluded spot with grass and water they had passed coming in. There they would leave their horses and go to the village on foot. They made a small sweathouse where they prayed and cleansed their bodies, and redressed in their freshly smudged clothes. This would help to keep the village dogs from recognizing them as strangers and barking an alarm. After applying their war paint and securing their personal medicine, they returned to the village on foot. The young men left their guns with their horses, only taking their knives with them. They wanted to avoid a conflict if possible, but knew they could very well be killed if they were caught.

It was easy for Joseph's companions to each catch a good horse because there were no night guards with the herd. They would have liked to take more than one, but had agreed to only one apiece as their success depended on a fast flight, and they would be caught if they were encumbered by too many horses. Meanwhile Joseph had entered the village, gliding silently among the tipis, going directly to where the stud was picketed.

With the skill of an experienced horseman he gently reassured the horse all was well as he slipped on his war bridle and cut the picket rope, then quickly swung onto the stallion's back. Instead of quietly riding away, he let out his Flathead war cry. His astonished companions listened as he raced among the tipis, the full length of the entire village, giving his war cry all the way. Fear and anticipation caused their hearts to race when they heard several rifle shots. They turned their mounts towards their war camp, praying Joseph's medicine was strong. When his two excited companions reached their meeting place or war camp, they found Joseph already there, safe and smiling. They quickly gathered their horses and belongings and headed for home. They rode the rest of the night, and all the next day, switching horses when one tired. When both of their horses played out, they let them rest and eat before continuing their flight. Their pursuers never caught up to them, and lost their tracks when they reached the Bitterroot Valley. Here it was easy for the raiders to hide their tracks with all the livestock and activity going on in the valley.

Alex Que-Que-Suh, grandson of Joseph.

This story is one of many I listened to as a boy when the old full-blood elders related them to my father. I wish I knew the names of Joseph's companions on the horse raid. I don't remember Joseph, I was only two years old when he walked on, but I knew three of his sons, Eneas, Joseph Jr., and Antoine, who were elders when I was a boy. I grew up living just three miles from the Que que sah's. They had a lot of cattle, as well as horses then. Alex Que que sah is still our neighbor, and is a big strong man, well liked and respected. Noted for preserving the old ways and language, Alex inherited many of his grandfather Joseph's characteristics, and I'm sure Joseph would be proud of him.

THE FLATHEAD WAR CHIEFS OF THE 1800's

The Flatheads, as they were called, were made up of two tribes, the Bitterroot Salish and the upper Pend d'Oreille, who lived in the Mission Valley, the Plains, and Hot Springs areas. The Flatheads were noted for their extreme bravery and fighting ability. They were most often outnumbered in battle but endured due in part to the example and bravery of their great war chiefs.

Chief Adolph, who died at the agency in 1887 at the age of seventy-eight, was the head war chief. Other noted names of war chiefs of that period were Chief Big Canoe, Chief Moiese, who died in 1868 from wounds he received in an earlier battle with the Blackfeet, Chief Ambrose, Chief Moses, and the last Flathead War Chief, Arlee.

The next time you drive up Evaro Canyon, west and north of Missoula, you might let your mind drift back in time, as this area is rich in Montana history. The canyon was first called Coriacan (Coviaca) Defile, later was known as O'Keefe's Defile and now Evaro Hill, or canyon.

Antoine Ninepipes.

Through the years there were many tragedies in this area, from horse and wagon wrecks to car and train wrecks. One of the first recorded incidents in the canyon's history took place in about 1837, where the Marant railroad trestle is now. Chief Factor Kitson of the Hudson's Bay Company came from his post at present day Thompson Falls on the Pend d'Oreille River, to what is now Missoula, Montana. He came with a large pack string and his party of packers and traders to trade with the Flatheads. The bands of Flathead people had gathered together in a big village for this event. After days of trading and the usual festivities of dancing, horse racing, and games, the traders prepared for an early morning start on the three to four day trip back to their post.

Two packers left first, with their pack string loaded with furs, buffalo tongues, hides, dried meat and buckskin. The rest of the party was some distance behind, which was lucky for them. When the first two men and their pack strings started up the Evaro Canyon, they were ambushed by a large war party of about 100 Gros Ventres Indians. These Indians were a long way from their homeland in north-central Montana. The two packers were killed and when Kitson saw what was happening, he and the rest of the party escaped back to the Flathead village. If they had not been lagging behind they would have shared the same fate as the two packers. Escaping with their lives, they lost all their trade goods. They gave the alarm to the Flatheads and you can imagine what kind of turmoil the village was in, with news that the Gros Ventres were in the valley.

Adolph and Arlee led the warriors in a charge on the Gros Ventres' camp. Although they fought bravely, the Gros Ventres were no match for the Flatheads. They retreated and there was a running fight for many miles, with the Gros Ventres making a final stand at Savallie Creek. They suffered heavy losses and finally escaped, but not before about half their party were killed and scalped by the Flatheads. A different account of this battle stated nearly eighty of the invaders were killed. It was certainly a major battle and victory for the Flatheads. There was great celebrating in the Flathead village, and the war chiefs were given much praise and honor.

When I drive up Evaro Canyon my mind often drifts back to that fateful day. If you really listen on a quiet spring morning, you too might hear the war cries echoing through the canyon as I do.

Information for this story was taken from the journals of Major Owens, *"Wilderness Kingdom"* by Father Nicolas Point, *"Flathead Indian Nation"* by Major Peter Ronan, and Eneas Conko recollections. Although in some accounts of this incident it was thought the invaders were Blackfeet, another said they were Assiniboine. I believe Major Peter Ronan to be right, as he heard the story directly from some of the participants of the battle. Eneas Conko, who was born in 1874, said the elders told of a great battle at Evaro where the Gros Ventres were defeated.

JACQUES HOULE (HOOLE)
'Louis Capois Houle'

Jacques Houle was born in France in about 1722 and joined the French army at a young age. He fought in Scotland, was wounded and taken prisoner. He was part of a prisoner exchange and was sent to Canada, probably in 1746, where he was engaged in the American

War. In 1759, as an army sergeant he fought in the battle of Abraham's Plains at Quebec. Houle was one of the soldiers that carried the mortally wounded General Louis Marquis de Montcalm off the battlefield. In 1775 he fought in the battles during the siege of Quebec, where he was wounded, and would walk with a limp the rest of his life. Because of family problems and an unfaithful wife, he left Ontario, Canada, in 1776 for the western frontier, never to return. He spent the rest of his life as a free trapper in the Northwest.

Not much is known of his life during the thirty-eight years he spent in the West. We do know he ended up in what is now northwest Montana, in the Libby, Montana, area. It is quite likely he came south from Canada with the Kootenai Indians in the late 1700's, and was in the area when Lewis and Clark made their journey to the Pacific. The old Kootenais said Jacques was the first known white man in this country. He was known by them as White Head, and was liked and respected by all the Indians in the area. He was here in 1807 when David Thompson of the North West Fur Company arrived. Ross Cox of the Pacific Fur Co. wrote in his journals of meeting him in 1812-13. Cox wrote that "Pe`re" as he was called, was a long-time resident of the area. He said the Canadians treated Jacques with much respect and greeted him *"Bon jour, Pe`re."* (Good day Father) He would answer *"Merci, Merci, mon fils."* (Thank you, thank you, my son). Cox again mentioned him in his journal in 1814, saying they had news that Pe`re had been murdered by the Blackfeet Indians.

Jacques was killed in 1814 at the age of 92 by a Blackfeet Indian war party. Some Flathead Indians found him by a beaver dam with a bullet through his head. He was scalped, and all his belongings, guns, traps and horses had been taken. So ended the life of a tough mountain man.

How I would have loved to had a chance to visit with this amazing old man. The Houle name is well known in the Flathead Indian Reservation. Joe Houle and two sons, Louie and Fred, were cowboys on the Allard-Pablo buffalo roundup. In 1908 the Flathead Agency listed the names of seventeen Houles on the rolls. It is not known if these were descendants of old Pe`re Houle, or maybe descendants of his son or other relatives who came later with the Hudson's Bay Company.

An interesting piece of Montana history. I hope you enjoyed it.

FLATHEAD INDIANS AND AMAZING TALES OF HORSEMANSHIP

In 1805 when Lewis and Clark met the Flathead Indians at Ross's Hole, now the Sula area of the upper Bitterroot Valley, there was a young boy present who would later become a noted Flathead chief. The boy was very impressed by William Clark and his red hair. He held Clark in high regard all of his life. Little Chief, Insula or Ensila (his name was recorded differently in some journals) was famous for his horsemanship and bravery.

In 1834, he led a party of Flatheads through enemy territory, engaging in several battles on their way to the Green River Rendezvous in what is now Wyoming. They had heard there were some Black Robes coming, and they hoped to persuade them to come to the Flathead country. They were disappointed because it was the Whitman party of Protestant missionaries, not their cherished Black Robes. William M. Anderson notes in his journal about meeting Little Chief, and how impressed he was with him. Anderson had accompanied William L. Sublette of the Rocky Mountain Fur Co. on his expedition from Independence, Missouri, to the Rocky Mountains. He was at the Green River rendezvous when the Flatheads arrived. Anderson, who was a towhead, was introduced to Little Chief, who was very interested in his hair. When Sublette told Little Chief that Anderson was related to William Clark, Little Chief hugged Anderson and related his story of meeting Clark.

A few days later a grizzly was accidentally scared into the encampment, scattering women and children in all directions. The bear took refuge in a dense patch of tall willow brush. Little Chief went into the brush; they heard a gunshot, then the Flathead war cry, and they knew the bear was dead. Later that night Little Chief presented the hide with head and claws attached to Anderson. He told Anderson he was giving him the bear in honor of the great red-haired Chief Clark.

At another time, Little Chief mounted a freshly caught wild horse with a small robe in one hand and a hand drum in the other. The horse was turned loose. Holding on only with his moccasin-covered feet, he stuck to the wild, pitching horse. Little Chief used the drum to slap the horse on the side of the head to control the direction of the horse, and covered the horse's head with the robe when he wanted to slow its speed. He did this until the horse was exhausted and easily ridden back to camp.

On another occasion at the encampment, there was a great commotion as Bull's Head, a Nez Perce Indian, came driving a big bull buffalo into camp, riding his tired horse, and waving his robe. A dozen arrows quickly dispatched the buffalo to the cheers of all. Bull's Head had made good on his promise to drive a buffalo bull though camp for Captain Sublette's pleasure.

In later years a great horseman named Jackson Sundown won the world champion bronc-riding title in 1916 at the age of fifty-three. Jackson was born in Montana about 1863. As a boy of fourteen years he was a horse wrangler for the Chiefs Joseph, Looking Glass, and White Bird when they made their famous flight through Montana. He escaped into Canada at the battle of the Bear Paws. Sundown came back to Montana and lived on the Flathead Reservation where he married and had three children. He was soon well known for his riding ability. Just for show, he rode a wild horse bareback, with just a mane hold and a silver dollar under the heel of each moccasin. When they slipped the blind off the horse, it went wild, trying to buck Jackson off. When it finally played out and stopped, Sundown still had both silver dollars under his heels. It was said no one had ever seen or known of Jackson getting bucked off.

Jackson Sundown on his war horse.

This kind of amazing horsemanship was commonplace to the Northwest Plains horse tribes. The women and girls were just as much at home on horseback as the men.

Wouldn't it be great to have witnessed some of these amazing feats firsthand?

JACKSON SUNDOWN AND THE NEZ PERCE WAR

The following is a brief history of the Nez Perce War and a great horseman who was part of it. I know many of you already know this tragic story, and for those who don't, it might encourage you to read one of the many books written about it. Duncan McDonald, the son of the famous Hudson's Bay Factor, Angus McDonald, and the great uncle of Joe McDonald, who is the recently retired president of Salish-Kootenai College, gave an accurate account of the Nez Perce War. Duncan's mother was a sister of Eagle-of-the-Light. Her father was half French, half Iroquois and she was also related to Chief White Bird. I think my favorite book on this event is "Yellow Wolf" by Lucullius McWhorter. The following story is dedicated to my old friend Pat Adams, and his mother, Red Sky, the grandson and daughter of Sundown.

The Nez Perce war began June 15, 1877, with the Battle of White Bird Canyon, where the Army and some volunteers under the command of Captain Perry were badly defeated. Thirty-four soldiers were killed and many more wounded, while the Indians had five wounded and no one killed. This was the first battle of many in the one thousand three hundred mile trek, lasting almost four months, as the Nez Perce tried to reach Canada.

This long, tragic fight could have been avoided if General Howard would have used a little diplomacy in trying to get the non-treaty Nez Perce on a reservation instead of trying to strong arm them onto it. Neither Chief Joseph or Chief Looking Glass wanted a war with the Whites. Tensions were running high when three hothead Indians, ignoring their chief's orders not to kill any whites, killed four white men. Seventeen more young men joined them, and they all went on a wild raid against the white settlers, burning and killing them, including two women and two children. Even though the Indians had good reasons for some of their actions, this was the beginning of a no win war for the non-treaty Nez Perce. Joseph had a heavy heart! He knew this could not end well, but he now had to do the best he could for his people.

They outmaneuvered, and outfought General Howard on a number of engagements, crossing back and forth over the swollen river, leaving the Army behind when they were unable to follow. They did this with about seven hundred fifty people; only two hundred were warriors, the rest were women and children. This remarkable feat was done while herding close to three thousand horses. Looking Glass wanted to escape to the buffalo country on the Montana plains, and on July 16th they headed north over the Lolo Trail.

Just before reaching the Bitterroot Valley they were detained by Captain Rawn who only had thirty-five soldiers, along with fifty volunteers at what was later called Fort Fizzle. The captain's force was too small to stop the Indians, and Looking Glass did not want to fight anybody in Montana as they passed through. The Indians went up over the ridge, around the barricade and continued up the valley without a shot being fired. The Nez Perce purchased supplies, paying for everything as they traveled through the valley. Because many of the Whites were sympathetic to the Indians' plight, Looking Glass stopped and shook hands with many of the settlers, telling them he wanted only peace with them. Looking Glass was a good man, but not a good war chief. Joseph's brother Ollokot, and Chief White Bird were the real war chiefs, while Joseph was charged with protecting the women, the children and the horse herd.

As they traveled though the Bitterroot there was another band of Nez Perce camped there and they joined the hostiles, increasing their numbers to about eight hundred. Chief Charlo of the Bitterroot Salish Tribe stayed neutral in the conflict, but had warned the Nez Perce if they caused any trouble in his country he would send his warriors against them. The Nez Perce continued up the valley, camping at Ross Hole, then crossing the divide into the Big Hole Valley the next day.

On Aug. 7, 1877, the non-treaty Nez Perce bands under the leadership of Chief Looking Glass, as well as Chief White Bird and Young Chief Joseph, set up their tipis on the edge of the Big Hole Valley. They knew they were a long way ahead of General Howard, so they decided to rest and cut some new tipi poles.

They were unaware that Colonel J. Gibbons from Fort Shaw, along with Fort Missoula soldiers were just one day's march behind them. Chief White Bird warned them not to stay, that death was on their trail. Also, Wah-Lit-its, a medicine man with special powers warned them not to stay there another day, for many would die, including himself. Chief Looking Glass, who had been voted head chief at the start of the flight north, counseled to stay, as he believed they were safe.

Colonel Gibbons moved his troops in to position the evening of August 8th, and before daylight on August 9th he attacked the camp. They killed seventy-eight Indians as they slept. Thirty were men, the rest were women, and children. The medicine man, Wah-Lit-its, who predicted this was one of the men killed.

There were that many more wounded. Some historians put the total death number at eighty-eight Indians. The Army had thirty-six soldiers, including seven officers and volunteers, killed, with forty more wounded. The Bannock Indian scouts with the army scalped and mutilated the Nez Perce bodies, even digging them out of their shallow graves to do so. The Nez Perce had to fight the Assiniboines, the Bannocks, the Cheyennes, and even their old friends, the Crows, besides five different army units during this long running battle north. The only Indians that showed them some kindness during their flight were the Crees in northern Montana.

Two fourteen-year-old boys, Jackson Sundown and his cousin, Samel Tilden, had been asleep in a tipi, covered with buffalo robes, and were not seen by the troopers when their tipi was set on fire. The boys escaped the burning tipi, and with some of the women and children hid in the brush until they could get to the horse herd and help secure them. The two boys were both expert horseman, doing men's work herding the huge herd of horses during this long-running battle. With White Bird, Ollokot and Joseph encouraging them, the warriors quickly rallied and drove the soldiers back. Still, this was a terrible blow to the Nez Perce, and the only major mistake they made on their amazing flight to Canada. It was to be a fatal one for them; they never recovered from this great loss. If they would have had guards out that night or had kept moving like White Bird counseled, most of them probably would have made it to Canada.

The Nez Perce were unaware that Colonel Nelson Miles was coming from the east to intercept them. He caught up with the Indians at the Bear Paw Mountains, just forty miles from Canada.

At the battle of the Bear Paw Chief Joseph surrendered to Colonel Miles. Chief Looking Glass was dead, as well as Ollokot, and Joseph was considered the head chief by the army. Chief White Bird and about two hundred or more men, women and children, including Jackson Sundown, who was wounded, escaped to Canada. Joseph and a number of warriors stayed with the sick, the wounded, the old, and the women and children that could not get away. The Nez Perce lost between one hundred fifty-five to two hundred women, children, and warriors, with about that many more wounded in this long flight to safety in Canada. The Army lost about one hundred twenty-five men as well as roughly fifty-five civilian fighters, and that many more wounded.

Jackson Sundown's Indian name was Waaya-Tonnah-Toesit-Kahn,

meaning Earth-Left-by-the-Setting Sun. He was a nephew of Chief Joseph, and for a number of years he was called Buffalo Jackson, but later was known by all as Jackson Sundown. Sundown was born in 1863 in Montana while his mother was with a band of Nez Perce on a horse stealing foray against the Flathead Indians. After escaping from the Bear Paw Mountains to Canada he stayed there about two years, at the Sitting Bull camp. He returned to Washington Territory for a short while, then went to Montana where he was married Indian fashion to Annie Pewlosap. He was given an allotment on the Flathead Reservation where he and Annie had three daughters. Only one, Red Sky (Adeline), born in 1896, lived to adulthood.

Sundown had earned a reputation as a great horseman, and often demonstrated his skills riding the wild bucking horses in the Valley. A few miles from the Ninepipes Museum there is a rounded depression in the ground where the locals used to have rodeos. They built a corral in the bottom, and the people could sit on the sloping sides, with a good view. Jackson sometimes rode exhibition there and my father, when he was a small boy, watched him ride.

In 1910 Annie and Jackson split up and he moved to Idaho, and later married a young Nez Perce widow, Cecelia Wapshela. In 1912 Jackson entered a number of rodeos in Canada, Montana, Idaho, and Washington. There is no record of him ever being bucked off of any horse. He was so good some riders would not sign up for a show if Jackson was there because they knew he would win the money.

Jackson Sundown.

In 1914 he entered the Cul-de-sac Round-Up, but the other top riders would not ride if Jackson was riding, protesting that they wouldn't have a chance against Sundown. The rodeo promoters then signed him up to ride Exhibition. He was paid fifty dollars a day to ride in the three day show, and the crowd loved him. Jackson also signed up for the Pendleton Round-Up that year, and again in 1915, winning third place.

It was said he should have won first place both years, but politics kept the judges from scoring him the points he had really earned. Jackson was then disillusioned with rodeo, and decided to quit riding.

Artist and sculptor A. P. Proctor, who was using Jackson as a model for some of his famous bronzes, urged Jackson to enter the 1916 Round-Up. Proctor offered to pay the entry fee if Jackson would ride, so he did. The fifty-three-year-old Jackson, wearing orange with black spotted woolies chaps, a high crown reservation hat with a flowing ribbon, and a long silk neckerchief with his traditional braids made an impressive sight.

Jackson drew the great bucking horse, Angel for his championship ride. The crowd went wild as he rode, hat in hand, fanning the horse. With shouts, whistles, and thunderous applause, the crowd screamed "Ride 'em, Sundown!"

Jackson Sundown, World Champion at Pendleton Roundup.

It was quite clear who had won. When the ride was over the cowboys rushed up to Sundown to congratulate him, and he tossed his hat in the air with joy. He was given a horse with a beautiful handmade saddle, which he rode around the arena while the crowd cheered wildly. In 1972 he was voted into the Pendleton Round-Up Hall of Fame. His daughter Adeline (Red Sky) Adams from Ronan, Montana, was there to accept the award. The famous living legend, Jackson Sundown died of pneumonia in 1923 at the age of sixty.

Sundown's allotment was close to our home when I grew up. His daughter, Red Sky, and his grandson, Patrick, were our neighbors. Pat, my sister, Ola and I rode the school bus together. We were the first kids on the bus in the morning and the last ones off at night. Pat was a special person; handsome, a good worker, honest, and always had a smile on his face. He was a excellent Indian dancer and one of a few that could perform the hoop dance, and with such grace. He was a good man, and like his father he loved horses.

Pat died too young of a heart attack, and I often think of what he told me a few years before he died. I was doing some work out by the gravel road one day when Pat drove by, and I waved as always, and went back to my work, Pat stopped and backed up, got out and walked over to where I was working. He told me, "Bud you are always working, you are too busy, you never take time to talk to a old friend. You always wave to me, but hardly ever stop and visit. You need to take more time for your friends and to enjoy life." What he said was so true, and this has always been one of my faults.

Center, Jackson Sundown's daughter, Mrs Red Sky Adams, receiving his plaque.

Pat Adams and Dorothy Felsman.

Pat, I bet you had time for a good visit with your Grandfather, Jackson Sundown, when you reached the other side. I'm sure he was as proud of you as you were of him. A few years ago I saw a cloud formation that looked like a hoop dancer, and I like to think it was Pat.

MAJOR JOHN OWEN

Major John Owen of Fort Owen in the Bitterroot Valley was the Indian Agent from 1856 to 1861. His diaries are very important to the study of Montana history. He was truly compassionate to the plight of the Indians, and many times used his own money to feed them when the Government didn't respond to an emergency as they should have. This story will give you a real glimpse of the Tribal warfare of the mid-1800 period.

Owen to Geary in Description of the Defeat of Chief Alexander by the Assiniboines and His Aid to the Beaten Indians, December 21, 1860:
Sir,
I returned last evening after an absence of two weeks to the Jocko Reservation. While there I heard of Alexander's approach with his defeated & scattered camp. I went to see him. My feelings were shocked at the scene his camp presented. Women with their children slung upon their backs had traversed the whole 400 miles on foot from the point on the Milk River where they had been defeated. They were literally worn out and exhausted. The loss of horses they sustained by the attack of the Assiniboine's & Cree was so great that most of their camp equipage had to be abandoned on the battlefield. They were destitute of provisions & clothing. I immediately ordered the Indian Dept pack train from the Jocko to this place for stores. I issued them four head of oxen. Alexander had lost a son in the fight, a young man of much promise, some 20 years of age. He found his son's body in a horribly mutilated state, scalped, stripped and heart cut out. Some of the wounded have since died. Dr. Mullan was prompt & efficient in rendering assistance to the wounded that succeeded in reaching home. Some fifteen operations of difficult nature had to be performed. Extracting arrow points, bullets, &c. The Pend'd Oreilles had twenty-five wounded (five of the latter since dead) and lost 290 head of horses. Ogden, a ½ breed who was one of the party, gave me a thrilling & interesting account of the attack & the battle. He says the Assiniboines numbered some two hundred, or thereabouts. They were a War party all on foot & unencumbered with families, lodges, horses, &c. Nothing in the world saved the complete & entire extermination of Alexander's Camp but the amt. of plunder the attacking party had come in possession of. The 290 head of horses, which they were eager to secure, beyond a doubt. The Pend d' Oreilles made every effort that a brave and gallant band could do to recover some

of the animals they had lost. But they were overcome by numbers & had to quietly submit to their fate & beat a retreat toward their far distant home. It was hard. They had just reached the buffalo. They were in fine spirits. On the evening of the night of the attack the tired Camp, on bended knees, offered their thanks to almighty God for the prospect then before them. Alexander in a short harangue told his camp that "Here we will make our winter's meat & return. Secure you fleet horses for tomorrow's chase, &c &c. Little did the unsuspecting Camp know what awaited them. Before the dawn the Camp was surrounded & between the report of the rifle, the wailings of the women, the neighing of the horses at the picket, & the sheet of fire that encircled the Camp from the rifles of the attacking party, you can form but a slight conception of what followed. Mr. Odgen says it was about one hour before day when the attack was made. Alexander's camp was still asleep. The attacking party approached the lodges, cut an opening with the knife through which they thrust their rifles and discharged their deadly contents. The heart bleeds at the thrilling story. Alexander thirsts for revenge. He talked to me with moistened eyes. He says he must visit the Sleeping place of his son & people. I tell him I appreciate his feelings. I sympathize deeply with him. I had a long talk with him. I have no doubt myself, but there will be a large war party in the field this spring. I have had to purchase ammunition for camp, none having been sent up with the annuity goods from the East.

Respect &c

John Owen, Ind. SubAgent &c &c W.T.

THE END OF A WAY OF LIFE
By Josephine Chevre

This story is a fictionalized account of an actual event that took place in 1886. Eneas Michel Conko and Philip Pierre were horse tenders on this raid, and Motlemon, later known as Charlie Mollman, was believed to have been the leader. There is no written documentation about this event, but the story that Motlemon tells about the big horse raid of 1863 is documented in history books. Montlemon was actually on this raid. The oral story about Michel and Pierre has been told and collaborated by several sources, and to the best of the author's knowledge, her interpretation follows this oral history.

The two boys could hardly contain their excitement. Sworn to secrecy and honored by being chosen to be horse tenders on the raid, the youths imagined themselves seasoned warriors, and stood proudly in the shadows as they waited for further instructions. At fourteen, Michel's young shoulders were broadening into manhood, and his voice had deepened, a fact that nettled his friend Pierre, who at twelve was still small and willowy. His mother had promised him he would soon begin to grow like his friend, but she smiled as she turned back to her work, because Pierre's face was round and innocent, and his voice still childishly sweet. All the same, he showed a steady and determined nature, which complimented that of his fiery, strong willed friend.

The men's voices held a note of excitement as they discussed the horse raid. Tired of the restrictions of reservation life, a group of young hot-bloods of the Upper Pend d'Oreille had persuaded an older, seasoned warrior, Motlemon, to lead them across the mountains to Blackfeet Country. Motelmon had advised the young men to plan the raid in the good green grass time, when the Blackfeet Nation held their annual sacred Sun Dance celebration. Many different bands would be traveling to this special event, so their group would arouse little suspicion of they were seen by someone, and the Blackfeet would be preoccupied with preparations for the ceremony. Great care was taken to ensure that the plan remained a secret to anyone outside the group. If work of the raid should reach the ears of Indian

Charlie Mollman.

Agent Peter Ronan, he would certainly feel obliged to stop it.

In this year of 1886, the settling of the western frontier was an undeniable reality, yet perhaps only Motlemon guessed that this would be the last horse stealing raid against their old enemy, the Blackfeet. Gazing at the two young boys, he wondered if they would hold this experience as a memory of a boy's journey into manhood, a marker on the path from careless childhood to the responsibilities and obligations of an adult within the tribe. And in the long season ahead, he wondered, would they pity their own sons, who would have no such path to follow, no such accomplishment to be sung in the summer camps while family and friend praised their daring?

Along with tending the horses, it was Pierre's and Michel's task to provide water for the warriors on the raid, and the two boys took their role seriously, keeping the skin bags full of fresh water, and exercising caution each time they left the group to refill the bags. But water was not a difficulty on the first leg of the journey, these mountains were full of springs and glacial spills. The raiders had started out long before daybreak, through what some day would be called North Crow Canyon, crossing over into the Swan Range and on through Little Salmon Pass, all the while avoiding the most heavily traveled passes. They would ride on up the White River, crossing the great rock wall north of Camp Creek, where the Blackfeet has ambushed a Pend d'Oreille camp years earlier. When the mountains met the prairie, they would be in Blackfeet country. From there they would travel cautiously for two or three days to where the Blackfeet came together on Willow Creek.

On the fourth night Motlemon permitted a cooking fire, as they were still half a day's ride from the open grass country, and discovery was not yet a danger. Although they had firearms, Motlemon had taken a mule deer with his bow, not only to avoid arousing attention from a rifle report, but also because he disdained using anything that came from the White Man. Let these young braves notice how they themselves forgot the way of the bow.

After they had cooked the meal and hung strips of uneaten meat to dry over the fire, Motlemon decided it was a good time to fire the young men's blood. He began an account of the big horse raid in which he had been a participant more than twenty years before. "Back then," Motlemon explained, "the Gros Ventre were allies with the Blackfeet, but after this raid became bitter enemies. We had raided the Gros Ventre camp and come away with many, many fine horses. Our enemies pursued us into the land of the Blackfeet, and might have called upon them for help, had it not been for the cunning of our own leader.

We came across a herd of Blackfeet horses, but instead of raiding them as well, we left the lame and worthless ones we had captured among the Blackfeet herd in the night and rode away. Soon the Gros Ventre caught up with this herd and seeing their own horses grazing with the Blackfeet mounts, they became enraged, thinking their allies had stolen from them. They killed two of the boys tending the horses, but the third escaped to warn his people that the Gros Ventre had broken the alliance. The Gros Ventre and the Blackfeet fought, and many were killed, but not one Pend d' Oreille was lost. We came home with a great many horses to the joyful trilling of our women."

Pierre and Michel nudged each other in the darkness, stirred to excitement by Motlemon's story. The other young warriors laughed and joked, each privately dreaming that he too, would show such cunning and daring, and be dancing his own account of this raid in the flickering light of the home fires. For the moment, at least, the log buildings of the Indian Agency did not exist for them.

They were in Buffalo Country, yet now the great herds roamed only in the minds of the travelers, the rich stories of days of the buffalo hunts blossoming in the young men's imaginations. They stared around themselves in awe, marveling not only at the vastness of space, but at the fact that the absence of bison on the plain somehow made them feel curiously empty inside. Michel and Pierre glanced nervously around them. This landscape of grass and sky, hill and butte, where the giant cloud people swept their shadows across the earth in proud silence seemed to swallow them, yet they felt exposed to any Blackfeet scout that might be scanning the horizon. The group kept to the draws and coulees as much as possible, utilizing every bit of sparse cover and avoiding the skyline where they might be spotted. Acting on Montlemon's instruction, they had changed their soft soled moccasins for pairs sewn with rawhide bottoms to protect their feet from prickly pear cactus. They made note of small bands of horses they passed, with the intention of capturing them on the return trip. They gave the Two Medicine River Mission a wide berth, traveling mostly at night as they cautiously made their way north toward the Willow Creek encampment, tension mounting with each mile they covered.

It took the party three days to reach the place of the Sun Dance gathering. The men put on their paint and called upon their personal medicine, making ready to fight and die honorably if that should be their fate. They waited until dark to slip in closer to the camp. Finally, from the vantage point of a low ridge, flat on their bellies, hearts pounding to the distant drums, the boys were allowed to look down on the plain where hundreds of lighted tepees, orange from camp fires, seemed to float on an upside down night sky. The two boys breathed their amazement in silent wonder. Never had they seen such a camp as the one spread before them. A light touch from the warriors next to them sent the boys slipping silently back to their horses. Although there were horses grazing everywhere, the men decided not to risk taking any near the encampment. Instead they retraced their steps, gathering some of the bands they had passed earlier. Running them into a small canyon, they picked out the best of the herd, and headed them home, taking only what they could easily handle.

They had only gone a few miles with the stolen horses when a scout signaled that a party of armed riders was approaching. Motlemon's eyes flashed and his lips drew back across his teeth in a fierce grin. Thinking that they were caught, the men prepared to fight, leaving the two boys with the horses, ordering them to flee home if it went badly.

Trying to swallow their fear, Michel and Pierre vowed to each other to fight bravely to keep the horses, even if the warriors did not return to them. The sound of hoofbeats was suddenly loud as the oncoming party started down the hill, and Motlemon and his young warriors readied themselves to give their war cries. But upon seeing the Pend d'Oreilles standing before them painted for war, the other group turned sharply and raced back over the hill. The Pend d'Oreilles looked at each other, surprise, relief and disappointment mingling on their faces. Finally, they determined that the retreating horsemen were Crow intent on the same endeavor, and so posed no threat of exposure for Motlemon's group.

The rest of the trip was uneventful, and once they were again in the mountains, they hunted down several deer and enjoyed a much needed feast before returning home to celebrate their success with trusted family and friends. Two boy in the midst of singing and dancing walked proudly, seeing something new about one another, something they both carried inside of them, and recognizing that their relatives saw it too, and approved. Thereafter these two young men would spend a lifetime fighting to help their people walk into a new and difficult century. They would travel across the plains, and across a continent to do battle in the halls of the White House, to hold the rights of the people and demand their voice be heard. They would live out their lives in a place known as the Flathead Indian Reservation, and die with their own truths still firm in their hearts, leaving their grandchildren to continue the story.

THE BLACKFEET WINTER RAID AT WILD PLUM CAMP

The following story was told to Dad when he was a boy by Eneas Conko. Twenty years later, when I was a young boy, Phillip Pierre told it to Dad again. We were sitting on blocks of wood at the wood pile where Dad was sharpening a crosscut saw. Both storytellers were Pend d' Oreilles, and told almost the same story. They did not know the date but said it was before Lewis and Clark or any white men, probably about 1750, before they had guns. Bows, arrows and war clubs were their only fighting weapons.

A large band of Pend d' Oreilles were in winter camp in the wild plum area, now Dixon, Montana. It had been a long cold winter; so cold Flathead Lake to the north was completely frozen over. Their supply of dried buffalo was getting low, and all the able-bodied men were out hunting instead of telling stories by the fires. On this particular fateful day the hunters were gone on a hunt. All the deer and elk close to camp had been killed so they had to travel a dozen miles or so to the southeast to hunt. They were unaware that a couple of Blackfeet scouts were watching the Pend d' Oreille camp. These scouts hurried back to their hidden camp to give the word; their medicine was strong and now was the time to attack the Pend d' Oreilles.

The Blackfeet war party had come over Marias Pass, down through Bad Rock Canyon and crossed Flathead Lake on the ice. This was a big war party of about forty or more warriors, traveling on foot as usual. Horses could not get through the deep snow on the pass in the wintertime.

The war party was upon the winter village with wild war cries, taking them by complete surprise, killing many of the old men, and boys, also any woman that tried to fight. The battle was over quickly. The Blackfeet took what plunder they could easily carry, taking many scalps. They gathered up the village horse herd, and taking a couple dozen younger women and girls captive they made a hasty exist. They rode the stolen horses twenty-five miles to the iced-over lake, then abandoned them, as the ice was not fit for horse travel. They started the long trek across the lake with their captives. When they were about three-fourths of the way they could see the Pend d' Oreille men in the distance, coming in pursuit. A number of the captive women were carrying their babies and were slowing the raiders' retreat. They took the babies away from their mothers and holding them by their feet they swung them down, smashing their heads on the ice, killing them. The mothers fought them, and they killed a couple of them; a death warning to the rest to keep up or die.

When the Pend d' Oreilles got to this bloody spot they swore revenge, saying they would fight to the death. With renewed strength they took up the chase, gaining all the time. When the Blackfeet reached Bad Rock Canyon they could see that their pursuers were going to catch up to them. They set up an ambush in the canyon, sending a few of the party on, herding the women ahead of them. The Pend d' Oreilles knew this place, and were expecting the ambush. A great battle took place with many casualties but the Blackfeet were defeated, and the remaining women and girls were rescued. Phillip said the lake had a different name then but after this incident they referred to the lake as Flathead because of the smashed heads. He thought some of the old ones, when telling Lewis and Clark about the big Flathead Lake had been misunderstood, and because of poor translation, Lewis and Clark thought they were describing themselves as Flatheads. That's why they called the Salish and Pend d' Oreilles "Flathead Indians."

This story has remained in my mind all my life and I have tried to relate it just as I heard it. To me, as a boy, there was no braver or better fighters than the Flatheads. I used to tell Dad, "I wish I had Flathead blood instead of Iroquois." Now in my winter years I know it's not what tribe or what blood is in your veins, but what's in your heart that matters. In 1946 when I was ten years old, the family was going from Ronan to Martin City when we had a flat tire going through Bad Rock Canyon. This was a usual thing in those days – every one always had flats. While Dad changed the tire my sister Ola and I climbed up the side of the canyon. We found a cave-like rock crevice which we crawled into, and in the back sticking partially out from under a packrat nest Ola found a war club. To me, this was a special find, as I had heard the story the year before of the battle here. This war club made my imagination run wild with visions of the battle.

A few years later my brother Kenny and I were rummaging around at an old burned-down trading post. Most of one log wall was still standing and under some of the debris along that wall we found many treasures including arrowheads, spear points, a calvary buckle, knives, axe heads, a buffalo horn, and other things. Most of it had been ruined by age and fire but some things were as good as new, and I was hooked forever on western history, and collecting. My love of history was enhanced by my ancestors in both my father's and mother's families. On my mother's side our great-grandfather, George Rogers' sister Rachel Ann married John Clark. Their two sons, George Rogers Clark of the French and Indian War and William Rogers Clark of the Lewis and Clark Expedition were my American heroes. I have spent a lot of time throughout my life, trying to save Montana treasures for the future. You can view the results of my efforts in the Ninepipes Museum of Early Montana that Laurie and I founded in 1996.

Chapter Seven

WRAPPING IT UP

We were just notified that my dad, Bud Cheff Sr., has been inducted into the Montana Cowboy Hall of Fame. He easily met all the needed qualifications. He was first and always a cowboy, a noted wilderness outfitter and woodsman, a historian, a teacher and story-teller. He was truly a Montana legend.

One More Ride

With a rainbow as his reins
And stars as his spurs
He rode a bolt of lightnin'
And flashed across the sky.
He forgot his aches and pains
And mustered all his nerve,
His grip was ever tightnin',
And resolve was in his eye.
This was no ride in a wains,
And never twice occurs.
To him it's not that fright'nin
And you won't hear him cry.
Across Montana's open plains
And high over mountain firs,
The end begins to brighten
And he dismounts with a sigh,
….He's home.

Bud Cheff III

Bud Cheff Sr., at the age of 93 breaking a horse, a true cowboy throughout his entire life.

AFTERWORD

Thank you for joining me in my desire to share a little of my life and some of the history of our great state.

Bud Cheff Jr.